BERLITZ®

DISCOVER
PRAGUE

Edited and Designed by
D & N Publishing,
Lambourn, Berkshire

Cartography by
Carte Blanche,
Basingstoke, Hampshire.

Although we have made every effort to ensure the accuracy of all the information in this book, changes occur incessantly. We cannot therefore take responsibility for facts, addresses and circumstances in general that are constantly subject to alteration.

 The Berlitz tick is used to indicate places or events of particular interest.

Phototypeset by Wyvern Typesetting Ltd., Bristol.

Printed by C. S. Graphics, Singapore.

Acknowledgements

I would like to thank the Press Centre for Foreign Journalists and the Čedok offices for their helpful co-operation. Thanks are also due to Derek Draper, Helen Conor, and the kind co-operation of the International Union of Students. I am particularly grateful to Louise Morriss for her help in editing this guide. A debt is owed to Dagmar Žáková, Vladimír Matějovský, Tamara Smolová, Milan Sládek and Otto Klikar for introducing me to Prague, and to Bernie Higgins for tireless assistance with photography, accommodation and planning. Thanks also to Andy Osborne, Pat O'Flaherty, Ken Biggs, Jenny Letham, Tanya White and Rebecca Dumphy. In the later stages of preparation the assistance of Lee Hall was invaluable, and it is to him that I owe the essay on Prague's musical background.

Photographic Acknowledgements

Front cover: Charles Bridge; reproduced courtesy of Pictor International.

Back cover: Building in Tyn Square, by Claude Huber; © Berlitz Publishing Company Ltd.

All inside photographs by the author except for those on the following pages: © Berlitz Publishing Company Ltd.: 6, 23, 29, 38, 48, 65, 66, 67, 72/73, 83, 87 (upper), 120, 122, 125, 145, 162, 165, 175.

Dedication
To Bernie Higgins.

If you have any new information, suggestions or corrections to contribute to this guide, we would like to hear from you. Please write to Berlitz Publishing at the above address.

BERLITZ®

DISCOVER
PRAGUE

Mark Corner

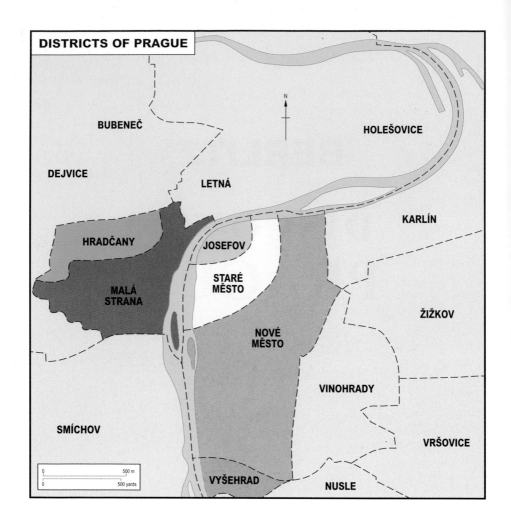

DISTRICTS OF PRAGUE

N

BUBENEČ

HOLEŠOVICE

DEJVICE

LETNÁ

KARLÍN

HRADČANY

JOSEFOV

STARÉ
MĚSTO

ŽIŽKOV

MALÁ
STRANA

NOVÉ
MĚSTO

VINOHRADY

SMÍCHOV

VRŠOVICE

0   500 m
0   500 yards

VYŠEHRAD

NUSLE

Contents

An Ounce of Prevention

For advice on how to make the best of your holiday, here are the very basics: money matters, accommodation, transport, communication and health matters. The rest should be pure pleasure.

When To Go

Prague has quite a changeable climate. Mild weather and freezing weather can easily alternate with one another in the winter months, whilst heat and rain often alternate in the summer months. It can be very warm and pleasant just outside the main tourist season in March and October. The best thing to do is to come prepared: bring a light raincoat in summer, and some light (as well as warm and thick) clothes if you visit at any other time of year. The city is probably at its most beautiful in May.

St Vitus' Cathedral seen from the Petřín Hill.

So far as temperature is concerned, you can expect 27°C (80°F) and warm nights in summer, anything between 10°C (50°F) and 21°C (70°F) in spring and autumn, and anything between -6°C (20°F) and 10°C (50°F) in winter (when short bursts of mild weather alternate with short bursts well below freezing).

Time Differences

Central European Time is followed by Czechoslovakia, which is usually an hour ahead of the time in Britain (the two are briefly the same between September and October). From September to March Czechoslovakia is GMT (Greenwich Mean Time) + 1 hour, whilst from March to September it is GMT + 2.

GMT + 1 is 7 hours ahead of American Eastern Standard Time.

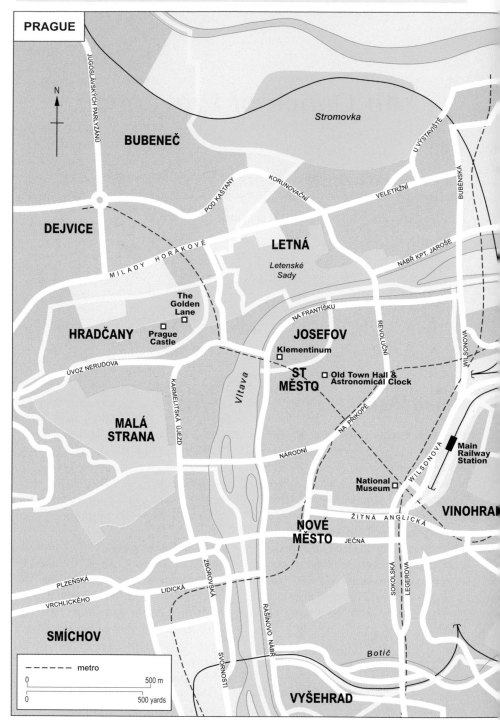

Customs and Entry Regulations

You cannot take Czech currency into or out of the country. Your passport must be valid for at least five months beyond the date of entry.

Visitors from Australia and New Zealand must obtain a visa from the Czech embassies in their countries. Those from Ireland, the UK or the USA and Canada need only a passport. Other nationalities should contact the Czech embassy in their country.

Two litres of wine, 1 litre of spirits and 250 cigarettes can be taken in or out. Clothes and jewellery should be purchased in Tuzex shops and receipts kept—but no one's going to worry about a few souvenirs. Cratefuls of the finest Bohemian glass are what the customs officers are concerned about.

Useful phrases:

I have nothing to declare.	**Nemám nic k proclení.**
It's for my personal use.	**To mám pro osobní potřebu.**

(Keep your souvenirs to the level where the above sentence is believable!)

Getting There

Airports

Prague's Ruzyně airport, about 20 km (12 miles) from the city centre, makes up in the speed with which it processes arrivals

T he city of Prague showing the main roads and sights.

and departures for the relative lack of facilities (at least by the standards of an international airport). There are daily flights to Prague from London (Heathrow) and New York. However, problems of visibility are not uncommon—you may find yourself landing in Nuremberg and facing a six or seven hour journey by train or bus!

Taxis or buses (every thirty minutes till 7.00 p.m.) take you into the centre of Prague within half an hour.

For the information service at the airport telephone 36 77 60.

If you want to travel by ČSA (Czechoslovak airlines), they have offices in all the major capitals.

In London the address is:
72, Margaret St
London W1N 7LF
Tel. (071) 255 1898

In New York the address is:
545 Fifth Avenue
New York 10017
Tel. (212) 682 7541

Currency

Czech money comes in crowns. There are notes to the value of 10, 20, 50, 100, 500 and 1,000 crowns, and the crown (koruna) is itself sub-divided into 100 heller (there are coins to the value of 5, 10, 20, and 50 heller, and to the value of 1, 2 and 5 crowns). Prices will be advertised with the letters kčs after them (meaning Czech crowns).

Changing Money

Do *not* change money on the black market. It is illegal, you'll be cheated, and you can do just as well in a bank. A favourite trick is to offer you enticing rates of exchange, take you into some alley-way, show you a bundle of notes, count them out, hand you an entirely different bundle worth much less by a clever sleight of hand, and then waltz off, perhaps with an accomplice to distract you. Don't be a fool.

The reason this happens (apart from the gullibility of tourists) is that it is very difficult to obtain hard currency in Czechoslovakia. There is something to be said for taking some into the country—particularly German marks, but American dollars, British pounds or any Western currency will do—since they can be used in a number of places which do not accept crowns for cash payment (e.g. the Tuzex shops which sell items that only deal in hard currency—*see* SHOPPING below). Czech people who want to use such facilities themselves may also welcome payment in hard currency. On the other hand, with an increasing use of credit cards and the possibility of using traveller's cheques in Tuzex shops it is not essential to bring in hard currency. Remember, however, that you may not be able to obtain it again until you leave Czechoslovakia.

There are exchange offices all over the place, particularly around Wenceslas Square, some of which are open all night. Avoid them—they will not give you the best deal. Go to the bank to cash traveller's cheques or to change hard currency into crowns. The Czechoslovak State Bank (Státní banka Československa), at Na přikopě 28 (about 200m—220 yds—from the bottom of Wenceslas Square as you head towards náměstí Republiky) is open from 8.00 a.m. to 5.00 p.m. Monday to Friday and on Saturday mornings. Of course, you may have to use an exchange office if you are needing to change money outside those hours, but after the fee you'll receive about 10 per cent less. The same will be true if you use hotels or Čedok offices.

As a rough guide, for every pound you change you should come away with about 50 crowns, for each German mark about 17 crowns, and for each American dollar about 30 crowns—but that's on 1992 exchange rates.

Getting Around

Cars

Arriving and Leaving by Car

If you come from southern Germany then you can simply follow the E-12 from Frankfurt via Nuremberg to Plzeň (the border crossing is at Waidhaus–Rozvadov). If you come down from the North on the E-15 from Berlin, then the border is at Schmilka–Hřensko. A third route from Bayreuth crosses at Schirnding–Pomezí. The roads become decidedly narrower (although less busy, since only one Czech in ten is a car owner) once you reach Czechoslovakia, and you will be grateful for the occasional stretch of dual carriageway. If you are hitching, the E-12 is best, although you shouldn't have too much trouble on any of the routes.

Drivers should have the following essential items with them:
1. Registration document
2. International driving licence.
3. International insurance certificate.
4. First aid kit.
5. Replacement bulbs.
6. Red warning triangle.
7. National identification sticker.

*P*olitical whitewash? *Advertising comes to Wenceslas Square.*

Tips on Driving

On motorways keep within 110 kph (about 70 mph); in built-up areas keep to 60 kph (about 35–40 mph) Motorbikes cannot exceed 80 kph (50 mph) anywhere.

If you break down ring 154. This puts you in touch with Autoturist's "Yellow Angels"!

Seat belts are compulsory. Children under 12 should be in the back. *Any* drinking and driving is illegal.

There isn't much in the way of road markings or signs, but a yellow diamond means that you have right of way.

The following specialist garages can repair your vehicle:

BMW/Volkswagen—Severni XI Praha 4 (Tel. 76 67 52).

Citroen—Za opravnou 1, Praha 5 (Tel. 52 26 51).

Fiat—Na strži 35, Praha 4 (Tel. 42 66 14).

Ford—Osiková 2, Praha 3 (Tel. 82 95 00).

Renault—Ďáblicka 2, Praha 8 (Tel. 88 78 03).

Petrol

You have to buy petrol coupons in advance at border crossings, at the state bank, at travel offices and at certain hotels. For diesel fuel you need special vouchers from the state bank. Since the amount of fuel sent across to Czechoslovakia at highly subsidised prices from the former Soviet Union has gone down considerably since the Velvet Revolution, there is a shortage which may mean long queues. Petrol in Czech is *benzín*, and you can get "super" at 96 octane or "special" at 90 octane. The word for diesel is *nafta*. Unleaded petrol, known as natural or *bezolovnatý*, is only available from some petrol stations. Although some stations are open 24 hours a day, most close at 8.00 p.m. and there are not many, so do not allow fuel levels to fall too far. You can import up to four gallons (20 litres) duty free.

Car Hire

This is expensive and you may be asked to pay in hard currency or by credit card. Many of the hotels will organize this for you. Alternatively you can rent from:

Pragocar
Štěpánská 42
Praha 1
Tel. 235 28 25 or 235 28 09

or organize the hire via an international car hire agency like Avis or Hertz before you leave for Czechoslovakia. You pay for the time of hire, not for the mileage covered. The cost will range from upwards of about £200 per week, making it cheaper to hire the car in Germany and drive over the border!

Driving in Prague

Since the city is compact and has an excellent public transport system running throughout the day and night, this should not be necessary. You will not find it easy to park in the city centre, and may find it necessary to leave the car at your hotel or at the railway station (and at one or two metro stations away from the centre—a kind of Park and Ride approach).

Some useful words:

Entrance	**Vchod**
Exit	**Východ**
No Entry	**Vstup zakázáno**
Left	**Vlevo**
Right	**Vpravo**
Straight On	**Hned**
Near	**Blízko**
Far	**Daleko**
Danger!	**Pozor!** (also **Nebezpečí!**)
Full tank please.	**Plnou nádrž, prosím.**
Please check the oil/tyres/battery.	**Prosím, zkontrolujte mi olej/ pneumatiky/ baterii.**
I have broken down.	**Mám poruchu.**
There's been an accident.	**Stala se nehoda.**
May I park here?	**Mohu zde parkovat?**

Road Signs:

One way	**Jednosměrný provoz**
Road works	**Na silnici se pracuje**
No entry	**Nevstupujte**
Diversion	**Objížďka**
Caution	**Opatrně**
Pedestrian zone	**Pěší zóna**
Slow down	**Snížit rychlost** (also **zpomalit**)

Taxis

Taxi fares are close to western prices, partly because of a petrol shortage. They are easy to find by day or night (there are always some at the bottom of Wenceslas Square), particularly outside hotels and stations. An unoccupied taxi has a lit-up sign and can be flagged down. Private enterprise has moved into the taxi business in a big way since the Velvet Revolution. Not everyone is scrupulous, so make sure that there is a meter running and that the driver doesn't give you a guided tour of Prague by night on the way home.

The trams continue to roll in Prague— but with their familiar red increasingly supplanted by advertisements.

Public Transport

This is undoubtedly the best legacy of communist rule. Prague has a cheap and superb public transport system, something that many western nations are struggling to reproduce in city centres choked by traffic fumes. The underground runs on three lines from 5.00 a.m.

13

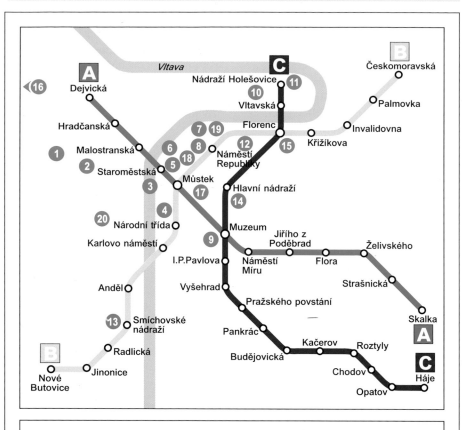

1 Pražský hrad (Prague Castle)	**11** Nádraží Holešovice (Holešovice Railway Station)
2 chrám sv. Mikuláše na Malé Straně (Church of St.Nicholas in the Lesser Town)	**12** Masarykovo nádraží (Masaryk Railway Station)
3 Karlův most (Charles Bridge)	**13** Nádraží Smíchov (Smíchov Railway Station)
4 Národní divadlo (National Theatre)	**14** Praha-hlavní nádraží (Prague-Main Railway Station)
5 Staroměstské náměstí (Old Town Square)	**15** Autobusové nádraží Florenc (Florenc Bus Station)
6 Židovský hřbitov (Jewish Cemetery)	**16** letiště (Airport)
7 Anežský klášter (Convent of St.Agnes)	**17** hlavní pošta (Main Post Office)
8 Prašná brána (Powder Tower)	**18** Státní banka Československá (Czechoslovak State Bank)
9 Národní muzeum (National Museum)	**19** obchodní dům Kotva (Kotva Department Store)
10 Výstaviště (Exhibition Grounds)	**20** lanová dráha Újezd-Petřín (Újezd-Petřín Funicular)

to midnight. Stations are tidy, some of them with space-age designs, and the trains run every four minutes (with a clock to tell you the length of time since the last one arrived!). A recorded voice on the train announces the next station. The trams run on a similar schedule, most of them at ten-minute intervals or more frequently. After 11.00 p.m. a number of "night trams" continue to run throughout the night at intervals of twenty minutes.

For trips further out from the centre which are not on tram routes, you can catch an appropriate bus from a connecting tram.

Fares are based on the number of journeys, not their length. You pay a fixed amount per trip, wherever you go. Tickets are usable on both tram and metro (and the funicular railway). In 1990 the cost was 1 crown per journey. By 1991 it had risen to 4 crowns, and held at that price into 1992. By any accounts it is still a very cheap system.

You cannot purchase tickets on the trams or at the stations—you must buy them in advance from newstands (PNS), tobacconists and some metro stations. You can buy sets of five or ten. A very useful thing to do is to buy a pass for up to five days which entitles you to unlimited travel. When you board the tram punch a ticket into the machine by the door. Do the same at the entrance to metro stations. It is unwise to try to escape without paying. If stopped (often by inspectors in plain clothes), you will end up paying fines at Western prices!

*P*rague's metro system also indicating positions of the main sights.

Useful words and phrases:

Bus	Autobus
Bus stop	Zastavká
Can I get off?	Můžu vystoupit?
Emergency exit	Nouzový východ (východ exit)
Entrance	Vchod
No entrance	Vstup zakazán
How much?	Kolik?
Ticket	Lístek
Tram	Tramvaj
Underground	Metro
Station	Stanice
Platform	Nástupiště
Direction	Směr
How many stops is it?	Kolik stanic je do?

Balloons

If you feel like a more exotic way of seeing the city than is offered by various modes of transport at ground level, contact:
Prag Tourist Ballooning
Trojanova 18
120 00 Praha 2
Tel. 296 851 or 276 552

They offer daily flights over Prague in a hot air balloon. Champagne is served as you glide over the city—but the cost is hardly cheap!

Consulates and Embassies

Canada
Mickiewiczova 6
Praha 6 Tel. 31 20 25 1-4.
UK
Thunovská 14
Praha 1. Tel. 53 33 47.
USA
Tržiště 15
Praha 1. Tel. 53 66 41.

Health

Getting Treatment

Obviously most hotels will arrange this for you. Otherwise you should call 5292 2146 for medical assistance on weekdays and 5292 1111 evenings and weekends. For children's medical assistance call 5292 2025.

There is a modern Diplomatic Health Centre for Foreigners at Na homolce 724, Prague 5. It offers 24-hour emergency care as well as 24-hour dental services, and has a women's clinic from 8.00 a.m. to 12.00 noon on Tuesdays which offers pregnancy testing, birth control, abortion and pre-natal care.

Emergency treatment is free. An examination by a doctor will require a deposit of about 1,000 crowns (£20 or $35). It will cost about the same to have a couple of dental fillings. Overnight stays in a hospital cost about 2,000 crowns per night.

If you are visiting the Diplomatic Health Centre, take bus 167 from metro station Anděl to the stop Sídliště homolka. You can't miss the large building opposite. *Take your passport.*

If your problem can be dealt with adequately by a chemist, there are a number open 24 hours a day. The most convenient for the centre of town is Na přikopě 7, Praha 1 (Tel. 22 00 81) which is close to the bottom of Wenceslas Square. Alternatively there is Ječná 1, Praha 2 (Tel. 26 71 81) or Pod marjánkou 12, Břevnov, Praha 6 (Tel. 35 09 67).

Health Spas

Places like Karlovy Vary (Karlsbad) have been famous for the beneficial effects of "taking the waters" for centuries. If you want a course of treatment at a Western Bohemian health spa, you can either book through Čedok or contact:
Balnea
Pařížská 11
Praha 1
Tel. 23 23 76.

Tips for Health

Take clothes for a climate where temperatures vary in every season. Drink bottled water.

Useful words:

Chemist	**Lekárna**
Hospital	**Nemocnice**
Toothache	**Bolest zubů**
Headache	**Bolest hlavy**
I have a sore throat.	**Bolí mě v krku.**
I'm in great pain.	**Mám velké bolesti.**

Contraception

Condoms are readily on sale now, not only at chemists but also from machines. Look out for machines marked "Men's Shop" at the entrance to metro stations. AIDS was hardly spoken of under the communists, but there are now wide campaigns to encourage safer sex.

Tampons

Sanitary towels are called *vložky*. Tampons (*tampóny*) are fortunately much more available than they used to be. It may, however, be best to bring a supply.

Disabled Visitors

Prague is only beginning to cater for groups like disabled people whose needs were not catered for by the communist regime. It is notably the newer hotels that offer accommodation for disabled guests. Many of the sights lack adaptations, although there is ramp access to much of Prague Castle area and the tower of the Old Town Hall has a lift. But this is totally unsatisfactory when viewed with the many sights, shops, restaurants and public transport system that have no wheelchair accesses. This will change in time, and it is already being established as an issue, but at the moment disabled visitors will face a lot of inconvenience. The official national organization for the disabled with its headquarters on Karlínské náměstí 12, Praha 8.

from Australia—0011422;
from Ireland—16422;
from New Zealand—00422;
from the UK—010422;
from the USA and Canada—001.

You can always book accommodation through Čedok, the main tourist agency for Czechoslovakia and before the Velvet Revolution a state monopoly through which every visitor was compulsorily directed to a range of over-priced hotels. Čedok has branches in London:
17–18 Old Bond Street
London W1X 4RB Tel. (071) 629 6058.

Where to Stay

Accommodation

Two years ago, in the immediate aftermath of the Velvet Revolution, Prague was totally unable to cope with the sudden increase in foreign visitors. Although at certain times during the year the system is still strained, it no longer looks as if it might break down. At the top end of the scale new hotels have been and are being built, whilst at the other end a wide range of private flats and houses (some of them quite luxurious) have become available for rent as Praguers take advantage of new opportunities for private enterprise. Although it is true that accommodation is the one area in which Czech prices match Western ones, both the cost and the problems of availability can be exaggerated.

Telephone (and where available fax) numbers of agencies are given below. If you are ringing from outside Prague, of course, you will have to add a prefix. The appropriate prefix from English-speaking countries is as follows:

The main Čedok accommodation bureau in the New Town, with the Týn Church in the background.

*P*rague offers a range of hotel choices, from the ultra-modern Hotel Forum to the more traditional Hotel Central, and not forgetting the "botels" like the Albatros.

And New York
10 East 40th Street, New York, NY 10016; Tel. (212) 689 9720.

Alternatively, you may want to arrive first and then book. Čedok has offices in many parts of Prague, but the main office is a few yards from Wenceslas Square, near to Můstek metro station at:

Na příkopé 18
Praha 1.

At this office you can book theatre tickets and sightseeing tours at the same time. Čedok no longer has a monopoly on accommodation, however, and a number of other agencies are mentioned below. For a selection of hotels available in Prague, see the list at the end of the book.

Botels

If you fancy sleeping on the river, then you may be attracted to the idea of a "botel", although these "hotel barges" are not particularly cheap.

Cheap Accommodation

Before the Velvet Revolution at the end of 1989 a section on cheap accommodation could not have existed. Since then, however, there has been an explosion of private enterprise as Praguers have thrown themselves into the tourism business. A large number of people now offer their homes for foreign visitors, particularly during the summer months when they vacate Prague for their *dachas* in the country, go on holiday themselves, or stay with friends in order to supplement their income. Guide books written before 1991 will say that at certain times during the year it is impossible to find accommodation in Prague. If you are happy to be at the cheap end of the market, that is no longer true. You can arrive in August without a booking and find somewhere to stay in a few minutes. A number of people will hang around at the railway station or come up to you in the street offering a spare room in their homes. This can be an interesting, if risky, offer to take up. Safer and more reliable is the excellent AVE travel agency, which offers accommodation in Prague at prices from 20 German Marks (£7 or $12) per person per night.

Agencies to Help You

AVE Ltd. travel agency is situated at the main railway station (Hlavní nádraží) Wilsonova 80 120 00 Praha 2.

It can also be found at the airport and at Holešovice railway station (which you may arrive at if you travel to Prague from Berlin). The office at the main railway station is open from 6.00 a.m. to 11.00 p.m. daily throughout the year, but at Holešovice these hours only apply during the summer (May to September). For the rest of the year it is open from 6.00 a.m. until 4.00 p.m. AVE will arrange for you to stay in a private apartment—which can include shower, bath, television, washing-machine and a kitchen with oven and fridge (so that you can buy and cook your own food if you wish to). In many ways this is much nicer than a hotel, and a lot cheaper if you are staying for more than a day or two (and even if you aren't!). AVE will also help with guides, reservations, renting cars and booking sightseeing tours.

You can telephone AVE and make a reservation if you don't like the idea of arriving without pre-planned accommodation. Their numbers are 236 25 60, 236 30 75, or 236 25 41. They will also be able to advise you on hotel accommodation.

Apart from AVE, you can also make use of Čedok's accommodation bureau at:

Panská 5
Praha 1
Tel. 22 56 57 or 22 70 04.
open from 9.00 a.m. to 5.00 p.m. daily.

Pragotour, located at:
U Obecního domu 23
Tel. 232 72 81
also offers private accommodation.

Top Tour started up recently at:
Rybná 3
110 00 Praha 1
Tel. 232 10 77 or Fax. 232 08 60.

Dozens of other operators will probably be working by the time you arrive! Look for signs strapped to lamp-posts or fly-sheets being distributed in the street.

Young People

Young people (anyone under 30!) can stay at a Juniorhotel at:
Žitna 12
Praha 2
Tel. 29 99 49.

The Youth Travel Agency at the same address can provide help with accommodation if the Juniorhotel is full.

Camping

Finally, some people may fancy camping. If you do take this option, expect the sites to be full and don't expect to find bottled gas or methylated spirit. Some campsites have bungalows for hire—they are:
Sportcamp
V podháji
Praha 5
Tel 52 18 02.

Kotva Bránik
U ledáren 55
Praha 4
Tel. 46 13 97.

and Transit which is next to the airport at:
Ruzyně
25 února 197
Praha 6
Tel. 36 71 08.

Others vary from a couple of toilets next to rough ground to *Autokempinky* (motor camps) with shower and toilet facilities, that may sell food. Try Caravan-camp at:
Plzeňská
Praha 5
Tel 52 47 14,

The futuristic Kotva department store.

or
Na Vlachove
Rudé armády 217
Praha 8
Tel. 84 12 90.

To make inquiries or to reserve places contact the Autoturist Organisation at:
Na Rybničku 16
Praha 2
Tel. 22 48 28.

Shopping

Prague's large pedestrianized area and compact city centre make it a pleasure to shop in. It may not have the range of

consumer goods that Western cities have (although that has changed to some extent since 1989), but it has a number of excellent speciality items which are listed below.

Department Stores

The futuristic Kotva store (náměstí Republiky 8), and the Máj department store (Národní 26) are both close to the centre and contain a wide range of basic goods. Dětský dům at Na přikopě 15 specializes in children's goods.

Specialist Stores

Glassware

Bohemian glassware is world-famous. Bohemia Moser at Na přikopé 12 has the widest range, but Bohemia Glass at Pařížská 2 or Krystal at Celetná 20 have a wide range of porcelain goods. Some items may only be purchased in hard currency.

Antiques

There are a variety of places to try. Celetná 12, Národní 22 and many other stores are worth a visit.

Books

Some of the best art books are available at exhibitions, on sale alongside postcards, posters etc., or at art galleries such as the Galerie Na Můstku at 28 řijna 16. For general literature try Knikupectví Melantrich, at Na přikopě 3-5, Praha 1. For rare books and original prints and drawings try the Charles Bridge Bookstore and Gallery, Antikvariát U Karlova Mostu, next to the Charles Bridge (Tel. 26 56 72). Books are relatively cheap by Western standards, many of them beautifully bound and illustrated.

Sports Equipment

Try Dům sportu, Jungmannova 28, Praha 1.

Records

Jungmannova 20, just off Wenceslas Square, has a wide range. Apart from a selection of the local classical favourites, Smetana, Dvořak and Janáček, there is a range of Czech and Slovak folk music. Clubs like the new and attractive Agartha Jazz Club at Krakovská 5 off Wenceslas Square sell a range of jazz records.

Food

Paris-Praha in Jindřišska, opposite the main post office, specializes in French food and wine (which is admittedly a rather despairing piece of advice since you're visiting Prague!). For a sample of Czech food, wine and spirits you could begin by visiting any *potraviny* (food-store). Dům potravin, at number 59 Wenceslas Square, has a range of goods. There isn't the range of a western delicatessen, and until recently fresh fruit and vegetables were in noticeably short supply, but this is rapidly changing. The open-air market area beside Havelská is worth a visit for fresh food.

Drink

Everyone mentions the omnipresent liqueur *Becherovka* and the plum brandy *Slivovice*, and certainly these are worth tasting. But speaking personally, if you are returning abroad with a maximum of a couple of litres or so then I would recommend, where liqueurs are concerned, *Staré Myslivecká* (it should have a label featuring a far-gone white-haired gent with a pipe), and a bottle of the red(!) champagne. There is a range of fine

Moravian wines too (*see* the Mělnik wine-tasting expedition later in the book).

Tuzex Shops

These sell a range of Czech and imported goods, but can only be paid for in hard currency. Keep your receipts so that they can pass through customs. A number specialise in particular items—for instance Benetton at Revoluční 2 sells clothes, Železná 18 sells cameras, Náměstí Míru 3 sells food and drink, Rytířska 13 sells jewellery, Va smečkách 24 cosmetics and Skořepka 4 car accessories. They are useful when you run out of something practical that can't be purchased easily in Czechoslovakia, but seem to attract a range of people who can't bear the thought of a week away from home without being able to shop in a Benetton.

Useful words and phrases:
Cash desk   **Pokladna**
How much?   **Kolik?**

The following shop-names are common:
Confectionery	**Cukrárna**
Gift-shop	**Dárky**
Drug-store/	**Drogerie/**
Chemist	**Lekárna**
Bookshop	**Knihkupectvi**
Food-store	**Potraviny**
Drinks	**Nápoje**
Refreshments	**Občerstveni**
Meat/Salami	**Uzeniny**
Milk	**Mléko**
Cheese	**Sýr**
Bread	**Chléb**
Baked goods	**Pečivo**
Delicatessen	**Lahůdky**
Fruit/Veg	**Ovoce/Zelenina**
Large/Small	**Velký/Malý**
Open/Closed	**Otevřeno/Zavřeno**
Excuse me	**Promiňte**

Cigarettes

Czech cigarettes are cheap but many smokers find the taste too harsh. Sparta, decorated with an ancient Greek trireme, are probably the best; the President has popularized Petra by smoking forty a day. You may prefer to buy western brands at western prices. Czech cigarettes cost anything from 18 to 30 crowns per pack; western cigarettes from 55 to 70 crowns per pack. Non-smokers will not find many places that are free of smoke, but look out for the sign *koužení zakázáno*. Smokers should note that there is no smoking either at railway stations or on the underground.

Useful words:
Matches	**Sirky**
Cigarettes	**Cigarety**
Cigar	**Doutník**
Lighter	**Zapalovač**

Tourist Offices

The numerous Čedok offices will answer any queries and provide extra services like theatre tickets, changing money and reserving places on organised excursions. The Pražská informační služba (Prague Information Service), at Panská 4, Praha 1 (Tel. 22 34 11 or 22 43 11) is very helpful, and will have copies of English-language information bulletins (in effect they are newspapers).

Photography

Enormous progress has been made in the last two or three years to provide the ever-increasing number of tourists with the apparatus and facilities they need. You can

Lost in Prague.

now easily obtain good modern film like Kodachrome, a high standard of developing and even spare parts like batteries for most makes of camera.

Useful words:

Camera	**Fotoaparát**
Photograph	**Fotografie**
Film	**Film**
Colour film	**Barevny film**
Black and white film	**Černobílý film**
Is it allowed to photograph here?	**Může se zde fotografovat?**
Develop a film	**Vyvolat film**

Maps and Guides

Make sure you get one that is up-to-date, because the names of a large number of streets and stations have changed since the Velvet Revolution. Any map with anything named after Klement Gottwald is definitely out of date!

Opinions vary as to which map is best. One of the most straightforward is contained within the *Prague Guide*, a monthly booklet whose centre pages contain a map of the central area. This has the advantage of being newly compiled, easy to fold and free (just pick up the guide from a Čedok office or tourist information centre).

The best map is the *Falk plan*, which is both easy to fold and comes with separate sections for the underground, the city centre and a road map for an 80-km (50-mile) radius around Prague. Don't buy anything earlier than the eighth edition.

There will be plenty of guides on sale in the street. Beware the Olympia guides—these were written before the Velvet Revolution, and whilst they contain a mine of useful information (for instance how many live in a particular "workers' estate" on the edge of the city), they are now out of date.

Whatever you buy should have been produced since the Velvet Revolution of November 1989, and given the significant changes over the last two years you should buy what is most up-to-date.

Invaluable as a source of information are the English-language newspapers such as *The Prague Post* and *Prognosis*, which contains a Visitors' Guide. This contains reviews of places to eat and drink, as well as listings for films and plays, together with interesting articles on social and political issues of the day. These are usually much more informative than the accounts in foreign newspapers.

Useful phrases:

City Plan	**Plán Města**
Guide-book	**Průvodce**

Communications

Posting letters and cards

Post boxes are an unmistakable orange (with a dash of blue). Stamps can be bought in some hotels and newsagents, or you can visit the main post office at Jindřišská 14 just off Wenceslas Square (Tel. 26 48 41 or 26 41 93). The building is open 24 hours a day, although not after 6.00 pm for stamps. There are dozens of confusing kiosks in the place, each with a different function, so look out for the word *známky* (stamps). Currently stamps are on sale from kiosks 20–24. You should also ensure you buy stamps for posting abroad (some newsagents only sell stamps for destinations within Czechoslovakia). Cards and letters should be delivered to European destinations within a week.

Poste Restante

There is a kiosk in the main post office for collecting mail sent in this fashion (you may be asked to prove your identity). If sending mail to Prague by this means, write your own name and address on the back. Send the letter to the main post office (Pošta 1), at the address given above.

Using a Telephone

Until recently, international calls had to be made from the main post office or the main railway station. There are a few telephones in the city centre now which will connect you with the outside world, but the best thing is still to go to the main post office (this part is open 24 hours a day). You simply pay a deposit and then go to a booth where the amount you've paid appears as a number of units on a screen. When you've finished you can collect change or pay extra. The similar facility at the main railway station closes at 6.00 p.m.

A number of telephones now take phonecards. You can buy them in the main post office at kiosks 20-24. Ask for *Telecart*.

Dialling codes for calls to English-speaking countries from Prague are as follows: UK-00144; US/Canada-001; Australia-0061; Ireland-00353; New Zealand-0064.

International calls are not cheap and 200 crowns will give you less than ten minutes. You can, of course, ring from many hotels—but watch for the surcharge on top of what is already an expensive call!

National calls can theoretically be made from any telephone, but Prague still needs to get most of them working! Try the ones in metro stations where there are usually a couple that function.

Telegrams

These can be sent from post offices and many hotels.

Useful words:

Phone	**Telefon**
Post office	**Pošta**
Stamps (stamp)	**Známky (znamka)**
Letters (letter)	**Dopisy (dopis)**
Registered letter	**Doporučeny dopis**
Parcel	**Balík**
To post by airmail	**Poslat letecky**
What is your number?	**Jaké máte číslo telefonu?**

Newspapers, Magazines and Television

The main foreign newspapers are on sale in a range of newsagents, particularly in the vicinity of Wenceslas Square. The *International Herald Tribune* and the *International Guardian* are easily available.

With the demise of communism there is an outburst of poorly produced soft porn flooding the magazine market. At the same time, there are some interesting magazines like *Expres* which carry one or two articles in English. There is a tendency even for serious magazines to contain the odd gratuitous nude, simply because the communists would have banned them. English-speaking magazines like *The Economist* and *Time* are available—others are not easy to get hold of unless you like reading *Playboy*.

There is a 24-hour news programme called CNN which is available in hotels and on a number of private television channels. It's hardly in-depth coverage, but if you're worried about whether World War III has broken out it will probably tell you. For a much higher standard of coverage, tune in to the BBC World Service on the radio.

Crime

This has been on the increase since the Velvet Revolution, but the extent of it can be exaggerated. Prague is safe by the standard of western cities.

In case of emergency ring 158.

If you want to contact the police, the address (aptly enough!) is:
Konviktská 14
Praha 1
Tel. 21 21 11 11.

Useful words and phrases:

I want to report a theft.	Chci ohlásit krádež.
Passport	Pas
Money	Peníze
Wallet	Náprsní taška
Handbag	Kabelka
Ticket	lístek
Traveller's cheque	Cestovní šek
Camera	Fotoaparát
Jewel	Šperk

Lost Property
Main Office:
Bolzanova 5
Praha 1 (Tel. 24 84 30).

Documents:
Olšanska 2
Praha 3 (Tel. 24 51 84).

Electricity

Prague electricity is distributed at 220 volt on a 50 cycle AC circuit. Shavers should take a standard continental adaptor with square pins.

Laundry

Launderettes are in the process of getting established, but you will probably have to rely on a *čistírna*, where you can get a service wash and dry cleaning within a couple of days. There is, however, a recently-opened Laundromat called Laundry Kings at Devická 16, 160 00 Praha 6, Tel. 312 37 43. The more up-market hotels, of course, will have appropriate facilities. If you are renting a private apartment from AVE or another agency, you can ask whether it contains a washing-machine.

Toilets

There are not many public ones. The best bet is the larger metro stations. Look out for the sign WC or for the words *Muži* or *Páni* (Men) and *Ženy* or *Dámy* (Women). In some restaurants you may find a cloak-room attendant, who will dispense a par-simonious quantity of toilet paper for a couple of crowns.

Useful phrases:

Do you have any more, please?	**Máte víc, prosím?**
Where are the toilets?	**Kde jso su toalety?**

Tipping

This is common. Cloakroom attendants tend to receive a couple of coins; taxi drivers and waiters tend to receive about 10 per cent.

Emergencies

Ambulance-333.
Doctor-158.
Fire-150.
Police-158.

Useful words:

Help!	**Pomoc**
Doctor	**Lékař/Doktor**
Ambulance	**Sanitka**
Police	**Policie**
Fire extinguisher	**Hasicí přistroj**
Hospital	**Nemocnice**

Public Holidays

Apart from Christmas, New Year and Easter Monday, there are holidays on the first of May (at present!) and the ninth of May (National Day).

Eating and Drinking Out

In the last three years there has been an explosion of fast food in the city. As the tanks went rolling out, McDonald's came rolling in. There is still, however, a welter of atmospheric pubs and restaurants where you can dine very well for a modest sum. However, you must book in most cases—although a number of places exist where you can get a snack or a modest meal without reserving, you will almost certainly not be able to get a good meal without booking in advance.

Eating Out

Czechoslovak cuisine does not rate very highly internationally. Many visitors to Prague return home talking of a choice between different slabs of meat and a few desultory vegetables. It is important to emphasize, firstly that Czech cuisine has its own variety and merits, secondly that since the Velvet Revolution there has been a significant increase in the range of international cuisine on offer in the capital (although a lot of it is down-market fast food), and thirdly that (once again since the Velvet Revolution) there is now much more fresh fruit and vegetables available than a few years back. Snacks are readily available for tired tourists in need of a little refreshment, and although life isn't as easy for vegetarians as it should be, it's not impossible and becoming easier.

The old meets the new. Prague's first McDonald's.

For a selection of restaurants catering to most tastes and pockets, see the selection at the end of the book.

Snacks

There are many places to buy ice-cream (*zmrzlína*) and (more tastily) waffles (*vafle*), and an increasing number of outlets for chips. Up and down Wenceslas Square there's a roaring nightly trade in sausages with a dollop of mustard and a lump of brown bread. Vegetarians should look out for *smažený sýr* (fried cheese). One of the best snack bars is tucked away at a side of the Old Town Square. Called Gyros, it is next to the grassy area between the Old Town Hall and St Nicholas' Church, and serves kebabs (with a generous portion of salad or salad on their own).

If you are out late at night and fancy a snack, then there's always Rebecca, open 9.00 a.m. to 8.00 p.m. and 9.00 p.m. to 7.00 a.m., and easily recognizable from the sign *Non-Stop Snack Bar* in purple letters. Salads, sandwiches and pastas are available through the night, together with coffee, wine and liqueur. The only problem (apart from the purple and black decor) is that it's a mile from the city centre, at Olšanské náměstí 8. But the night tram number 58 runs there every 40 minutes. Ask for Táboritská. Alternatively, it's only fifteen minutes' walk, so why not work up an appetite at three in the morning?

Vegetarians

Two years ago vegetarians in Prague lost either weight or their principles. Nowadays many more restaurants recognise that they will have a number of vegetarian customers to cater for, and most menus now have a range of options that are "*bez masa*" (without meat). Having said that, there are still a number of establishments with little understanding of vegetarianism, and supposedly meat-free dishes regularly turn up with something fleshy floating in them.

One of the best places for vegetarians to eat is the *Palace Hotel Cafeteria* (Panská 12), which is open from 12.00 noon to 9.00 p.m. It has the best salad bar in town, and although self-service the standard of food is high. It is also a non-smoking restaurant.

Vegetárka, at Celetná 3, is not vegetarian, but an easy-going café looking like a student union snack-bar (and usually sounding like one), where you can get a range of permutations of beans, chips,

sausages, egg and one or two other things. It is only open at lunch-times.

There is a good selection of meatless dishes in *Crazy Daisy*, and some good mushroom dishes in *U šupů*, located in Spálená, although meat creeps into most of them.

The Czechoslovak Vegetarian Association was founded in September 1989, and a Czech Vegetarian Society runs on a shoe-string from Kubelikova 17. They desperately need funds and office equipment according to the 1991 Vegetarian Travel Guide.

Particularly recommended for vegetarians is U Góvindy, a new Hare Krishna (Haré Krna) club which promotes Indian philosophy and culture as well as providing meals from 11.00 am to 5.00 pm, Monday to Friday. U Góvindy is situated at Na hrázi 5, Praha 8 (Tel. 821 438). Take metro line B to Palmovka, walk about a hundred metres down Rudé armády, and Na hrázi is on your right.

Drinking Out

Prague offers a wonderful selection of places to drink—and very many of them will provide light (or in some cases heavy) meals as well. The architectural richness of the city ensures a range of superb settings, added to which the thriving café society of the early twentieth century, which lay dormant under communist rule, has an opportunity now to re-emerge. Unfortunately the big bucks business people moving in on the city today are not keen on traditions which extol the idea of sitting for a whole evening with a single coffee, and the cafés will have difficulty surviving. From being dens of suspected free-thinking dissidence under communism they are now regarded as insufficient "earners" under capitalism.

Looking for business at one of the restaurants in Nerudova

Places of refreshment come in various kinds. There is what is sometimes described as the equivalent of the English pub, but is in fact less kitsch and tacky, perhaps best described as a simple beer hall. Focussed on beer and the intake of alcohol, this combination of plaid tablecloths and plywood walls is known as a "*pivnice*". Then there is the equivalent of the continental café, which is focussed upon coffee, wine and liqueurs rather than beer (which it may not serve). This is the "*kavárna*", (although the French word café is quite widely used). Finally, there is the "*cukrárna*", (literally "sweetshop"), which may well provide coffee and something sweet, a useful resource for a break during days of sight-seeing. A dozen of the best (or in some cases most infamous) places together with some description of each is given at the end of the book.

29

Resilient and Resourceful, Prague and its People have Emerged from Invasion and Repression into a New Freedom

From its position at the heart of Europe, Prague has seen empires and ideologies come and go. It has been at the centre of continental wars, and yet has been miraculously preserved from their devastation. Its beauty is largely untouched, its unique atmosphere cannot be missed, and now in the 1990s it is fast becoming a vibrant modern metropolis as well as a city steeped in history.

Prague is a magical city which invites easy superlatives, especially from the writers of guide-books! The French writer Guillaume Apollinaire's description of "a golden ship sailing majestically on the Vltava" has perhaps been used often enough. But Prague is not merely beautiful: it is alluring. Time and again, people find that their first visit is only the first of many. Before they know what has happened, a casual acquaintance has become a love affair.

An example of a house sign from the Malá Strana area.

Until the Velvet Revolution in 1989 and the general disorders in so-called Eastern Europe drew attention to that part of the continent, the most popular cities in Europe tended to be the Western European capitals like London and Paris or the famous Italian cities of Venice, Florence and Rome. The "Iron Curtain" came down on the rest of Europe and for all but the most intrepid hid it from sight.

Now that curtain has been raised. The beauty and cultural sophistication of places like Budapest and Prague is once more being acknowledged. Doubtless there is always the danger of overkill when the intensive media spotlight turns upon something new. There can always be one "Prague: Czech It Out" T-shirt too many! But few would doubt that in the new interest shown in this part of the world an imbalance is being put right. Prague has always deserved more of the world's attention than it ever received during the 40-or-so years of communist rule in the post-war period.

Geography

It is a city at the heart of Europe. Any map of the continent will show that Prague is more aptly described by the old German term *Mitteleuropa* (Middle Europe) than by the more recent Eastern Europe, a term imposed more by history than by geography. It may be a surprise to hear that Prague is only 1,200 km (745 miles) from London, about the same distance as from one end of the British Isles to the other!

There is also an historical and cultural aspect to Prague's Middle European character. It is the capital of Czechoslovakia,

*P*rague and its position in Czechoslovakia and in relation to the surrounding countries.

a land-locked country bordered by Austria and Hungary to the south, while Germany and Poland lie to the north and west. It has a narrow border with the former Soviet Union at its eastern tip. Trapped like a squashed sausage between these other countries, Czechoslovakia covers a far greater distance from west to east than from north to south, and there are strong regional differences between its western part, Bohemia and Moravia, and its eastern half, Slovakia. The tensions between Czechs and Slovaks are not on the scale of those seen in the recent history of Yugoslavia when tension between Serbs and Croats erupted into violence, but they do present problems for the new post-communist government.

The city of Prague is very firmly located in the culture and attitudes of the "Czech" or western half of the country. Visitors here will probably not feel that they are part of a "Slavic" culture, in the way that visitors to the eastern half of the country will. The tall turn-of-the-century buildings which adorn so much of Prague will suggest Western cities like Trieste rather than anything further east. It is the old central European Austro-Hungarian

Prague

One of the most powerful descriptions of the city comes from *Prague Farewell* by Heda Margolius Kovaly, a brilliant analysis of life initially under Nazi and then under communist domination by a woman who survived the concentration camp only to see her Jewish husband later executed by Stalin after the notorious Slansky trial:

"Springtimes in Prague—who could forget them? Forsythias on the Letná Plain. The flowering hills of Strahov. The chestnuts of Zofin. The gulls on Jirasek Bridge. There is no other city like Prague. It is not only the beauty of the buildings, of the towers and bridges, though it is that too.

They rise up from the slopes and riverbanks in such harmony that it seems nature created them alongside its trees and flowers. But what is unique about Prague is the relation between the city and its people. Prague is not an uncaring backdrop which stands impassive, ignoring happiness and suffering alike. Prague lives in the lives of her people and they repay her with the love we usually reserve for other human beings. Prague is not an aggregate of buildings where people are born, work, and die. She is alive, sad and brave, and when she smiles with spring, her smile glistens like a tear."

Empire, tying closely together great cities like Prague and Vienna, which can be recognized in much of its appearance. In its life and art it is progressive and liberal, although racked by considerable social tensions in the post-revolutionary period. For all the dangers of generalization, there is something "Bohemian" about this part of Bohemia!

"This Little Mother"

Prague had the good fortune, unlike Berlin or Warsaw, to survive the last war virtually undamaged, although there were some terrible atrocities like the Nazis' deliberate destruction of a large part of the Old Town Hall one day before the end of the war. Under the post-war rule of the communists, it was preserved as a show-piece city. Whilst historic buildings in other parts of the country were destroyed or left to grow derelict, those in Prague were left untouched or carefully repaired, often by a painstakingly slow process brought on by a lack of resources. In many parts of Prague the scaffolding around

certain sites looks almost as historic as the buildings it is designed to preserve.

A visitor to this show-piece city in the 1980s would have encountered a strange atmosphere. There would have been a restful, coffee-house atmosphere and a nostalgic hint of past imperial glories, but little to suggest a vibrant metropolis. Visiting Prague was like stepping inside a huge open air museum. On the one hand, its fine architectural landscape remained largely untouched either by warfare or by the planning policies of the post-war communist regime, which sought to expand on the outskirts of the city rather than in its historic centre. On the other hand, repressive social policies severely constrained the extent to which it could express the lively cultural and artistic imagination that had clearly been present in the Prague of the early 20th century.

Since 1989, the city has been able to come to life in a way that was not previously possible, save perhaps in the late 1960s when the "Prague Spring" offered the first dawn of freedom of expression. The city no longer suggests anything remotely like a museum. Still fresh with the heady memories of a bloodless revolution, Prague has exploded back into vibrant life. The centre and the underground stations are full of temporary stalls either selling books, magazines and pamphlets or handing out leaflets about a new jazz club, art display or gallery. Occasionally memorabilia from the past, like communist party membership cards, busts of Stalin (the pink ones are rather attractive) or badges from the days of the Velvet Revolution are on sale. Prague still remembers the events of 1989, but can now turn on its past with humour. Some of the articles on sale reflect the seamy side of western freedom—

Changing times: after the revolution, Praguers are encouraged to become share-owners and to join the investment fund.

for instance pornography—and there is little sign in Prague of the insights which the feminist movement has brought to the West. However, the general excitement at a new-found freedom is thoroughly captivating all the same.

Walk through Prague in the 1990s and you trip over exhibitions of previously neglected talents, many of them rediscovering earlier movements from the 1910s and 1920s. Since the current president, Václav Havel, is a playwright, many of whose works were formerly banned, there is unsurprisingly a great deal of contemporary drama and fiction. Movements in art and architecture from the first half of the century and before, Art Nouveau, cubist, modernist and surreal, are being rediscovered and enhanced by contemporary work. Exhibitions explode into life in a range of venues and it is not uncommon to find a gallery dedicated to one particular subject containing a floor taken over temporarily by an exhibition from a different period or entirely separate art form.

At the same time, it would be wrong to present the change as lacking in dangers. For all their narrow-minded social policies, the communist government did preserve those cultural forms of which they approved. They also lacked the financial resources to destroy the city with development. There is a danger that the sophisticated culture of Prague may not find it easy to survive commercial pressures, and that art forms will become debased into tacky imitations designed to satisfy a tourist market.

These dangers, however, should not be exaggerated. There may be a few more pizza parlours than there used to be; there may be some hotels, like the giant Hotel Forum built by a French-based consortium and dominating the skyline of Karlín and

Žižkov, which hardly blend in with their surroundings. There is also a determination to preserve the historic character of Prague and indeed to open it up further as restoration work proceeds apace. Prague has coped far better than many other cities with a four-fold increase in foreign visitors within a single year. It knows it is now on the map, and it is not going to destroy the very things that have put it there.

Whatever the many cultural and architectural glories of a city that is made up out of centuries of development and different styles: Romanesque, Gothic, Renaissance, Baroque, Neo-Renaissance, Art Nouveau and Cubist, to name but a few; it is the atmosphere of a city that counts. The magic of Prague lies in a whole range of ingredients. There are the tumbling streets of the Malá Strana (Lesser Quarter), recently highlighted as the setting for Miloš Forman's film *Amadeus*. There are the steep lanes and steps of the paths leading up to the Castle, or the glorious archways, statues and doorways of the Old Town, where every turn in the road leads to another unexpectedly beautiful facade. There is the grand boulevard which is incongruously called Wenceslas Square, lined with hotels decked out with Art Nouveau features and topped by a self-conscious Neo-Renaissance National Museum, and there are the copper-roofed churches of the "city of a hundred towers" looked down upon from the top of the Petřin Hill above the West bank. It is a cacophony of styles but there is also a quality of wholeness about this compact city, in places stunning and awesome; in others mellow and homely. One of Prague's greatest writers, Franz Kafka, wrote of the place from which he could never escape: "Prague does not let go, either of you or of me.

This little mother has claws. There is nothing for it but to give in."

There is also an exciting political and social atmosphere about the city. Of course it has its problems, both financial and social. Crime has risen, there are bitter arguments about immigration, and occasional outbreaks of racist violence, although not as pronounced as in Germany, and the familiar problem of rising unemployment and inflation which has hit the former communist societies of Eastern Europe. But there is also an unpretentious enthusiasm for and confidence in the future. And it is still undoubtedly a safer city to walk around in by day or night than most Western cities.

There can be few countries which, like Czechoslovakia, have come to be ruled by a former absurdist playwright. Indeed President Václav Havel was reluctant to

You can't go far in Prague without seeing a picture of Václav Havel, President since the revolution of 1989.

give up the theatre for the world stage, and refused to live in the presidential palace in Hradčany Castle after his victory in 1989, preferring a riverside apartment block that was part of a terrace built by his grandfather! At the nearby fish restaurant Na Rybárne on Gorazdova in the New Town they keep a table reserved for him, and he frequently eats there. It gives him more of an entitlement to be called a "man of the people" than the leaders of the "people's republic" who preceded him and preferred to occupy the presidential apartments up in the castle.

The political humour of Prague is well pronounced, and stretches back through decades of poster art and cartoons. It can be seen in Havel himself. When he became President he exchanged black motorcades for multi-coloured ones, and

Václav Havel: From Absurdist Playwright to President
Born in Prague in 1936, Havel assumed power in the best way possible—reluctantly, rather than sacrificing everybody and everything in a bid for glory. In the 1960s he worked as a playwright at the Divadlo na zábradlí (Anenské náměstí), during the years of social and political thaw that led to the brief Prague Spring. Two of the poems he wrote then, and published in his Antíkody, provide a commentary upon the "normalization" process that was to follow the crushing of the Prague Spring by Red Army tanks in 1968.

1. FORWARD.

FORWARD

FORWARD   FORWARD

FORWARD   FORWARD

FORWARD   FORWARD

FORWARD   FORWARD

FORWARD   FORWARD

FORWARD   FORWARD

FORWARD   FORWARD

FORWARD

2. STALINIST PHILOSOPHY.
!!!!!!!!!!!!!!!!!!!!!!!!
!!!!!!!!!!!!!!!!!!!!!!!!
!!!!!!!!!!!!!!!!!!!!!!!!
!!!!!!!!!!!!!!!!!!!!!!!!
!!!!!!!!!!!!!!!!!!!!!!!!
!!!!!!!!!!!!!!!!!?!!!!!!
!!!!!!!!!!!!!!!!!!!!!!!!

decked out the national guard in new Ruritanian-style uniforms, designed by a film costumier friend of his to replace the drab brown of the communist years.

A brief and unfortunately rapidly reversed decision, following a night on the town with Frank Zappa and Lou Reed in 1990, to make Frank Zappa the Czechoslovakian cultural envoy at large, might also be taken to illustrate the President's political humour, although some of us would see it merely as good taste!

The tank is a familiar theme of Prague humour, for obvious reasons. The city was liberated by Soviet tanks in 1945, and then its spirit was crushed by tanks from the same source in 1968. In 1990 posters appeared all over the city advertising the Rolling Stones concert which was to take place in the Spartakiádní Stadion, once the venue for huge communist rallies, bearing the words "The tanks are rolling out. The Stones are rolling in." A cardboard tank appeared at the same time in Wenceslas Square, an excellent climbing frame for children and focus for graffiti artists. A year later the Soviet tank placed on a stone plinth in the Smíchov district to commemorate the city's liberation by the Red Army in May 1945 disappeared after the bemused authorities discovered that it had been painted pink overnight and hung with the label "Trojský Kůň", Trojan Horse. Most people in the city remember the tanks which rolled in twenty-three years later, in 1968, to crush the "Prague Spring", more than they recall the genuine liberation of 1945. An absurdist and sometimes black political humour, born of years underground during the period of communist rule, now offers a more public commentary on events.

Compared with many others, Prague is not a large capital. Its total population is barely 1¼ million, and its main sights are contained in a compact central region around the River Vltava, all of them well within walking range. Its dimensions are more those of an Amsterdam than a London or a Paris, but no one should be in any doubt that there is enough within those dimensions to satisfy a visit of several days.

In addition to this convenience, a superb public transport system connects all parts of the city day and night. The latter facility is useful as Prague's night-life has opened up since the Revolution of 1989, and there are plenty of bars, jazz clubs, discotheques and casinos open until the early hours. They are growing at such a rate that the listings you find when out there will almost certainly be a necessary addition to the information in this guide. Prague has a unique combination of ease of discovery and a wealth of things to discover. Its wonderful atmosphere continues through street after unforgettable street. Its beauty grips because it is both real and surreal. On the one hand, no one can deny the wealth of architectural glory that any guide-book can happily list: cathedral, castle, churches, bridges, streets and so on. On the other hand, there are the images of a world that is not so real-where people live a "Bohemian" life ("If people hear you're from Prague, they take it for granted that you're a writer", commented popular journalist Egon Erwin Kisch at the beginning of the century) in a city topped with a fairyland castle and full of numerous architectural eccentricities wrought by a millenium of change.

Prague is a city that holds the imagination both as reality and as fantasy. To return to the thoughts of Czech writer Egon Erwin Kisch (1885–1948), author of *Prague Adventures* and *Tales from Prague's Streets and Nights*:

*B*oating on the Vltava.

"Prague is magic, something that ties you down and holds you and always brings you back. You can never forget."

History

Prague was founded over a thousand years ago because of a woman's dream on a hilltop now known as Vyšehrad. Since then it has experienced periods of fame and times of obscurity. In the 14th century it was treated as the heart of his empire by Charles IV. In the 17th century it was treated as a provincial city in their empire by the Hapsburg rulers. Now, at the end of the 20th century, it has won its independence from the Stalinist empire of the former Soviet Union, and is set to flourish as an independent city at the heart of Europe.

The historical sections for the different areas of Prague described later in the guide fill out much of the detail of Prague's development. What is offered here is a short summary of the city's history.

The Origins of Prague

The oldest settlements in the area date back thousands of years, when roving tribes moved to and fro in Bohemia through the hills alongside the River Vltava. Small trading settlements formed at various points on the banks of the river in the centuries before Christ, particularly on the western side in what are now the Castle and Lesser Quarter areas. The origins of the city, however, lie at the point when these settlements became permanent enough to look for ways of fortifying themselves against attack, in a period around the 8th or 9th centuries AD.

Tradition is that the city was founded by Princess Libuše, youngest daughter of Prince Krok, who was endowed with the gift of prophecy. She foretold a city whose glory would "touch the stars":

"The time will come when two golden olive trees will grow in this city. Their tops will reach the seventh heaven and they will shine throughout the world through signs and wonders."

According to legend, her followers went to the place she described, and there founded the city of Prague. One interpretation identifies the spot as one where a ploughman (*přemysl*) was building the door-sill (*práh*) of his house, an explanation both of the name of the city and of the Přemyslid dynasty which was to rule Bohemia until the 14th century. It explains the name of the dynasty because Krok had three daughters but no son; and Libuše, prone to throwing her lovers off the cliff at Vyšehrad, was finally wed to the sturdy ploughman who was too heavy to throw off the cliff and by whom she bore sons.

A more prosaic view is that the city was the outcome of a power struggle between rival groups in Bohemia, the Slavnik and the Přemyslid tribes. The Přemyslids eventually prevailed and sealed their supremacy by establishing a fortified settlement on the relatively impenetrable outcrop on the banks of the Vltava that is the present site of Prague Castle.

Under the Přemyslids, Prague took advantage of its strategic position on the Central European trading routes and developed a tendency which it has always possessed, that of looking Westwards rather than Eastwards. The Magyars (fore-

runners of modern Hungarians) were expelled, and links with the West reaching as far as Rome were cultivated. In the 10th century its status was enhanced by the granting of a bishopric, and by the 13th century merchants from all over Europe were settling here.

Another tendency which was to last developed in this period too, namely hostility between Germans and Czechs. Under the reign of King Wenceslas I in the mid-13th century, German merchants were invited to Prague and given a measure of self-government, a facility which came under the scrutiny of the local nobility. Malá Strana was founded later in the century for the German traders, at the expense of a Jewish community which was unceremoniously thrown out, and the feeling of colonization intensified among those native to Bohemia.

*S*tatue of Charles IV at the Old Town entrance to the Charles Bridge.

The Golden Age and After

Prague's first golden age came in the 14th century under the Holy Roman Emperor Charles IV, whose name is associated with the foundation of so much of the city—its university, its cathedral (the bishopric was now raised to an archbishopric); several religious establishments; a new bridge over the Vltava River (which has survived 600 years of torrents and floods) and the New Town area. This area was originally conceived as student accommodation to cope with the influx of people to the new university, which was the first university in Central Europe, attracting large numbers from as far away as England. Charles chose Prague as his imperial residence and spared no effort in developing its international importance, whilst at the same time promoting the Czech language and the historical traditions of the city associated with the Přemyslids and Wenceslas. Artists and scholars flocked to the new "Rome of the North". By this time the population of Prague had reached 40,000, a sizeable figure by medieval standards.

After the death of Charles IV, however, a period of turmoil and decline followed. The Hussite movement, named after reformer Jan Hus, forerunner of many of the ideas of Martin Luther a century later, developed a radical social and religious programme. This led among other things, to the first of Prague's many "defenestrations", giving a whole new meaning to the idea of asking someone you disagree with to "leave the room". For over a century the Hussites provided dogged resistance to imperial forces right across parts of what are now Germany, Austria and Czechoslovakia, but the resistance in Bohemia was always the most effective and dangerous.

In the end, however, the Hussite forces were overcome, and Prague suffered for its association with them. The imperial Hapsburg dynasty increasingly dominated the area, and were making it clear that once they'd dealt with the Turks, recalcitrant forces in Bohemia would be next! When, in the early 17th century, the Czech Princes rose up against the Hapsburgs, things were finally settled by the Battle of the White Mountain (*bílá hora*).

The philosopher Descartes was a mercenary with the Catholic forces at the time, and legend has it that he was wounded. On recovering consciousness, his first words on realising that he was alive and not dead were: "I think, therefore I am". The sort of obvious statement which wouldn't turn a hair in a bus queue will get philosophers scribbling for centuries.

In subsequent years Prague lost its independence and was effectively subordinated to the Austro-Hungarian Empire for 300 years. This was a remnant of the old Holy Roman Empire which had dominated Western and Central Europe. Vienna's star waxed as that of Prague waned, although the city saw the construction of some of its finest Baroque buildings during this period, much of it overseen by the Jesuits who arrived in 1600 to Catholicize an overwhelmingly Protestant population. In this endeavour they succeeded remarkably well.

By 1800 the population of the city had only doubled to 80,000 from its heyday four centuries earlier. The 19th century, however, saw an influx of people from rural areas to Prague as part of the impact of the European industrial revolution. At the same time, a rising tide of national consciousness, expressed in heavy Neo-Renaissance buildings like the National Theatre and the National Museum, made it a symbol of the struggle for national recognition. Efforts were made to redevelop the Czech language, which had virtually died out after the Battle of the White Mountain, to be replaced by the ever-present and ever-resented German. There was a sense that time was on the side of the Czechs. The Austro-Hungarian empire was in a state of collapse, whereas the Bohemian soul was being stirred as never before by Dvořák, Smetana and writers like František Palacký.

Recent Events

That said, the historical situation was not a simple one. Some further developments were necessary before Bohemia became incorporated into what is now Czechoslovakia. In the east of the country the Slovakians protested against Hungarian rule. The new country was born as the product of two communities, Czechs and Slovaks, with a joint experience of external rule but with little else in common.

In 1918 Prague finally became the centre of an independent, newly-formed Czechoslovak state. It rapidly increased in size and significance until the arrival of German troops, as a consequence of the Munich agreement, once more threw the country back into occupation by outside forces. The one fortunate outcome of this process was that Prague, unlike other great European capitals, was largely untouched by the devastation of war.

Tho Tanks Roll In . . .

The city was liberated by the Red Army in 1945, four days after the Prague uprising against Nazi rule which left part of the Old Town Hall burned down and thousands of people dead. The 3,000,000-strong German-speaking minority was expelled. Three years later Czechoslovakia became a socialist republic (ČSSR) under

*S*tanislav Sucharda's extravagant Art Nouveau monument to 19th-century Czech historian and nationalist František Palacký.

41

communist control, effectively controlled by the former Soviet Union. When the notorious Klement Gottwald took over as President in 1948, he did the time-honoured thing with his leading political opponent, foreign minister Jan Masaryk, son of Tomaš Masaryk who effectively founded Czechoslovakia by persuading American President Woodrow Wilson to support it. Masaryk hit the ground after a "fall" from his office window from which there was no hope of recovery.

Czechoslovakia settled down to a period of repression. Gottwald went to Stalin's funeral in 1953, caught pneumonia and died (they called it "Moscow flu"), but it was not until a decade later that the first liberalising tendencies that were to issue in the "Prague Spring" came to the fore. They were short-lived. Armies from five Warsaw Pact countries (Rumania refused) invaded, and in place of Dubček "resistance hero" Gustáv Husák was installed to begin the process of "normalisation".

The 1977 human rights manifesto, Charter 77, showed that liberalism had not been extinguished, but the level of opposition to the puppet government was slight. Ironically, the Velvet Revolution was partly unleashed by the impact of events in Germany, the country which Czechoslovakia had for so long regarded as a virtual colonizer. It was the destruction of the Berlin Wall, and the flood of East German refugees into the West German embassy in Prague in early November 1989, that sparked off the upsurge of popular protest which was to bring the communist government down.

. . . and Out Again

After ten days of turmoil the communist party finally resigned. A new coalition government, Obšanské Fórum, under former playwright and dissident Václav Havel, assumed power in November 1989. However, any coalition tends to lose its unity when it ceases to have a common enemy, and there is a great deal of conflict in government circles today. Slovak nationalists, right-wing monetarists, and liberals like Havel, occasionally looking a little less liberal than he is supposed to be, fight it out for supremacy. But one thing is clear. There can be no turning back. The fissiparous tendencies in Eastern Europe and in the former Soviet Union itself have put Czechoslovakia's independence beyond doubt. Prague is once more a free city in a free country-although not without many of the problems which freedom brings.

For most of its history, therefore, Prague has been the centre of a country which has been part of a wider Empire, whether the Austro-Hungarian Hapsburg Empire of the 17th to 19th centuries or the communist empire of the 20th. Before that it knew periods of greatness based on royal patronage (during the reign of Charles IV), or the prosperity generated by its trading situation (as in earlier centuries), but its position in these times was always precarious, subject to plunder, invasion and neglect.

This increasingly lively and vibrant capital, which throughout its history has maintained strong links with the West, whether commercial, cultural or artistic, will almost certainly enter the 21st century as one of the most exciting places to live in and to visit. Whatever bitter memories of the past there may be, there is no shortage of humour or of confidence about the times to come in a city that still feels the heady thrill of liberation, however uncertain the future may be.

Religion

Whether or not under communist rule, Prague's life and its history have been full of religion. It has also had its fair share of the most basic of Christian conflicts, that between Protestant and Catholic.

Throughout the medieval period, when Roman Catholicism was the required religion of all loyal citizens (for political and religious affiliation were regarded as inseparable), there were sporadic outbreaks of protest against various church practices. One of these came from Jan Hus, Rector of Charles University in Prague from 1402.

Hus would always have seen himself as a Catholic. Many of his beliefs, however, such as the right to preach in his native tongue rather than in Latin, or to administer wine as well as bread to the congregation at the Eucharist or communion service, enraged the ecclesiastical authorities. He was summoned to explain himself before a General Council of the Church at Constance. Promised a safe conduct, he soon found himself locked up, and on 6 July 1416 burned at the stake. His ashes were poured out over the Rhine. The burning of Hus doubtless contributed to the feelings that led to Prague's first defenestration four years later, when a number of Catholic councillors were thrown out of a window in Prague and killed with pikes if they survived the fall.

Hus had many ideas which anticipated those of Martin Luther and the rise of Protestantism a century later. By the mid-16th century Protestant feeling was strong in Bohemia, although always laced with nationalistic opposition to the Hapsburgs. By the early 1600s something like 90 per cent of the city was Protestant, but the next century was to see a resurgence of Catholicism, the "Counter-Reformation", particularly after the Battle of the White Mountain in 1620. By a combination of brutal repression and beautification (beheading on the one hand, Baroque on the other), the Hapsburgs consolidated their position in their way, with a single religion (Catholicism) for a single European empire.

But Christianity has never simply been a matter of Protestants and Catholics—that is how the Western Church views it, but Prague, at the heart of Europe, also has experience of Eastern Christendom. To understand the full range of Christian belief in the city, one must also recognize the importance of the Orthodox.

The Orthodox Church emerged in the 11th century after a dispute between Rome and Constantinople, ostensibly over the right of the Bishop of Rome to possess more than a "first among equals" authority. Orthodoxy is particularly prevalent in what was Eastern Europe and the Soviet Union—originally it took hold in the Greek-speaking as opposed to the Latin-speaking part of the Holy Roman Empire. If anything, it is liturgically and doctrinally more conservative than Catholicism, but because of its particular opposition to the primacy of one bishop, that of Rome, it exists as a federation of Orthodox churches: Russian Orthodox; Greek Orthodox; Syrian Orthodox and so on. An example of an orthodox church in Prague is the Church of Saints Cyril and Methodius in Resslova near Charles Square in the New Town.

Just to complicate things further, there exist Uniate Churches in Prague, as in other parts of Eastern Europe, which have the distinctive rites of the Orthodox churches whilst remaining in communion with the Church of Rome—a kind of halfway house between Catholicism and Orthodoxy. An example of a Uniate Church in Prague is St Clement's (sv. Kliment) in Karlova, next to the Klementinum, a short distance into the Old

Modernist church built by Jože Plečnik in George of Poděbrady Square.

Town across the road from the Charles Bridge.

The 20th century has seen a more complicated picture emerge. Early nationalist trends saw a re-emphasis upon Protestantism, and in 1918 the Unity of Czech Brethren or Czech national church was formed-the best example is the Church of St Nicholas in the Old Town Square. This church can ultimately be traced back to Hussite ideas via the earlier Unity of Bohemian Brethren.

Communist persecution drove religious feeling underground but did not destroy it. A number of churches were looted and closed, and children had to learn "scientific atheism", a subject which would even make religious studies sound like an interesting subject at school.

Since the Velvet Revolution it has not only been churches but also sects which have taken advantage of the new freedom to proselytize. In the summer of 1991 Prague was full of thousands of Jehovah's Witnesses, sporting badges and smiling nicely. The previous year the Dalai Lama visited Prague and spent a day meditating for peace with the President. Seventh-Day Adventists have a church in the city at Korunni 60.

Unlike Poland, where Catholicism was a focus for opposition to communist repression, Prague with its traditions of Hussitism knows that Catholicism has itself been repressive. Prague's liberal traditions were less attuned to religious fervour anyway, and whilst in 1990 a lot of young people wore crucifixes to express the triumph over communism in the previous year, by 1991 that habit had largely died out. Many people in Prague, not least because of Czech hostility to deeply Catholic Slovakia, would as little like to see Catholicism dominant again in the city as communism.

No account of religion in Prague should omit Judaism. Whilst the details are covered in the section on Josefov, it should be noted that Prague's Jews now number under a thousand. In 1700 one in four of the population was Jewish, and in 1939 one in twenty. The figure is now less than one in a thousand, a mark of the terrible destruction wrought by the Nazis upon a city's life and culture.

The shrine to Mary, focus of the Loreto complex.

Just the Essentials

This choice of the really best places to go in Prague is, inevitably, subjective, but it may help you decide on an itinerary. On a first-time visit you may be overwhelmed by the wealth of choice you have wherever you start. The major landmarks and places to see are proposed here to help you establish priorities.

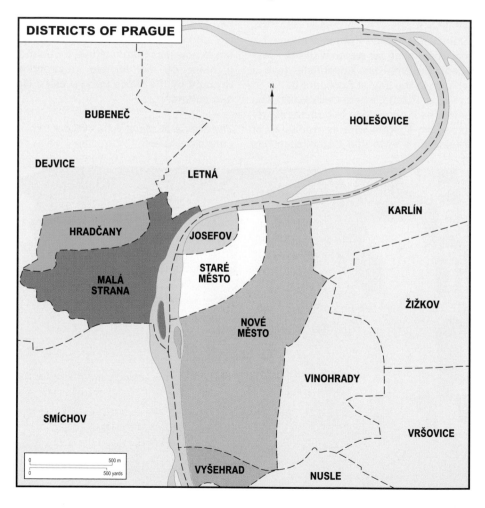

DISTRICTS OF PRAGUE

BUBENEČ

HOLEŠOVICE

DEJVICE

LETNÁ

KARLÍN

HRADČANY

JOSEFOV

STARÉ
MĚSTO

MALÁ
STRANA

ŽIŽKOV

NOVÉ
MĚSTO

VINOHRADY

SMÍCHOV

VRŠOVICE

VYŠEHRAD

NUSLE

Josefov

Old-New Synagogue: oldest surviving synagogue in Europe; still used for worship.

Old Jewish Cemetery: crowded and fascinating; oldest tombstone dated 1439.

"House of Ceremonies": 19th-century house; display of children's artwork from concentration camp.

Prague Castle

St Vitus' Cathedral: large and impressive, the product of many different styles of architecture.

Royal Palace: Vladislav Hall and views from the palace.

Convent of St George: old Bohemian art collection.

Powder Tower: houses variety of exhibitions and reconstruction of alchemist's laboratory.

Royal Gardens: Belvedere Palace.

Sternberg Palace: wonderful collection of art.

Strahov Monastery.

Malá Strana

Charles Bridge over the River Vltava.

Lesser Town Square: Church of St Nicholas.

Nebozízek: first stop on funicular for finest views of city.

Nerudova: house signs and views.

Nové Město

Wenceslas Square: especially a drink at the Hotel Evropa.

Municipal House: Art Nouveau treasure trove.

National Theatre: expression of Czech pride and national identity.

Vila Amerika: Dvořák Museum.

Staré Město

Old Town Square, arguably the best sight in Prague.

Astronomical Clock.

Týn Church, especially the portal of the entrance to the north side nave.

Estates (Tyl) Theatre: the oldest theatre building in Prague.

Ethnological Museum.

Klementinum: former Jesuit college.

Rott Haus: neo-Renaissance house.

Convent of St Agnes.

Vyšehrad

Vyšehrad gardens overlooking the River Vltava.

Slavin Cemetery: full of distinguished representatives of Czech art and culture.

A walk along the fortress walls.

30 Neklanova: one of the best examples of Prague's Cubist architecture.

Other Districts

Výstaviště: exhibition centre and amusement park.

Troja Palace: late 17th-century model of an Italian country residence.

Around Prague

Kutná Hora: Cathedral of St Barbara; Ossuary with remains of about 10,000 people; many made into pieces of modern art.

Mělník.

Karlovy Vary: spa town.

Karlštejn Castle.

Going Somewhere with Something Special in Mind

Despite its relatively small size for a capital city, Prague has an abundance of sights, and one way of organising your visit is to plan it around particular themes. These are a few suggestions about how to do so.

Panoramic Prague

With a "fairy tale castle" on a hill, the winding river Vltava down below and a mass of towers and domes on either side of it, Prague offers amazing views from several vantage-points. Here are some of the best.

1 LETNÁ PLAIN

The site of the former Stalin Monument on the edge of the Letná Plain is an ideal spot to look down on the rest of Prague from the point where the watchful granite countenance of "Uncle Joe" once

An exhibit on display in the National Gallery, part of Prague's rich artistic heritage.

surveyed the city. A giant metronome now stands in place of Stalin.

2 NEBOZÍZEK

First stop on the funicular railway up the Petřín Hill in Malá Strana is Nebozízek, where an excellent café provides food and refreshments. Some of the best views of Prague, both across the river to the Old Town and over the gardens and orchards of the Petřín Hill towards the castle, are to be found at this spot.

3 KE HRADU

If you've made the steep climb to the castle up Nerudova or via the steep castle steps (Zámecké schody), don't forget to look back when you reach the top. There is a breathtaking view of Prague from several of vantage-points in this area.

4 VYŠEHRAD

There is nowhere in Prague more suffused with legend and mythology than the craggy edge of the park which looks out over the River Vltava at the spot known as Libuse's Bath. The path along the edge of the rock offers one of the most beautiful views in the city.

5 VYŠEHRAD

This is nother striking panorama in Vyšehrad, this time looking in the opposite direction over the Botič valley towards the red domes of the New Town. It is right next to the metro station, on the concrete promenade outside the Palace of Culture.

6 NATIONAL MONUMENT

Formerly a communist mausoleum, this ugly granite building in the heart of Žižkov has very little to recommend it, but it does provide some good views of the city and will almost certainly offer you a quiet walk away from the tourist throng.

7 OLD TOWN HALL

The view from the top of the Old Town Hall provides not only a wonderful panorama of the whole city, but an interesting perspective on the Old Town Square itself. Look down on those steep daddled Gothic roofs which are otherwise hidden from view behind the Baroque façades that are all that is visible at ground level. The surreal quality of Prague's many jumbled-up periods and styles is very striking from a height.

8 POWDER TOWER

Another view which requires a climb, and providing a similar perspective to that offered by the Old Town Hall.

The Architecture of Prague

The city of Prague contains an enormous variety of architectural styles—indeed this is true of many of its buildings, which have often been rebuilt or partially replaced at a later period in another form. Rather than concentrate on particular styles, this section offers examples of the diversity of Prague.

9 CHARLES BRIDGE

Gothic gateways lead onto a 14th-century bridge decorated with Baroque statues designed to popularize the Counter-Reformation onslaught on Protestantism. Strangely, the Prague magic has made of this bizarre architectural mixture something unique and awesome.

10 ST NICHOLAS' CHURCH, MALÁ STRANA

This church spanned the heyday of Baroque and ended up with a twirl or two of Rococo. It is probably Prague's most impressive church.

11 ST VITUS' CATHEDRAL

Largely Gothic, but with some Baroque additions and a smattering of Romanesque. Rather crunched up inside the castle walls, but still a very impressive part of the sky-line and with a fascinating interior.

12 BELVEDERE PALACE

Probably the finest example of Renaissance architecture in the city, the Belvedere summer-house is situated at the far end of the Royal Gardens. It was designed by Paolo della Stella, a Genovese architect who settled in the city in the 16th century.

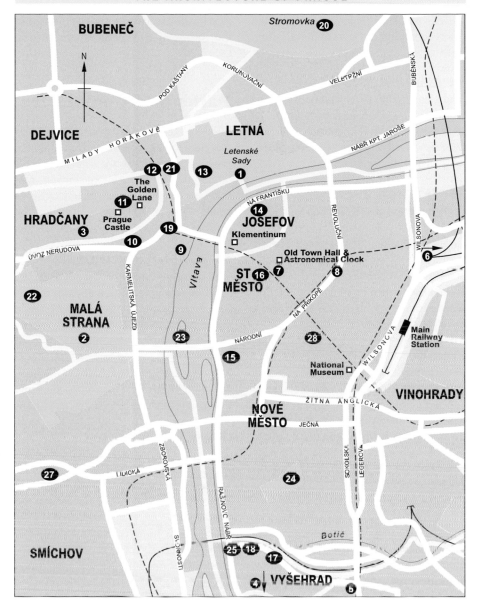

BUBENEČ

Stromovka 20

N

KORUMOVAČNÍ

POD KAŠTANY

VELETRŽNÍ

BUBENSKÁ

DEJVICE

MILADY HORÁKOVĚ

LETNÁ

Letenské Sady

NÁBŘ KPT. JAROŠE

12 21 13 1

The Golden Lane

11

NA FRANTIŠKU

14

JOSEFOV

REVOLUČNÍ

WILSONOVA

HRADČANY 3

Prague Castle

19

Klementinum

10

9

Vltava

Old Town Hall & Astronomical Clock

6

ÚVOZ NERUDOVA

KARMELITSKÁ ÚJEZD

ST 16 7 **MĚSTO**

8

22

MALÁ STRANA 2

23

NÁRODNÍ

NA PŘÍKOPĚ

28

WILSONOVA

Main Railway Station

15

National Museum

VINOHRADY

ŽITNÁ ANGLICKÁ

NOVÉ MĚSTO

JEČNÁ

ZBOROVSKÁ

SOKOLSKÁ

LEGEROVA

27

LIDICKÁ

24

RAŠÍNOVC NÁBŘ

SVORNOSTI

Botič

SMÍCHOV

25 18

17

VYŠEHRAD 6

13 HANAVA PAVILION

No visit to Prague can ignore its Art Nouveau architecture. This Art Nouveau exhibition piece, cast from iron in the foundries of the Prince of Hanava (hence its name), was built for the Jubilee Exhibition of 1891. It was transferred to its

*P*anoramic views, and the main architectural sights and parks in Prague.

present parkland location in 1898, and offers some superb views of the city from its terrace.

14 OLD-NEW SYNAGOGUE

Completed in the 14th-century, this is the oldest surviving synagogue in Europe. Its early Gothic South Hall is much older, and the five-ribbed vaulting is unique in Bohemian architecture.

15 NATIONAL THEATRE

Built in a heavy neo-Renaissance style reflecting self-conscious 19th-century Czech nationalism, the National Theatre is similar in style to the National Museum at the top of Wenceslas Square. Make sure you manage to see its sumptuous interior, whether or not you're an avid fan of opera.

16 HOUSE OF THE LORDS OF KUNŠTÁT AND PODĚBRADY

The Romanesque style in Prague is largely hidden, partly because it is its oldest style and partly because it was buried in the mediaeval period by attempts to raise the level of the Old Town to avoid flooding. This building gives some idea of the original style of the Old Town before its "Gothicization".

17 ST MARTIN'S ROTUNDA

A beautiful 11th-century circular church, built in a style of Romanesque which was unique to the Czech lands. It is the oldest of the three rotundas still in existence, and represents the oldest complete church in Prague.

18 30 NEKLANOVA

The Cubist architecture of Prague is not to be missed. The corner block on Neklanova is a good example of this style, but note also number 2 at the end of the street and then the house with the zig-zag railings on the Rašínovo embankment overlooking the river.

Parks and Cemeteries

This is a "getting away from it all" section designed to help you find escape from the crowds. A cemetery may not be everyone's idea of relaxation, but in fact Prague's cemeteries are welcome areas of peace and quiet in what, for much of the year, is a bustling city.

19 WALDSTEIN GARDENS

One of many "secretive" gardens in the Malá Strana area. Reached from an entrance in Letenská, the gardens are a venue for chamber concerts in the summer months.

20 STROMOVKA PARK

Perfect for a stroll on the way to the Troja Château or the city's zoo, this large park was once a hunting ground for the castle nobility.

21 CHOTKOVY SADY

The name of Prague's first public park. It is next door to the Royal Gardens in the castle area, but unlike them is never packed with tourists. Relax next to the white marble figures carved in a rocky grotto to commemorate the poet Julius Zeyer.

22 STRAHOV GARDENS

All around the top of the Petřín Hill is attractive, but the best views are to be found on the winding paths around the Strahov monastery. You can either walk down to the Lesser Quarter or up through the orchards into the woods at the top.

23 STŘELECKÝ OSTROV (SHOOTER'S ISLAND)

Once a target area for shooting practice, and later on the scene for "spontaneous" May Day demonstrations, this island, reached from the most Legii, holds garden theatre during the summer months.

24 BOTANIC GARDENS

Not over-full of exotic flora, but not over-full of people either. A good place to relax and read.

25 VYŠEHRAD GARDENS

Always quiet, full of interesting objects like the devil's pillars and the monumental Myslbek statues, and offering superb views of the rest of the city. This is one of the best places in Prague for a half-day away from the crowds.

26 OLŠANY CEMETERY

One of many large cemeteries (off map) to the east of Vinohrady (note the New Jewish cemetery on its eastern edge). Well tended, architecturally diverse, and a good place to recall Prague's disappearing past.

27 LESSER TOWN CEMETERY

To be found in the Smíchov district of Prague, and can be tied in with a visit to Bertramka, the Mozart museum, which is probably the only other sight in the area.

28 FRANCISCAN GARDENS

Not large, but situated right in the heart of the city next to Wenceslas Square. The gardens are attached to the Church of Our Lady of the Snows, which is itself all too often missed by those scurrying along from the bottom of Wenceslas Square towards Národní (you can reach the blissfully quiet courtyard of the church from an opening on Jungmann Square).

Sport in Prague

Ice-hockey and tennis are probably the main areas of sporting success for which the Czechs are renowned, but this does not necessarily mean that facilities abound for visitors. If you're staying in a plush hotel then there will probably be a "fitness centre" and a number of sporting facilities. If not, the following facilities are available.

1 SWIMMING

Useful enough if you're visiting during the summer. The Czech for swimming-pool is *plovárna*, and there are a range to choose from. This one was built in 1840.

2 ROWING BOATS

These can be hired during the summer from Slovanský ostrov (Žofín island) near the National Theatre.

3 BOWLING

Try the Hotel Forum near Vyšehrad metro station (off map to the south). There is also a fitness centre and one of the city's few squash courts if you don't find bowling energetic enough.

4 TENNIS

There are tennis courts (tenisový dvorce) on the Letná Plain. Tel. 37 36 83 to reserve a place.

5 ICE SKATING

There is a rink on Štvanice island (ostrov Štvanice) on the edge of the New Town.

6 FITNESS CENTRE

Following the advice of the song, you can always try the YMCA! At Na Poříčí 12.

7 SOCCER

Sparta Prague is a football team of

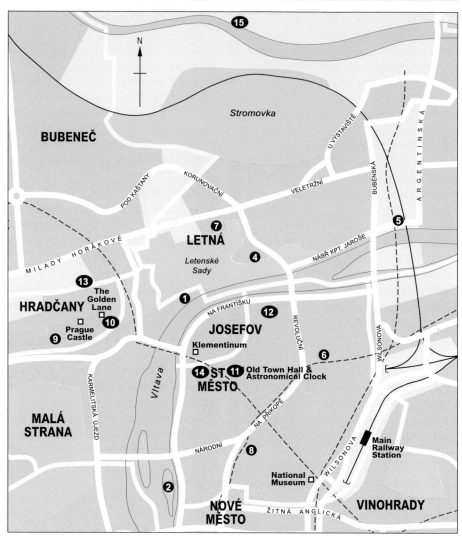

N

Stromovka

BUBENEČ

KORUNOVAČNÍ

POD KAŠTANY

VELETRŽNÍ

BUBENSKÁ

U VÝSTAVIŠTĚ

ARGENTINSKÁ

⑮

⑤

⑦

LETNÁ

Letenské
Sady

④

NÁBŘ KPT. JAROŠE

MILADY HORÁKOVÉ

⑬

The
Golden
Lane

HRADČANY Lane

①

NA FRANTIŠKU

⑫

JOSEFOV

REVOLUČNÍ

WILSONOVA

⑩

Prague
Castle

⑨

Klementinum

⑥

⑭ ST. ⑪ Old Town Hall &
MĚSTO   Astronomical Clock

KARMELITSKÁ ÚJEZD

Vltava

MALÁ
STRANA

NA PŘÍKOPĚ

NÁRODNÍ

⑧

Main
Railway
Station

WILSONOVA

②

National
Museum

NOVÉ
MĚSTO

ŽITNÁ   ANGLICKÁ

VINOHRADY

Exhibitions of Art

*S*porting venues and the
main art exhibition centres.

international renown. See them at the
Sparta Praha Stadion in Letná. The national team will play matches here also.

8 BUYING SPORTS EQUIPMENT

Head for Dům sportu on Jungmannova 28.

The main exhibition venues are all part of
Prague's National Gallery (Národní Galerie). Though they are listed elsewhere (in
the section on Art and Architecture), it
will be useful to identify some of them
here also.

9 EUROPEAN PAINTERS

The Sternberg Palace close to Prague

Castle has a wide-ranging collection. The room devoted to French art and sculpture in the 19th and 20th centuries is particularly fine. Doze off happily in the courtyard afterwards.

10 CZECH GOTHIC AND BAROQUE ART
This may sound rather parochial, but in fact it's one of the most interesting exhibitions in Prague—especially the Gothic art. Located in St George's Convent, part of the castle complex.

11 GRAPHIC ART
The Golz-Kinsky Palace in the Old Town Square hosts a collection of interesting graphic art.

12 18TH AND 19TH CENTURY CZECH ART
The emphasis is very much on romantic art in a 19th century nationalist mode, but the setting in St Agnes' Convent is fine and there are some very good individual items.

13 and 14 MODERN ART
Temporary exhibitions abound in this recently liberated style. The excellent exhibition of Cubist art may still be continuing opposite the entrance to the Royal Gardens in the castle area (5), whilst the City Library (Městská knihovna) in Mariánské náměstí (6) contains exhibitions of modern art on its upper floors.

15 TROJA CHATEAU
The reason for including this is that Prague's only château contains some of the most interesting wall and ceiling paintings in the city (as well as sculptures in the gardens). Note in particular the Great Hall).

Drinking and "Clubbing" in Prague
There are many places to choose from, but this list is put together on the assumption that atmosphere will be your top priority.

1 CAFÉ SLAVIA
Opposite the National Theatre on Národní. A place to have a range of alcoholic or non-alcoholic drinks and snacks that can fill the gap. Good views from the window-seats, and the sort of place that always looks full but always has a free place somewhere.

2 EVROPA HOTEL
The terrace on the edge of Wenceslas Square is a great favourite, but for Art Nouveau decor you should venture inside.

3 OBECNÍ DŮM
The Art Nouveau elegance of the Municipal House makes it a fine venue for refreshment although you may find the service very slow. There is a night-club downstairs which is often the best place for drinks during the day.

4 U FLEKŮ
Horrifically tacky drinking den which will remain ever popular despite anything I could suggest if lines of tables jam packed with an international cast of beer-swillers is your idea of heaven, head for the clock at Křemencova 11

5 MAMMA KLUB
A wonderful den of iniquity, part-hippie, part-anarchist, but always relaxed and interesting. Small cover charge. Head for Elišky Krásnohorské 7 in Josefov. Great place for corrupted high school revolutionaries and the Allen Ginsberg fan club.

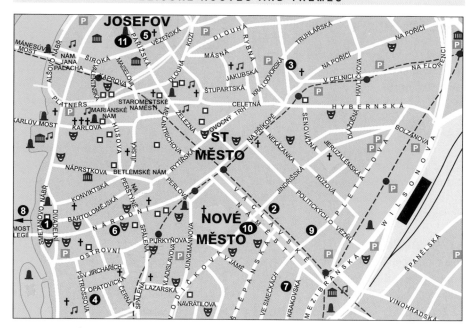

*A*tmospheric places to drink or "club".

6 NÁRODNÍ 20

The Reduta Jazz Club and the Rock Café are both here. Start with the Reduta, probably the best jazz club in town; then move on to the Rock Café which is open until 3.00 a.m.

7 AGARTHA JAZZ CENTRUM

Located at Krakovská 5 off the top of Wenceslas Square, this is a new jazz club with a pleasant atmosphere, open till midnight. Jazz records on sale at the entrance.

8 BORÁT

This "alternative" club only recently acquired a name—previously it was just known as Ujezd (the street where it is located, at number 18). Small entrance fee, many rooms, very friendly, and open late (2.00 a.m. at least).

9 SUPRACLUB

Situated just off Wenceslas Square at Opletalova 5, this club is very pleasant by night and day. There are jazz performances at week-ends.

10 F-CLUB

If you want to go night-clubbing in Wenceslas Square, this is your most atmospheric venue. Not sleazy, not packed with tourists and not a rip-off. You find it on the right-hand side of Wenceslas Square as you face the National Museum. Look for the sign on the wall.

11 PRESS JAZZ CLUB

A big barn of a place, but friendly and there's always a seat. Drinks, snacks and avant-garde jazz. Located on Pařížská.

12 U LORETY

If you're in the castle area (off map), this is the place for a seat outdoors with a drink and snack: Loreto Square at number 8.

Museums in Prague

The city has many fascinating museums, dedicated to subjects as varied as Musical Instruments, the Postal Service and War. What is offered below is a selection.

1 ANTONÍN DVOŘÁK MUSEUM

This Baroque villa is an oasis of calm, and a delight to walk around to the sound of Dvořák's works. Less hyped than the over-priced Mozart Museum in Smíchov, and with some fascinating memorabilia. Located at Ke Karlovu 20.

2 MUSEUM OF DECORATIVE ARTS

Very attractive display and surroundings. Although the jewellery and furniture are interesting, more of the posters (many of them Art Nouveau) and photographs currently locked away in the bowels of the building need to go on permanent display. Situated at 17 Listopadu 2.

3 NATIONAL TECHNICAL MUSEUM

All the better for being a little off the beaten track, with a grim exterior but a fascinating collection of old bicycles, aeroplanes, cameras and other "technical achievements" inside. You find it at the top of a gruelling walk up Kostelní towards the Letná Plain.

4 NATIONAL LITERATURE MUSEUM

Part of the Strahov monastery complex—look at the two wonderful libraries, the Philosophical and Theological Halls, while you're there.

5 STATE JEWISH MUSEUM

Many textiles, books, liturgical exotica and other aspects of Judaism were collected together here, initially by the Nazis in a gruesome bid to create the "Museum of an Extinct Race". The exhibitions are dotted about several synagogues. It is best to start from opposite the Old-New Synagogue.

6 MUSEUM OF THE CITY OF PRAGUE

Located just opposite Florenc metro station, the museum contains a model of the city and much interesting data on its history, including the events which lead up to the Russian invasion in 1968 and beyond.

7 MUSICAL INSTRUMENTS MUSEUM

Near the John Lennon Wall in Laženská, and sporting an interesting collection of instruments from around the world. There are concerts in the gardens during the summer months.

8 NÁPRSTEK MUSEUM OF ASIAN, AFRICAN AND AMERICAN CULTURES

Tends to perpetuate the myth that these peoples sit around in huts smoking peace-pipes or throwing spears at each other, but if you forget about any pretensions to anthropological accuracy it's entertaining.

9 MILITARY MUSEUM

The usual collection of deadly weapons through the centuries, becoming progressively deadlier as "civilization" progressed. Near the entrance to Prague Castle, with Sgraffito exterior which should not be missed.

10 POSTAGE STAMP MUSEUM

This is located in an old house on the edge

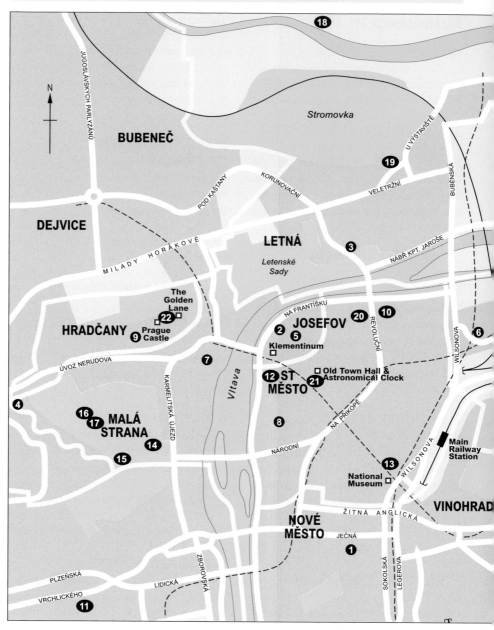

Museums and places of children's entertainment throughout Prague.

of the New Town in Nové mlýny, and is worth a visit if only because you'll be received like royalty. A philatelist's dream, and while he or she ploughs through pull-out displays of stamps you can go upstairs to look at the lithographs describing the life of a 19th-century postman.

11 MOZART MUSEUM

A delightful villa, Bertramka, in which Mozart completed *Don Giovanni* and enjoyed visiting a city in which his music was appreciated. Since the Velvet Revolution Mozart has been promoted in the city as if there were no Czech composers worth remembering, but this atmospheric house in leafy surroundings is well worth a visit.

12 SMETANA MUSEUM

Alongside Dvořák, one of the country's greatest composers. The museum is located on the edge of the river next to the Charles Bridge, and a bust of the composer stands next to a few benches for relaxing awhile outside afterwards.

13 NATIONAL MUSEUM

Located at the top of Wenceslas Square. A rather unimaginative collection of stuffed animals and rocks, but the Pantheon, salad bar and temporary exhibitions make it worth a visit.

Entertaining Children in Prague

The following suggestions may make it easier for you to visit the city as a family. Some of the museums above, especially 3 and 8, will be particularly fascinating for children.

14 UP THE FUNICULAR

Metro tickets will do for the ride, and there are donkey rides at the top.

15 ROYAL OBSERVATORY

Older children may like this, but there's a limit to what can be seen by day.

16 EIFFEL TOWER

In fact it's a replica for the Jubilee Exhibition of 1891, but the views are magnificent.

17 MIRROR MAZE

Good to lose the children, and a suitable come-uppance for any narcissus.

18 PRAGUE ZOO

Located close to the Troja Château. You can reach it at the end of a good wak through Stromovka Park, and then return by boat.

19 VÝSTAVIŠTĚ

Contains children's rides and a small roller-coaster, together with numerous exhibitions, a cinema, fountains and refreshments. A favourite week-end haunt for Prague families. Could be visited on the way to or from the zoo.

20 PUPPET SHOWS

There are a number of puppet and marionette shows in the city. This one is located at Dlouhá 39, at the Divadlo Jiřího Wolkra.

21 ASTRONOMICAL CLOCK

Arrive at a few minutes to the hour and see the figures emerge when it strikes. On the edge of the Old Town Square.

22 ESCAPING THE CHILDREN

Even the most responsible parent wants to do sometimes. The Czechoslovakian Children's House in Prague Castle will mind the children free of charge (in 1991!). Located on Jiřská.

A Wealth of History in a Tiny Corner of Prague

Jews have lived in Prague for a thousand years, during which time they have suffered the regular fate of their race in Europe—pogroms, banishments and restriction to the cramped quarters of the ghetto. Only about 1,000 Jews remain in Prague today but, partly because of Hitler's macabre wish to create a "Museum of an Extinct Race" in the city, their history has not entirely disappeared. In the synagogues, museums and cemetery that survive it is still possible to experience something of what it meant to be a European Jew during that troubled millennium.

History

The Old Jewish Town of Prague, **Josefov**, is recognized as an integral part of the city's history and heritage. Jews have struggled to settle in Prague for at least 900 years. During that time they have been restricted in space and persecuted at regular intervals. In the 19th century their living quarters were torn down by the Austro-Hungarian Empire as part of a town planning exercise, whilst in the 20th century they were ransacked and eventually decimated by the Nazis. Much of the history of their suffering has been chronicled and can be observed in the city's Jewish quarter today.

Jews initially settled on both sides of the river Vltava, but the settlement in the Lesser Quarter (Malá Strana) was destroyed, probably by Crusaders' attacks against the Jews in the 11th and 12th centuries. The others had to face increasingly stringent laws imposed by the medieval Catholic church. The Christian authorities regularly exploited the current myth that Jews spread the plague by poisoning wells. The fate of the Jews was very much at the mercy of particular rulers and their personal attitudes during these centuries. Ferdinand I in the early 16th century confined all Jews in Bohemia to Prague.

*T*he morning after the night before... statue of Moses beside the Old-New synagogue.

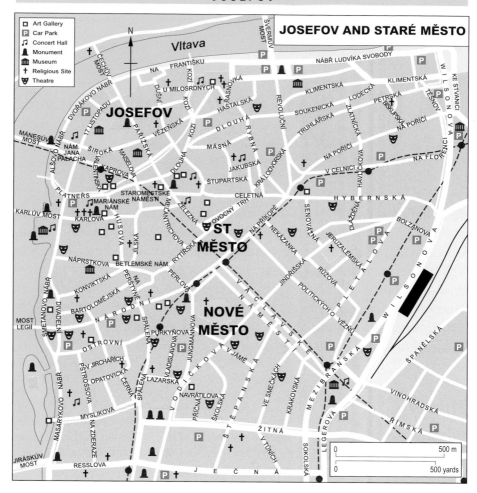

JOSEFOV AND STARÉ MĚSTO

*T*own plan of the Josefov
and Staré Město areas.

Maximilian II, on the other hand, and his successor Rudolph II, granted them many privileges, economic freedom and undisturbed residency. Indeed the late 16th and early 17th centuries are widely regarded as a golden age of Prague Jewry.

In the late 17th and 18th centuries, however, the fortunes of Prague's Jews changed for the worse. Efforts were made

to reduce both their numbers and the size of Josefov. Empress Maria Theresa in the 18th century banished them from the city, allowing their return only after pressure from the local nobility and representations from abroad, especially from England and the Netherlands. On top of this, Jesuit pressure ensured that their books were censored, and they were forced to take part in Christian worship.

Some measure of security for the Jewish quarter, hitherto at the mercy of rulers and their whims, was finally achieved only in the mid-19th century, when the

Jewish Town (since 1851 called Josefov) was incorporated into the covenant of the five towns of Prague, and became accepted at last as an integral part of the city's identity. Even then it was integration at a price. A "renewal project" carried out between 1893 and 1917 involved the destruction of large areas of Josefov, and elegant town apartments sprang up in streets like Pařižská which survive to this day in their turn-of-the-century form. They are certainly imposing, but they were constructed only through a forced requisitioning of much of the ghetto.

Then in 1939 the Nazis invaded Bohemia and Moravia, taking advantage of Neville Chamberlain's misplaced hopes for "peace in our time". They declared a protectorate of Bohemia and Moravia in the occupied territories and introduced anti-Jewish laws. The Jewish communities were abolished, and their members deported to the fortress of Terezín in northern Bohemia, which became a kind of distribution point for the Nazi death camps.

During the Second World War, the Nazis conceived the idea of collecting huge numbers of Jewish artefacts and concentrating them in Prague in order to build a "museum to an extinct race". They used Jewish experts to gather the material, before murdering most of them in the last year of the war. As a result, 1945 saw a huge number of manuscripts, books, textiles, sacred objects and other artefacts brought together in Prague, but very few Jews left to manage them. The only possibility was to turn them over to the new communist government and hope that it would take over the work of presenting them.

It can hardly be said that the communist authorities, who were not exactly immune to anti-semitism themselves, warmed to the task. Further progress has been made since the Velvet Revolution of 1989, and although at the end of 1991 two of the most famous synagogues in Josefov, the Spanish Synagogue and the Pinkas Synagogue, remained closed to the public, restoration work was clearly proceeding. It is quite possible from what is already open to understand a great deal about the history and significance of Prague's Jews.

A Tour of Josefov

The nearest metro stop is Staroměstská, from which it is necessary merely to walk away from the river via Valentinská and then Široká until you reach Pařižská. Alternatively you can walk from the **Staroměstské náměstí** (Old Town Square) down the length of Pařižská, which is scenic, if longer. Before you reach the end of Pařižská, about 90 m (100 yd) short of the affluent Intercontinental Hotel, you cannot miss the **Staronová synagóga** (Old-New Synagogue) on your left. If you do miss it, the statue of a weary Moses contemplating his navel in the synagogue garden, sculpted by František Bílek, should catch your eye. If you miss both, you are about to fall into the river Vltava, and should wake up.

Go down the steps on your left just before you reach the synagogue and your tour of Josefov begins. A useful map on the wall of the High Synagogue on your left tells you where everything is. It is important to realize that the often mentioned **Státní Židovský hřbitov** ("State Jewish Museum") is a collective noun referring to all the diverse sights in Josefov rather than to any particular display, although at the time of writing there was no single collective ticket admitting you to all of them.

63

*T*he sun sets behind Europe's oldest surviving synagogue, the Old-New.

The tour begins with the exhibits in the museum opposite the Old-New Synagogue, originally the **Vysoká synagóga** (High Synagogue), but now used to display part of a huge textile collection. Many of these were hand-made for religious festivals, often showing links between the rural folk art of Bohemia and Moravia on the one hand (hence the motifs of tulips, apples, animals and so on), and synagogical textile traditions from the cities on the other hand. There are a number of fascinating liturgical objects, such as the elaborate "Torah mantles", covered

parchment scrolls on which the text of the Pentateuch, the first five books of the "Old Testament" or Hebrew Bible, were written. "Torah", a Hebrew word meaning law or instruction, came to have the narrower meaning of the law as set down in those five books.

The Old-New Synagogue

The **Staronov á Synagóga** (Old-New Synagogue) is the oldest surviving synagogue in Europe and is still used for worship. Originally it was known as the New Synagogue, but its capacity to survive fire and tumult, supposedly under angelic protection, made it one of the oldest buildings in the area, and hence gave it its peculiarly ambivalent name.

Immediately on entering the building, the first area you reach is one of the two galleries from which women were allowed to view proceedings in the main hall, which was reserved exclusively for men. Pass through into the main two-aisled hall designed in Cistercian Gothic style—men are asked to purchase a paper cap for five crowns, or to improvise with a handkerchief or a scarf. The interior has virtually no natural light; low chandeliers form the main source of illumination and tend to obscure the stellar vaulting above. The lay-out is not dissimilar to that of pulpit and altar in a Christian church. In the centre a 15th-century iron grille surrounds a platform with a lectern used for reading from the Torah scrolls. On the eastern wall is the Torah shrine, flanked by two Renaissance pillars. Hebrew inscriptions cover the walls, largely to commemorate an early 16th-century renovation of the synagogue, and a battered flag at the centre sports a Star of David with a Swedish hat in the middle. This bears testimony to a rare moment in history when Jews were seen as loyal subjects rather than as political scapegoats. It was presented by the Emperor Ferdinand II in 1648 in recognition of the Jewish community's contribution to the fight against the Swedes during the Thirty Years' War.

At the back (or western end) of the synagogue is a glass cabinet filled with names underlined by light bulbs. On the anniversary of one of the named person's deaths their light bulb lights up—if you're a fan of Franz Kafka, visit on 3 July.

The Old-New Synagogue is not to everyone's taste—the Rough Guide to Czechoslovakia dubs it a "grubby medieval hall"—but some might see its gloomy interior as moving, a witness to faith enduring persecution, like Anne Frank's "grubby" quarters in Amsterdam.

Leaving the synagogue, turn right past the pink walls of the **Židovnická radnice** (Jewish Town Hall), of which the High Synagogue with its exhibition of textiles is a part. Look up to the top of the Town Hall (you will have to stand back a bit to do this), and you can see a wooden tower. Beneath the tower, on the north gable which faces you as you look at the Town Hall from the Old-New Synagogue, is a clock with Hebrew figures. The hands of this clock move in an anti-clockwise direction, although in a clockwise direction so far as Hebrew clocks are concerned, since Hebrew is read from right to left.

*C*rowded in life and death. For three centuries this was the only burial ground for thousands of Jews living in the Prague ghetto.

The Old Jewish Cemetery

Next port of call is the most famous site in Josefov and one of the wonders of Prague, the **Starý židovský hřbitov** (Old Jewish Cemetery), easily reached by a 90 m (100 yd) walk in the opposite direction to the steps down from Pařížská. Nothing

is so indicative of the cramped, ghetto-like existence of those who lived in Josefov than the means by which they coped with those who died there. The cemetery originated in about 1400 AD, and the oldest preserved tombstone is that of the scholar and poet Avigdor Karo, who died in 1439. Being insufficiently big to accommodate the needs of the overpopulated Jewish Town, it was progressively

Looking like rows of broken and decaying teeth from a distance, many of the tombstones in the Old Jewish Cemetery are seen from close up to have beautiful decorative motifs.

enlarged over the next four centuries. In spite of this, older graves had to be covered with a layer of new soil, which was then used for further burials, usually with the tombstones from the lower graves being elevated to the new "ground level". The result was the extreme density of grave memorials which characterizes the Old Jewish Cemetery. Since 1787, the date of the last funeral to be held in the cemetery, another site for burial of Jewish dead has been in use in the suburb of Žižkov, but even so there are 11,000 or 12,000 tombstones in the cemetery, and the number of graves must be well in excess of that.

A great deal can be discerned about the history of the ghetto from the Hebrew inscriptions and epitaphs on these tombstones, the latter of which would often contain a lengthy account of the good deeds of the deceased. At the same time, the often elaborate tombstone reliefs, displaying a rich sculptural decoration to be found nowhere else in such abundance, are themselves a living testimony to the history of art. The relatively flourishing late 16th and early 17th centuries saw sandstone give way to marble, and sarcophagi squashing their way in between simple tombstones. The Renaissance and Baroque periods saw a fashion for engraving with simple biblical motifs like crowns to symbolize wisdom or, more dubiously perhaps, grapes to symbolize learning. Animals might often be used to symbolize the name of the dead person, while other symbols might point to their profession—such as scissors for a tailor or books for a cantor (the leader of prayers in the synagogue). Other motifs may be purely decorative.

On many of the tombstones there are small collections of pebbles, which are left

---

Pebbles on Gravestones

The origin of the practice of leaving pebbles on gravestones is unclear, and appears to be unique to this graveyard. One suggestion is that it goes back to the Jewish tradition of the Exodus (told in the second book of the Hebrew Bible after the Book of Genesis), according to which rocks were used, when the Israelites escaped from Pharoah's Egypt into the wilderness, to mark desert graves. Certainly the practice of leaving a pile of stones to mark a grave is common to many societies.

The pebbles also provide a means of preventing small notes with scribbled messages from being blown away. The notes contain wishes which, it is hoped, some magical power associated with the interred person may be able to fulfil.

there as a mark of respect by relatives and friends. Sometimes notes are left under the pebbles, perhaps with a request for a prayer to be fulfilled — often at the tombstone of someone with a reputation for working miracles, such as Rabbi Löw (*see* page 69).

The multi-layered character of the graveyard makes it uneven and, in places, hilly. Although it can become crammed full with visitors, there is always somewhere peaceful within its cramped walls. The feeling of confinement only serves to emphasize its separation from the busy world outside. The powerful sense of a community overcrowded even in death is a reminder of the Jewish people's constant experience of being hemmed in by hostile forces, which continues to this day. At the same time the graveyard reveals in its testimonies and its decoration their extraordinary creativity in the face of adversity.

The "House of Ceremonies"

Next door to the cemetery entrance is the

Built in 1908, the Ceremonial House represents one more style of architecture to find in Prague: neo-Romanesque! It contains a harrowing collection of children's artwork and poetry from the concentration camp at Terezín, including a "camp magazine".

Obřadní síň (House of Ceremonies), a 19th-century house containing a harrowing exhibition of children's paintings and drawings from the concentration camp at

The Pinkas Synagogue on the south side of the cemetery contains a memorial to 80,000 Jews who died at the hands of the Nazis. In 1968 the communists closed it because of "problems with masonry". They had not solved these problems when the Velvet Revolution swept them from power in 1989.

Theresienstadt (Terezín), about 48 km (30 miles) north-west of Prague. It was to this camp that most of the Jews deported from the city were initially sent, as a kind of clearing-house for further deportation elsewhere. Between 1942 and 1944 alone approximately 15,000 Jewish children were sent there, and the drawings, mostly in simple pencil, represent their experience of life in crowded barracks on plank beds. There are pictures of what

they observed daily, such as executions, and of what they dreamed of seeing, things that might be imagined to be the natural subjects of children's drawings like trees, animals and trains. Extracts from a camp magazine, with poems and stories, are also on display. It is not possible to put into words the effect of these drawings.

The Pinkas Synagogue

On the edge of the cemetery the Pinkas Synagogue (which despite the hint in its name is yellow), is currently being renovated. It is a late-Renaissance building on the south side of the cemetery, although originally a part of a house bought in the 14th century from a Rabbi Pinkas. After the Second World War it became a memorial to Jews from Bohemia and Moravia killed by the Nazis. Their 77,297 names are inscribed on the walls of the synagogue, together with their dates of birth and of deportation to be exterminated.

Half of them came from Prague itself.

The Maisl Synagogue

The Pinkas synagogue is next to Široká, one of the streets running alongside the cemetery. Slightly further along Široká the road meets Maislova, and if you turn right at that point another synagogue, the Maisl synagogue, has now been re-opened after four years of restoration work. Founded in the late 16th century as a family synagogue in Renaissance style, and then subject, like so many of Prague's religious buildings, to additions and re-modellings in later styles—in this case turn of the century neo-Gothic—the synagogue is renowned for its exhibition of liturgical silver. Crowns, goblets, and candlesticks vie for attention with such delicacies as 19th-century circumcision sets and silver "pointers", silver fingers suspended from dressed Torah scrolls in order to help the reader keep the right place.

The Klaus Synagogue

Between the Old-New synagogue and the cemetery entrance is the Klaus synagogue, a late 17th-century Baroque building with some later additions, like the 18th-century rococo stucco ceiling. (Note especially the Baroque "Torah ark", roughly equivalent to the altar in a Christian church.) This synagogue, like several of the others, houses an exhibition, this time of the life and work of many of the scholars who lived in Josefov. Illustrated manuscripts, particularly of "haggadah", sacred texts recited at the Jewish Passover festival, and wood cuts show a fascinating fusion of folk art and religious symbolism similar to that of the textiles in the High Synagogue. Medieval Hebrew books on display tell the history of Jews in Prague since the 10th century. From later centuries the

life and work of famous Jewish astronomers and physicians is recalled, but one fascinating character stands out from all the others, Rabbi Löw (an abbreviation for the full name Rabbi Jehuda Liwa ben Betsalel).

Part of the exhibition in the Klaus (or Klausen) synagogue is devoted to the work of Rabbi Löw, together with that of other famous Jewish teachers. Astronomers such as David Gans, a 16th-century follower of Copernicus, and Solomon ben Elijahu Delmedigo, a disciple of Galileo, were leading figures in their day, as were the members of the Prague Enlightenment two centuries later, such as Peter Beer and Heinz Homberg. The exhibition demonstrates the richness of the Jewish contribution to Prague's intellectual and cultural life until the disaster of Nazism virtually destroyed it.

Rabbi Löw

Rabbi Löw was born about 1512 in Poznan, and did not come to live in Prague until 1573, where he eventually became Chief Rabbi. Although he is well-known

> **Rabbi Löw**
> According to another legend, Rabbi Löw went to the Old-New synagogue at the grand age of 96 in order to fight with a sword-waving apparition that was threatening to destroy the whole Jewish community. He ripped a scroll containing the names of all those who were to die from the apparition's "hands", but it managed to keep a small scrap of the scroll between its fingers. That scrap contained the name of Rabbi Löw.
>
> Such stories can be read at the level of pure fantasy, but they also represent an imaginative projection of the Jewish community's real experience of persecution and longing for a protector.

as a teacher and leader of Prague's Jewish community, his fame derives above all from stories (some probably apocryphal!), which circulated about his special powers. He lived to a great age (by most accounts nearly 100 years), apparently because the Angel of Death was unable to match his wisdom and so eventually had to conceal itself in a flower handed to the Rabbi by his granddaughter. Rabbi Löw succumbed to the grim reaper by sniffing a rose, but this was not the end of his powers. According to legend, he reacted to the crowded conditions in the Old Jewish Cemetery by shifting his own tombstone to make room for his grandson Samuel to lie beside him! A sarcophagus carved with the figures of lions (the figure of a lion symbolizes the name Je-huda), today marks Rabbi Löw's tomb in the cemetery.

Rabbi Löw was one of many supposedly miracle-working individuals who sought to unveil divine secrets by way of alchemy, astrology and magic (see the story of the Golem below). Such people were much talked about in the "mysterious ghetto" which was the Jewish quarter of Prague during the 16th-century Renaissance period. It appears at this time to have been a kind of "fantasy Prague", full of magical tales and claims to semi-divine powers.

The Spanish Synagogue

There is one other synagogue in Josefov to mention, the **Španělská synagóga** (Spanish synagogue). To reach this return

---

The Golem

The Golem was an artificial being in human form, supposedly made out of clay or mud, whose creation is one of the many miraculous works attributed to Rabbi Löw.

According to the legend, Rabbi Löw breathed life into the Golem with a magic word, the "Shem", which he obtained from a parchment scroll containing the secret name of God. This idea goes back to ancient Jewish mystical writings, the Kabbala, not to mention Jewish Creation stories in the Hebrew Bible or "Old Testament" which describe the creation of Adam by God—Genesis 2:7—"then the Lord God formed man of dust from the ground, and breathed into his nostrils the breath of life; and man became a living being".

The earliest accounts of the Golem, together with a kind of instruction manual on how to make one, date from the 13th century. Perhaps reflecting the situation of frequent persecution experienced by Jews, the Golem very quickly changed from its original conception as a kind of perfect butler to a protector, a kind of beat policeman who would protect the community from attack.

According to one version of the story dating from the 19th century, the Golem got out of control. Rabbi Löw was supposed to "put it to bed" each night by removing the sign of life from its mouth, but on one occasion forgot. As a consequence he had his house wrecked on the sabbath, and reacted to his own negligence somewhat unfairly by turning the creature back into mud and clay, the form in which it supposedly remains to this day underneath the Old-New synagogue in Josefov.

Many stories about Golem were well-known by the 18th century in Prague, although several were doubtless circulating before that, and will certainly have influenced that more commonly known tale of artificially-created human life from the 19th century, the story of Frankenstein. The silent film made of Gustav Meyrinck's novel *Der Golem* (based upon the Prague legends) was at least a partial contributor to the cinema genre of man-made monsters that is nowadays dominated by the Frankenstein legend.

*T*he intriguing design of the Spanish Synagogue recalls motifs also seen in the design of mosques. However, this potentially ecumenical building was closed down by the communists in 1980 for "electrical rewiring". This task proved too much for the government, and the synagogue remained shut until the Velvet Revolution closed down the communists.

along Maislova to Široká, turn right, go straight across Pařížská into Vězeňská, and the synagogue is about 180 m (200 yd) along on the left hand side. Unfortunately, the synagogue was shut in 1991, having been closed since 1980 for "electrical rewiring". To be fair to the new government of Václav Havel, there is now a genuine effort to open up and, where necessary, restore the remaining sights of Josefov, and the synagogue may soon be re-opened. It used to contain a large collection of Jewish textiles before a number of these were transferred to their present location in the High synagogue.

The Spanish synagogue receives its name from a group of Jews who fled the Inquisition in Spain and came to Prague. It was built on the site of an earlier synagogue known as the "Old Shul", reputedly the oldest synagogue in Prague but torn down in 1867. The Spanish synagogue was built in the following year by architects Ullmann and Niklas. Its style shows distinct Spanish, or more precisely Moorish, influences, with a central square plan and large cupola. The interior has low plaster arabesques with Islamic motifs, gilded and multi-coloured. The relative lightness of the interior and the striking mixture of designs that might be associated both with Judaism and with Islam make this one of the most interesting and distinctive of Prague's synagogues. It can only be hoped that the interior will be on display once again soon.

Refreshment

There are a number of interesting and very different places for refreshment in Josefov. For light refreshment, there are kosher snacks outside the Old-New synagogue, and at the top of the nearby steps on the corner of Pařížská is the Restaurace U staré synagogy, a lovely place for sitting

A decorative motif on a street corner in Josefov.

outside with a coffee watching the world go by. Unfortunately that is everyone's view and space may be limited. If this is the case, there is a café in the delicatessen on the opposite side of Pařižská. Here you can buy snacks at the counter such as

small platefuls of salad, or a variety of small open half-rolls with tasty spreads on them and retire to a high stool with a coffee. It may not be so idyllic, but it is one of Prague's few non-smoking areas if that is a problem to you.

A very different experience can be found in the Krušovická Pivnice at Široká 20 (just off Pařižská). This is a local bar for local people, and the perfect escape if you want to escape crowds of tourists for crowds of Czechs. It was known as "Uncle Joe's" in 1990 because it still displayed an old black-and-white postcard of Joseph Stalin (although the postcard had disappeared by 1991). This wonderful bar is basically a rectangular room with benches and tables. High-quality beer is brought by a waiter who delivers the pints as you drink them and chalks up the score on a piece of paper. There are no jukeboxes, no fruit machines, no carpets, no frills—just sturdy men, hard tables and big glasses of beer.

If you are looking for lunch, one of the best places to eat is the **Košer Jídelna** (Kosher restaurant) at Maislova 18, which is in fact part of the Jewish Town Hall, now the headquarters of Prague's Jewish community. Open from 11.00 a.m. until 2.00 p.m., this provides a filling three-course meal at what is admittedly "dollar prices", but you rarely have to queue for very long.

Museum of Decorative Arts

There are one or two other things to see which, whilst not connected with the Jewish community, can most conveniently be explored alongside the State Jewish Museum. Something not to miss is the **Umělecko-průmyslové muzeum** (Museum of Decorative Arts, sometimes called the Museum of Applied Art) to be found on 17 November Street (17 listopadu). This was the date of a demonstration against Nazis by students in 1939, and ironically one of the key dates during the students' protests which led to the downfall of the communist regime in

November 1989. The street is easy to find—it runs from the bottom of Pařižská beside the river back towards the Old Town—and the museum, recognizable as a large late-19th-century neo-Renaissance building, is close to the Staromětská underground.

Part of the museum is full of objects used to decorate human beings: necklaces, rings, fans, brooches, lockets, bracelets, pocket watches and a range of costumes, particularly dresses. Other parts contain objects to decorate rooms: decorative glassware, porcelain, tapestries and a range of furniture. The clocks are fascinating, including a grandfather clock that sprouts so many cherubs' heads and angels that you'd hardly remember to look at the time. If the exhibits grow tiring it is always possible to admire the decoration of the rooms they are exhibited in. Apart from the ceilings and doors there is the elaborate staircase area topped by stained glass windows. The ascent to the upper rooms requires you to walk between extraordinary decorative motifs where the naive might anticipate simple banisters. Men with horns facing women with scallop-shaped head bands can easily distract your step.

One thing that Prague must do in future years is to unloose its superb treasures of Art Nouveau. The best of these, in 1991, was pronounced by the museum staff to be "in the vaults". All museums tend to display only a part of their collections, but in this case the best is largely hidden. A superb and relatively cheap hard-backed catalogue is on sale at the **pokladna** (kiosk) looking at what the museum collected since its foundation in 1885. Although the book is in Czech it contains numerous fascinating illustrations, including a great deal of marvellous Art Nouveau

---

Jan Palach

Few areas of Prague have been so much the centre of ideological warfare as Jan Palach Square. In 1945 it was named Red Army Square and became a temporary burial ground for Soviet soldiers who died during the (genuine) liberation of Prague. A generation later Jan Palach burned himself to death in a public protest against the "liberation" of the city from the Prague Spring by Brezhnev's tanks. In response a large crowd gathered in the square and tore down the street signs, re-naming the square after the young martyr Palach who studied temporarily at the philosophy faculty there. The communist authorities swiftly restored the original signs, only for the Velvet Revolution twenty years later to turn the tables once again, and restore the square to Palach's memory. In 1992 the square was still being "redecorated", but it will hopefully re-open soon with a name that will last more than a generation!

---

and avant-garde material which is currently not on display.

Jan Palach Square

Another interesting area around Josefov, close to the Museum of Decorative Arts, is the formerly named **náměstí Krasnoarmejců** (Red Army Square), which used to sport a green lawn in the centre of which there was a large red star—the badge of the Red Army. The square has now been re-named **náměstí Jana Palacha** (a point which illustrates once again the need to have an up-to-date map), after the student Jan Palach who studied philosophy in the faculty building there. Jan Palach burned himself to death publicly, in protest at the invasion by Red Army tanks in August 1968, and became a symbol for 20 years of further resistance to Stalinist rule.

The square contains the House of Artists or Rudolfinum, another neo-Renaissance building which is nowadays used as a concert hall, although in its time it has also contained an art gallery and a museum. For 30 years from the formation of the Czech Republic in 1918 it was the seat of the new Parliament. Statues of lions and sphinxes beside the main entrance, and of outstanding composers and artists above, make for a grandiose building. Like some of the other notable neo-Renaissance buildings in the city like the National Museum and the National Theatre, it is perhaps slightly ponderous in its overall effect.

Kafka

The most famous character with whom Prague's Josefov is associated is probably the novelist Franz Kafka, a German-speaking Jew who spent most of his short life (1883-1924) in the area before failing to be cured of tuberculosis in Vienna. His three famous novels (*The Trial*, *The Castle*, and *America*) express a number of themes which have resonated with Czechoslovakia's 20th-century experience. The tanglings of individuals with an impossible bureaucracy reflect the later experience of state socialism, whilst *America* expresses some measure of disillusionment with the "American dream", a point of view which has been less fashionable since 1989. The claustrophobia of Josefov with its history of cramped confinement mixes with the claustrophobia of the individual at large in a crushingly bureaucratic society.

Kafka was banned by Nazis and communists alike, but since 1989 he has become the subject of exhibitions and plays on a grand scale. If you miss the bust at the bottom of Maislova, near to the Old Town Square, you will certainly not miss the T-shirts, "Kafka loved Prague" postcards (in fact it is doubtful whether Kafka loved anything), the posters or the type of shop which has been hastily converted into an "Expozice Franze Kafky".

Josefov is a relatively small and manageable area to see when compared, for instance, to the New Town, but it is one of the most atmospheric and historically rich parts of the city, surely deserving of a slower pace when it comes up on your itinerary. If, incidentally, you finish your visit to the area with an evening meal, the restaurant to plump for is U Golema (Maislova 8), which has a pleasant, intimate atmosphere although there are fewer Jewish specialities than some of the guides promise.

Josefov: Opening Times

1. Státní Židovské Muzeum (State Jewish Museum).
This is a collection of buildings rather than a single one, and includes the Starý Židovský Hřbitov (Old Jewish Cemetery).
Open 9.00 a.m. to 5.00 p.m. (Not Saturdays—the Jewish Sabbath.)
2. Umělecko-Průmyslové Muzeum (Museum of Applied or Decorative Arts).
Open 10.00 a.m. to 6.00 p.m. (Not Mondays.)

Highlights for Children

There is less for younger children in this part of the city than in others, although older children might well appreciate the historical and cultural significance of the area. Whilst the exhibition of paintings, poems and drawings from the children's concentration camp of Terezín is harrowing, it is after all an exhibition of children's work, and you may feel it to

Kafka

Franz Kafka, whose name was based upon the Czech word Kavka meaning jackdaw, was born into a community racked by national and racial tensions. Late 19th-century Prague was beset by bitter divisions between Germans and Czechs, and by a growing tide of anti-semitism. To be a German-speaking Jew in such a society was to enter the worst of both worlds and be everybody's victim. It is unsurprising that the physically frail Franz had to develop resources of inner strength and resilience in order to cope with a permanently hostile social environment. It is equally unsurprising that much of his most famous writing depicts menacing and repressive authorities.

Kafka was born on 3 July 1883, on the corner of Kaprova and Maislova, opposite to which there is a modern bust of the writer (it is to the left of St Nicholas' church as you face the church from the Old Town Square). His father was an ambitious, extrovert character called Hermann who ran a haberdasher's in the Old Town Square. He was constantly seeking to move up in the world, and his search for respectability led to five changes of house in six years. Meanwhile his mother, forced to spend a large amount of time in the shop, had to engage a nurse for the children. During the same period both of Franz Kafka's brothers died from measles and an ear infection. He rarely saw his parents outside meal-times.

At the age of six Kafka was sent to a German school, followed at ten by enrolment in what was reputed to be the strictest school in Prague, the Altstadter Deutsches Gymnasium. Nervous of his teachers, conscious of alienation from classmates and Prague society through his Jewishness, and unsupported by his bullying, ambitious father and his mother who would not stand up for her son against him, Kafka's burgeoning interest in literature and theatre was partly a retreat from the life around him. He was too frail for sport, hopeless at maths but from the age of 13 developed an all-absorbing interest in reading and drama.

At the age of 18 Kafka went to the university in Prague. Since 1882 the buildings had virtually been divided into two universities, one German and one Czech, reflecting the divisions of the age. Because Jews were rarely admitted to the army or civil service, Kafka was one of many who turned to the law, enrolling in the autumn of 1901 after a brief attempt to read chemistry.

In 1902 Kafka went on holiday in a village on the Elbe, Liboch, not far from Prague, where he met up with an uncle who had travelled over from Madrid since he was director general of the Spanish railways. His uncle encouraged Kafka to think of travelling, and suggested that he study at several universities. The suggestion only intensified what was to be a lifelong love-hate relationship with the city of Prague. Kafka considered going to Munich to study literature, but instead returned to his law degree in the Czech capital. Part of the reason was pressure from his father, but another part was pressure from the city itself. "This little mother has claws", he wrote, "one has to give in or else." Its "demonic magic" had enticed him back.

Whilst at university Kafka had a number of short stories published and met what was to be a lifelong friend, and posthumous biographer, Max Brod. But much of his time was devoted to the law degree with intermittent dreams of escape, which often centred around the idea that his Uncle Alfred would find him a job in Spain (a fantasy which he kept up by learning Spanish). On graduation he took unpaid employment working for the courts as a clerk, whilst learning

Italian in the evenings, since he entertained hopes of the firm sending him to Trieste. Indeed dreams of being sent abroad were the main source of hope in work that was routine and monotonous—although the experience gained from it was to contribute a great deal to his novels, particularly his most famous work *The Trial*.

Bust commemorating the birthplace of Franz Kafka beside St Nicholas Church just off the Old Town Square.

In March 1908 he had a collection of short stories published in the periodical *Hyperion*. His style was developing and the knowledge of his talents expanding, but he had to change jobs. Once again it was a friend who helped him, Ewald Pribram, whose father Otto ran the Workers' Accident Insurance Company for the Kingdom of Bohemia. That Otto was a Jew helped Kafka, as did the requirement, which Kafka could fulfil, of being thoroughly versed in both German and Czech. It meant some further courses, particularly in statistics which

he found hard, but he soon impressed his boss, and Kafka was to stay with the firm until forced to retire through ill-health in 1922, two years before his untimely death at the age of forty from tuberculosis.

Despite working for a large and bureaucratic organization, Kafka performed well at his job and at times seemed to enjoy it. He made friends more easily now than in the past, was often sent away on business trips which enabled him to dream again about leaving Prague permanently, and liked the thought of helping workers with injury claims to receive compensation.

In the spring of 1910 Kafka began to keep a diary, the perfect medium for what was already a characteristic of his writing, self-examination and the search for identity. His diary did not simply record events, it also sketched out fictional descriptions and became, in places, like the note-book for a novel. His friend Max Brod kept a diary too, and each prodded the other to write. They went on frequent holidays together around Europe, recording their impressions.

Kafka had various illnesses during these years including constipation, insomnia, and, more seriously, the weak lungs that eventually led to tuberculosis. He was also often lonely, finding it difficult to relate to women and occasionally visiting brothels, and since he was living at home, engagement and marriage obviously provided a potential means of escape from his parents. However, Kafka appeared to find it as hard to abandon his parents, difficult though he found them, as to abandon Prague itself.

In 1912 he met Felice Bauer, a woman from Berlin with whom he had probably his closest relationship, although marriage never took place despite two engagements. He got further toward the end of his life with Dora Dymant, with whom he lived for a short time in Berlin, thus managing to abandon both home and native city until driven back by terminal illness.

1912 was also the year in which Kafka published two stories, *The Judgment* and *Metamorphosis*, which are generally regarded as the beginning of his "mature" writing. To some extent they read like paranoid fantasies. *Metamorphosis*, for example, begins as follows:

"As Gregor Samsa woke up one morning out of uneasy dreams, he found that he had been transformed in his bed into an enormous insect."

But it soon becomes clear that there is more to them than this. The image of the insect in Metamorphosis, for instance, expresses both Kafka's alienation from his own body and his feelings towards a father and a society that treated the abnormal as repulsive. Many people like Kafka living in Prague were incapable of receiving any goodwill despite the fact that they did no active harm because of some characteristic beyond their control. Whether they were not tolerated because of accidents of birth, race, or physical appearance, the fact that they were treated like vermin and trodden on as if they were insects had to be recorded and interpreted. Kafka had suffered enough of this intolerance himself to know that it was not mere paranoia to draw attention to it.

Kafka began work on his most famous novel, *The Trial*, in the year that the First World War broke out. The simply-named Josef K. is suddenly arrested, for no apparent reason, and is immediately plunged into a nightmare world in which his initial anger and determination to right the "mistake" that has been made gradually turns into helpless subordination to the power of The Law. The individual's sense of justice pales into insignificance beside the omnipresent workings of the bureaucratic machine. This novel anticipates in a remarkable way aspects of life under bureaucracy in general, and communist bureaucracy in particular, during the 20th century.

The progression from defiant opposition to humble connivance in the face of repressive authority re-appears in *The Castle* too. The hero, simply called K., turns up in a village in order to take up a post as a land-surveyor. It soon turns out that no official, and in particular no representative of the castle in the village, can explain to him his position, what he is there to do (no land surveys are needed) or why he has been sent there. He finds a world which challenges all his expectations, refuses to answer any of his questions, and flattens his individual will.

The Castle is Kafka's most metaphysical work. The village is partly another bureaucratic nightmare like the legal system in *The Trial*, but it is also a metaphor for the state of the individual on earth as such, struggling under any system to understand why he or she is there and what sort of Creator, good or ill, might have put them there and for what purpose.

Kafka's most light-hearted and in some ways most accessible novel is *America*. The work describes the adventures of Karl Rossmann, shipped to America by unloving parents who want to avoid paying alimony to a servant-girl whom he has made pregnant. Once again there are the powerful descriptions of overwhelming systems, although in this case it is not faceless bureaucracy but the oppressive hierarchy of a hotel management that is described, with great comic effect. As in the other novels there are memorable descriptions, laced with humour, of the individual struggling to cope with mass society—

whether it's struggling to get food and drink from a packed restaurant, or watching a political rally from the roof of a balcony. But *America* also has a note of hope in it, perhaps reflecting Kafka's expectations for places he had never visited! Its view of American society is also particularly apt for the present day, when Prague has finally been liberated to receive as much "American culture" as it wants, and might be encouraged by Kafka's novel to be discerning in its reception.

America was an early work, written but never completed between 1911 and 1914 before *The Trial* and *The Castle*. By 1917, when he was working on and off on these two novels, (once again they were never in the form of completed manuscripts and were never published), Kafka started to cough up blood and was variously diagnosed. The doctor assured him that it wasn't tuberculosis. It was in fact just that.

Kafka had always had to write in the evenings, after his work in the factory, occasionally labouring all night. Now he had to contend with a worsening physical condition as well, losing weight and strength and suffering from a lot of pain. He moved through the spa towns of Europe seeking out remedies that failed to arrest his decline. He came within two days of marrying, this time to Julie Wohryzek, daughter of a Prague shoemaker and synagogue official, but pulled out when his plans for a flat fell through. Perhaps he interpreted the loss of the flat, like the appearance of illness, as a signal of disapproval from some higher authority.

The last love of Kafka's life, and in some ways the most fulfilling, was Dora Dymant, a young woman whom ho met at Muritz, one of many new places with supposed curative powers at which Kafka went through a familiar routine of initial improvement followed by relapse.

Dora was fascinated enough by Kafka to follow him around, whilst he noticed her scaling fish in a kitchen. This offended his vegetarianism: "such gentle hands and such bloody work". After meeting her every day in Muritz they agreed to live together in Berlin. Dora told him that his success in tearing himself away from Prague was his greatest achievement in life! But Berlin had its own problems. It was racked by inflation, their landlady was constantly antagonistic (especially about the electricity consumed by someone working through the night—in the end Dora bought him a paraffin lamp!), and he was still dreaming of settling in other places, particularly Palestine. After six weeks their landlady gave them notice to move, and they took off to another part of the city. Kafka spent the weeks writing *The Burrow*, a longish short story about a doomed animal tunnelling into another "Castle" as it unsuccessfully tries to escape its pursuers inside another impossible labyrinth.

His health deteriorated further. He returned temporarily to his parents in Prague, and then moved to a sanatorium near Vienna. As the illness became worse he demanded stronger drugs, including morphine. Dora remained with him, mediating between patient and doctor. In a final exchange of words with his doctor, Kafka ordered him not to go away from the room. "I'm not going away", the doctor assured him. "But I'm going away", Kafka replied. They were his last words.

After his death it was his friend Max Brod who edited his three major novels, all of which were published posthumously and were left deliberately unfinished. Kafka had left specific instructions that his unpublished works were to be destroyed, a demand that Brod ignored.

Despite the distaste which Kafka felt for his own work, it has repeatedly struck a chord in this century of personal doubt and mass organization. Kafka's hero is the individual, but the individual as victim rather than epic hero, resisting powers before which he or she is finally helpless, defeated but unyielding-and always finally perplexed.

Two years on from the Velvet Revolution, Prague is awash with exhibitions, posters, souvenirs, books, postcards-and of course T-shirts-celebrating one of its most famous literary sons. Despite the lack of outward drama and specific narratives in his writing, Kafka is frequently adapted for stage and screen, a mark of the chord which he strikes in contemporary thinking. There is bound to be a play about Kafka's life and work when you're in Prague, and you are bound to come across the memorable face with the Mr. Spock right ear-perhaps on a T-shirt with the words "Kafka didn't have much fun either" emblazoned on it.

Despite the unhappy character of his life, Kafka is much loved in Prague. His insights into bureaucracy and its overpowering ways speak to the modern mind, especially for those with experience of heavy state bureaucracies. He speaks out for the individual in an age which has all too often seen the individual subordinated to some undesirable collective will.

Kafka also represents two sides of Prague. On the one hand he reflects a feeling of claustrophobia, which would of course be especially pronounced in the cramped quarters of 19th-century Josefov but also in its high-sided streets and dark little alleyways. "This narrow circle encompasses my entire life", he said to a friend, pointing to the area within a square mile of the Old Town Square. Yet Prague was also always alluring, mysterious, attractive, drawing him back again and again. In the same conversation with a friend Kafka went on to say of the view from his flat above

the square, that it was "the most beautiful setting that has ever been seen on
this earth". To Franz Kafka the city remained the "little mother with claws" to
the end.

*Woodcutters preserve the surrounds
of Kafka's grave in the New Jewish
cemetery.*

The Ancient Seat of Power, a Stronghold Built to Keep Invaders Out

Visible from the rest of the city as a fairy-tale "castle in the air", Prague Castle turns out on closer inspection to be the size of a small town. All the trappings of religion and war, from cathedral and basilica on the one hand to powder tower and battlements on the other, are contained within its walls, whilst the area around it is well-endowed with palaces and gardens. Once housing no one but the President, the Castle area in high season is now effectively occupied by the rest of the world, and the President has gone off to live in the New Town.

Hradčany (the castle area) is the city's most famous and prominent landmark. Prague was founded here, and from here the kingdom of Bohemia, and for a time much of Europe, was governed for centuries.

History

The castle originated as a seat of tribal princes and kings, whose dynasty was known as the Přemyslids and who ruled Bohemia until 1306. It was founded in the late 9th century when the Přemyslids recognized the value of a stronghold in the centre of their territories, on a headland near a ford of the River Vltava, providing both military security and access to trade routes. They set out at once to fortify it with towers, moats, palisades and a bulwark. As a consequence the castle area in Prague, rather like the Kremlin in Moscow, soon became a virtual fortified town in its own right, containing churches, houses and palaces— one for the prince and one for the bishop. A few settlements, outside the fortifications but under their protective wing, were set up at the same time on either side of the river.

The castle was not impregnable. Destruction in 1041 was followed by rebuilding using dry stone walls, and further changes followed in the 12th century as

Samples from the cathedral treasury.

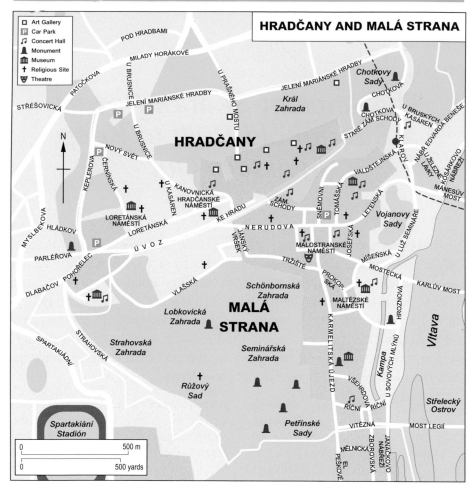

- □ Art Gallery
- P Car Park
- ♫ Concert Hall
- ▲ Monument
- 🏛 Museum
- † Religious Site
- ♛ Theatre

HRADČANY AND MALÁ STRANA

POD HRADBAMI

MILADY HORÁKOVÉ

STŘEŠOVICKÁ

PATOČKOVA

U BRUSNICE

JELENÍ MARIÁNSKÉ HRADBY

U PRAŠNÉHO MOSTU

JELENÍ MARIÁNSKÉ HRADBY

Chotkovy Sady

Král Zahrada

CHOTKOVA

CHOTKOVA

STARÉ ZÁM SCHODY

U BRUSKÝCH KASÁREN

NÁBŘ. EDVARDA BENEŠE

KLÁROV

N

NOVÝ SVĚT

U BRUSNICE

HRADČANY

KEPLEROVA

ČERNÍNSKÁ

KANOVNICKÁ

HRADČANSKÉ NÁMĚSTÍ

U KASÁREN

KE HRADU

ZÁM. SCHODY

SNĚMOVNÍ

TOMÁŠSKÁ

VALDŠTEJNSKÁ

LETENSKÁ

ŽELEZNÁ LÁVKY

KOŠÁRKOVO NÁBŘEŽÍ

MÁNESŮV MOST

MYSLBEKOVA

HLÁDKOV

LORETÁNSKÁ NÁMĚSTÍ

LORETÁNSKÁ

ÚVOZ

NERUDOVA

JÁNSKÝ VRŠEK

MALOSTRANSKÉ NÁMĚSTÍ

JOSEFSKÁ

MÍŠEŇSKÁ

U LUŽ SEMINÁŘE

Vojanovy Sady

PARLÉŘOVA

POHOŘELEC

DLABAČOV

VLAŠSKÁ

TRŽIŠTĚ

PROKOPSKÁ

MOSTECKÁ

KARLŮV MOST

Schönbornská Zahrada

MALTÉZSKÉ NÁMĚSTÍ

HROZNOVÁ

Lobkovická Zahrada

MALÁ STRANA

KARMELITSKÁ ÚJEZD

Vltava

SPARTAKIÁDNÍ

STRAHOVSKÁ

Strahovská Zahrada

Seminářská Zahrada

VŠEHRDOVA MLÝNŮ

U SOVOVÝCH MLÝNŮ

Kampa

Růžový Sad

ŘÍČNÍ

ŘÍČNÍ

Střelecký Ostrov

Spartakiání Stadión

Petřínské Sady

VÍTĚZNÁ

MOST LEGIÍ

MĚLNICKÁ

ZBOROVSKÁ

JANÁČKOVO NÁBŘEŽÍ

EL PEŠKOVÉ

| 0 | 500 m |
| 0 | 500 yards |

T own plan of Hradčany and Malá Strana areas.

the latest techniques of fortification, using limestone and mortar, were put to use. Damage and rebuilding was also engendered by that other great enemy of medieval towns, fire. The most important changes, however, took place in the 14th century when King Charles IV determined to put Prague on the map as a European Regional Capital. He was King of

Bohemia and also Holy Roman Emperor and therefore effectively the ruler of Europe. As part of his "Beecham" programme the castle became the Emperor's official residence, and a number of the most notable buildings in the castle area, such as St Vitus' Cathedral, were "upgraded" with a thorough High Gothic overhaul.

The castle survived capture by the Hussites in the 15th century and was extended in Renaissance style in the 16th, but in the 17th century it lost its importance as a focal point of European politics. After the

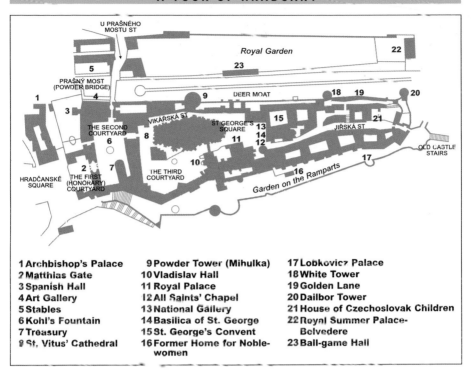

U PRAŠNÉHO MOSTU ST

Royal Garden — 22

23

5

PRAŠNÝ MOST (POWDER BRIDGE)

1

3

4

9

DEER MOAT

18 19 — 20

VIKÁŘSKÁ ST

THE SECOND COURTYARD

6

8

ST GEORGE'S SQUARE 13 14 11 12

15

JIŘSKÁ ST

21

OLD CASTLE STAIRS

2

7

THE FIRST (HONORARY) COURTYARD

THE THIRD COURTYARD

10

16

17

HRADČANSKÉ SQUARE

Garden on the Ramparts

1 Archbishop's Palace	9 Powder Tower (Mihulka)	17 Lobkovicz Palace
2 Matthias Gate	10 Vladislav Hall	18 White Tower
3 Spanish Hall	11 Royal Palace	19 Golden Lane
4 Art Gallery	12 All Saints' Chapel	20 Dailbor Tower
5 Stables	13 National Gallery	21 House of Czechoslovak Children
6 Kohl's Fountain	14 Basilica of St. George	22 Royal Summer Palace-
7 Treasury	15 St. George's Convent	Belvedere
8 St. Vitus' Cathedral	16 Former Home for Noble-	23 Ball-game Hall
	women	

*M*ap *of the castle area.*

Battle of the White Mountain in 1620, the Czech state effectively lost its independence and became absorbed in the wider Hapsburg Empire whose seat of government was Vienna rather than Prague. The castle was neglected for long periods, and during the late 18th century was put at the disposal of the army as a barracks, a move unlikely to improve its artistic merits. The 19th century, however, a time of rising Czech nationalism, heralded a new importance for the castle as a symbol of Bohemia's former glory. Groups sprang up like the "Association for the Completion of St Vitus' Cathedral", determined to restore the whole castle area.

These efforts bore fruit in 1918 with the achievement of an independent Czech republic after the First World War. The castle was once again the seat of a head of state. It was hardly damaged by the Second World War, and in 1945 was declared a national monument. It remained a centre of government under communist rule, and in 1989, when the government was brought down in the peaceful Velvet Revolution, Prague Castle was the focus of popular desire for political change, reflected in the slogan seen all over the city "Havel na Hrad" (Havel to the Castle).

A Tour of Hradčany

If you are feeling fit, the best approach to the castle is by one of the routes outlined at the end of our tour of Malá Strana.

From the Lesser Town Square the options are two-fold. One is to walk up Nerudova, and then go right where the street meets Úvoz and turn up Ke Hradu. You could also turn right earlier on as you ascend Nerudova, and tackle the steep, atmospheric but narrow Zámecká (Zámek is another word for castle, although usually used for something more like a château) coming out at Zámecké schody. The other option is to leave the Lesser Town Square by way of Sněmovní and Thunovská, which will also bring you to Zámecké schody. Schod is the Czech word for a step, which means that either route will entail flights of steps as well as a steep hill!

An alternative route is to take a metro or a tram to Hradčany, although it has to be emphasized that in neither case will you end up right outside the castle. The underground deposits you on the busy main road Milady Horákové, from which you have to walk up the hill on the far side of the road to Mariánské hradby. There are trams to Milady Horákové as well, but the number 22 takes you to the top of Mariánské hradby, which is the nearest point to the castle by public transport. From here it is a relatively short walk down U Prašného mostu to a side entrance of the castle. In the summer months a little tourist train, looking as if it's escaped from a seaside promenade, might be on hand to carry you right up to the entrance.

Courtyards of the Castle

The routes to the castle from the Lesser Town Square come out in **Hradčanské náměstí** (the castle square area). Enter the first courtyard of the castle through a wrought-iron gateway flanked by fighting giants, copies of statues by Ignatius Platzer the Elder. Posted beneath them are a

---

Changing of the Guard
Prior to the Velvet Revolution the guards sported a dull khaki outfit, which has since been replaced by costumes designed by Theodore Pištěk, a friend of the President and responsible for the outfits worn in Miloš Forman's film set in Prague about the life of Mozart, *Amadeus*. The new costumes have been described as "Ruritanian". They seem perfectly attuned to the surreal quality of Prague Castle—along with the brass band dressed in red which performs on Sunday mornings.

---

couple of sentries, looking by comparison with the titans above like toy soldiers, suffering endless camera-clicking distraction with a stony-faced self-control. Since the Revolution their uniform has been changed to that of the pre-war Czech Republic. A changing of the guard takes place every hour on the hour.

Passing between huge flagpoles made from Czech firs, the Matthias Gate leads into the second courtyard. As you pass through the arch of the gate a staircase to the right (which is not open to the public) leads to rooms traditionally occupied by the President. However, Havel prefers not to live in the presidential palace, and instead keeps a flat close to the river in the New Town area. The second courtyard is an austere combination of granite paving and plaster, with the Lion Fountain offering a little light relief. The **Kaple sv. Kříže** (Holy Cross Chapel), designed by Anselmo Lurago, contains a collection of priceless objects taken from St Vitus' Cathedral; such as reliquaries and golden chalices, and even if you aren't inspired by a collection of holy relics the interior decoration is worth the small entrance fee. The present system for visiting the castle involves paying a few crowns for everything from visiting the cathedral crypt to

The Changing of the Guard. After the Velvet Revolution the Palace Guard exchanges its khaki uniforms (left) for blue outfits (right) recalling the pre-communist Czech Republic (here in a winter version including fur hat)

a tour of the royal gardens, but the whole lot can be seen for the equivalent of an English pound or a couple of American dollars.

The north side of the courtyard contains the Plečnik Hall, the product of some 20th-century reconstruction of the interior. If open, it contains an exhibition of paintings collected by the Emperor Rudolf II, although when the imperial residence moved from Prague to Vienna much of the collection moved with it. About 70 paintings from the 16th to 18th centuries

remain, but despite the small number there are some that are particularly valuable: Tintoretto, Rubens, Veronese, not to mention those that reflect Czech art, such as the Bohemian Baroque artist Kupecky.

The third courtyard brings you right opposite St Vitus' Cathedral – so close to it, in fact, that it is hard not to wish that everything else would just disappear or at least recede to a respectful distance.

St Vitus' Cathedral

Chrám svatého Vita (St Vitus' Cathedral) is like so many other churches, bridges, castles, palaces and other buildings in Prague – it is the product of a history that includes many different styles. Although it is a magnificent building, the styles do not all gel with one another. In fact, despite its impressive size as the largest church in the city, there is something almost quaint about parts of it. Go, for instance, to the south end of the

Gothic topped with Baroque—an example of the mixture of styles in St Vitus' Cathedral.

building. Above the south door (the **Zlatá brána** or Golden Gate), on the triple-arched anteroom of the portal, there is a mosaic depicting The Day of Judgment by Italian artists of the 14th century. Stand back from the doorway, and look upwards

88

at the whole of the cathedral. A tower which in the 16th century was given a Renaissance top now sports a Baroque roof that was added two centuries later. Such a mixture of styles may be bizarre, but it makes the cathedral more "human", offsetting its grandeur with something almost comic.

It was founded by the ever-aspiring Emperor Charles IV in 1344, who employed a French architect, Matthias of Arras, to bring the fashionable Gothic style to Prague. It was continued by Peter Parler and his sons until the 15th-century Hussite wars intervened, and then continued in the 16th with the north tower and pillars of the main nave. In the next three centuries further Renaissance and Baroque additions were made, and in 1861 a "Union for the Completion of the Cathedral" was formed. The Neo-Gothic western end was completed only in 1929, since when only minor alterations and repairs have been carried out.

Inside the cathedral the first reaction will probably be to note its impressive size, especially when its 28 piers and 21 chapels are viewed from the centre. Beyond that, the mosaic effect of much of its relatively modern stained glass is very noticeable. Above the west door is a tracery window designed by F. Kysela dating from 1921 depicting the creation of the world. Kysela also designed the window in the Thun chapel, *Allegory of the Threat of Property* (third on the right from the west end), the decorative mosaic *Deeds of Mercy* in the Chapel of the Barton Family of Dobenin, and the painted window in the same chapel (first on the left from the west end).

Many of the other windows were painted during the inter-war years by leading Czech painters like Max

Švabinský, who designed the *Last Judgment* over the south door. However, the most well-known is the painted window by Alfons Mucha, *Saints Cyril and Methodius*, designed in 1931 and located in the New Archbishop's Chapel. This has contained the burial vault of the Prague archbishops since 1909 (third on the left from the west end). The style is suggestive of Art Nouveau (Mucha also designed Art Nouveau posters for Sarah Bernhardt), a strong contrast to the more abstract approach of Kysela.

On the north side of the transept (the part of the cathedral which bisects the long nave at the centre) is a wooden sculpture of the crucifixion by František Bílek (some of whose work is on permanent exhibition in Prague—*see* below) dating from 1899. Bílek, of whom more later, did several sculptures on religious themes, and biblical characters like Jesus or Mary are always portrayed in a very human way, as if the labour of the one or the crucifixion of the other involved real suffering.

The main attraction of the cathedral is always the Chapel of St Wenceslas (**sv Václav**), to be found on the south side of the cathedral next to the transept. In summer this is immediately recognisable from the crowds that gather around its two entrances, since it is not actually possible to go into it. Perhaps for this reason, seeing its gilded walls lit up by the light from bronze candelabra, walls that are inlaid with stones and decorated with frescoes beneath paintings depicting the life of St Wenceslas, is rather like gazing into a grotto. It is impressive enough, but seems out of place in a cathedral designed in a style of severe Gothic grandeur.

It pales into insignificance, however, beside the Tomb of St John of Nepomuk, designed in a fit of over-indulgence by

The Chapel of St Wenceslas

Like the Jesuits and Communists in future centuries, Charles IV knew the value of martyrdom and mythology to national unity. The grotto-like chapel, crammed with paintings, plasterwork and precious stones, is dedicated to the martyr Wenceslas who died at the hands of his brother Boleslav the Cruel in 935. In effect the grave was turned into a national shrine, and "Good King Wenceslas" (who despite the carol was a Prince) became a cult figure who could unite the nation (as he has remained to this day).

A good means of escape at this point is to descend—for a mere two crowns—into the crypt. This contains the remains of the walls of two Romanesque churches, usually festooned with coins which are customarily thrown in as if it were a wishing-well. This recalls once again the fact that a cathedral is not a single unity built in a short space of time, but the product of centuries-long building, often in very different styles, in a particular place. In this area are the sarcophagi of Charles IV, his children and his four wives and a few other

J.E. Fischer of Erlach in the 18th century. This Baroque extravaganza, situated near the east end of the cathedral, is composed of a tomb surrounded by a red marble balustrade topped with statues, over which four silver angels hold up a "baldachin", a ludicrous piece of drapery donated by the Empress Maria Theresa.

The interior courtyards of Prague Castle are an abundance of granite paving and plastered walls. This is the third courtyard which faces St Vitus' Cathedral.

notables. Look at the size to see how better diet has helped people to grow over the last 600 years! A number have been re-interred in modern imitations of the ancient sarcophagi, and there they lie under lights to be inspected by the streams of prying visitors.

Royal Palace

Across the courtyard from the south door of the cathedral is the **Královský palác** (Royal Palace), royal residence of the rulers of Bohemia until the 16th century. It was, however, relegated to the role of office and storage space under the Hapsburgs, when the centre of authority moved to another part of the castle.

The building is a conglomerate of different historical layers, with the oldest at the bottom. Thus the basement area contains remains of an original Romanesque palace dating from the 12th century, whilst the next two floors display sections of new palaces built in the next two centuries by Otakar II and the omnipresent Charles IV. These were reconstructed at the end of the 15th century, when a new floor was added by King Vladislav Jagellon. It is this third floor which contains the famous **Vladislavský sál** (Vladislav Hall), a masterpiece of Late Gothic architecture designed by Benedikt Ried, and at the time the largest secular hall in Prague.

Beneath the impressive rib-vaulting of this hall took place meetings, banquets, luxury markets and, in bad weather, indoor jousting tournaments. For these, the knights entered by the Riders' Staircase, recognizable by its width and gentle steps. Nowadays connected with the election of the President of the Czechoslovak Republic, it was here that Havel was sworn in at the end of 1989, when the hopes of "Havel na Hrad" were finally fulfilled.

As you enter the hall, the Riders' Staircase will be on your left and at the far end a short set of steps leads you to a balcony overlooking All Saints' Chapel, once again built above a Romanesque original in imitation of Saint-Chapelle in Paris, and then rebuilt again in a Renaissance design after a fire in the 16th century. Also on your left, beyond the Riders' Staircase, will be the Hall of the Diet, another imposing room and once again the work of Benedict Ried, but rebuilt 20 years later after a fire with some added Renaissance touches. It was here that the Supreme Court of Justice sat, and extra solemnity is conveyed by the portraits of famous Hapsburg rulers on the walls.

Surviving Defenestration

It was from a room in the tower here that two of the Emperor's Governors and their clerk were defenestrated in 1618 by angry Bohemian Protestant noblemen. Despite a fall of 15 m (50 ft) they survived with what one contemporary account called "only a few scratches". Their survival was hailed by the Catholic Church as a product of the miraculous intervention of the Virgin Mary. A more likely but prosaic explanation is that they had the good fortune to land in a dung-heap.

A few other rooms contain some 17th-century furniture, crests and emblems, and a smattering of historical memorabilia. It is worth breaking off from looking at the rooms however, and returning to what would be the top right hand corner of the Vladislav Hall opposite the entrance to the Hall of the Diet. It is possible to walk out onto a balcony here and see one of the finest views of Prague, looking down over red rooves towards the domes of the Old Town framed in the waters of the Vltava River, or across at the Petřín Hill above the Malá Strana. It is a magnificent sight.

The russet red of St George's Basilica in Prague Castle.

Basilica of St George

From the Royal Palace the next stop must be the twin-towered Romanesque **Basilica sv. Jiří** (Basilica of St George) facing the eastern end of the cathedral with its unmistakable red façade. It has the familiar history of medieval buildings.

Founded in the 10th century, it was burned down in the 12th, rebuilt and burned down again in the 16th, rebuilt again in Baroque style in the 18th century, and then restored in something designed to look Romanesque again in the 20th. Now used as a concert hall, it may strike you as having an air of soulless renovation, but at the back of the church there is a marvellous modern sculpture of the crucifixion designed by O. Hajek of Stuttgart (*Kristus z kmene stromu*).

Convent of St George

Next door to the basilica is the **Klášter sv. Jiří** (Convent of St George) which houses a collection of Old Bohemian Art. Although this might suggest a rather esoteric collection, it is in fact fascinating. A full two-volume guide in several languages, including English, can be borrowed from the ticket-desk. As with the buildings, Gothic Art is in the basement, Renaissance on the ground floor and Baroque on the first. If you are getting tired and hungry by now, a succession of madonnas with child might prove excessive, but the exhibition is really very interesting. The Gothic art reproduces themes from the gospels in vivid style, with lots of blood and devils. The room dedicated to the imperial painter Master Theodoric contains six intriguing panel-sections taken from a panel at nearby Karlštejn Castle. A mixture of colour, light and glazes makes the line of portraits stand out—a row of medieval figures designed with big heads and long noses, wide eyes and fleshy lips, all held up by short thick necks, and yet conveying a real spirituality.

Refreshment

At this point refreshment may be something of a necessity. There is a small coffee bar in the exhibition, but you may prefer to go to the nearby **Zlatá ulička** (Golden Lane), easily reached by going round the corner from the Convent a little further away from the cathedral. On the way you pass a restaurant/wine-bar (**U zlaté uličky**), which will almost

The Golden Lane

There are a number of theories about the origin of the street's name. One puts it down to alchemy, and argues that many of those who lived here devoted themselves to the alchemist's dream of turning base metals into gold. However, the alchemists didn't live in the street and had their laboratory in the Mihulkar Tower. An even less plausible suggestion is that the Emperor Rudolf II's infantrymen who were barracked in the lane found it difficult to cope with sharing only one toilet, and that the name of the street came from their unfortunate habit of relieving themselves in public! The obvious explanation that it derives from the fact that the emperor's goldsmiths were housed here (it was originally called Zlatnická ulice or Goldsmiths' Lane) is clearly too dull to be believable.

One of the City's more famous alleyways—the Golden Lane in Prague Castle.

certainly be full of panting tourists. Never mind—there's a drinking fountain nearby and if you continue into the Golden Lane and turn left there's another café on the left hand side at the top. This will always have space inside even if the tables outside are full, and it sports a rather decorous ceiling. The Golden Lane itself is an extraordinary piece of kitsch in pastel shades. Since there is only one entrance into what is in effect a blind alley, the Golden Lane becomes a tourist bottleneck throughout the summer. Some of the crowd is absorbed into the cottages to be plied with prints, cards and other mementoes, while the rest set to with cameras, only to find that pressure of numbers forces them inadvertently to take photographs of each other. January is the best time to see the Golden Lane, but even then it has an oppressively unreal air. No one lives in this Toytown which exists only for show.

It is possible to leave the castle here and descend to a point a few metres away from the Malostranská underground station by way of the **Staré zámecké schody** (literally Old Castle Steps). It is a wonderful walk on a relatively gentle incline (the steps are fairly far apart), the yellow wall on the left overhung with wild vines and the wall on the right low enough not to obscure the view of the city. Artists and "entrepreneurs" display their wares as you make the descent. Of course if you fancy a long but relatively gentle climb you can always approach the castle this way from the Malostranská metro station.

 ## Powder Tower

However, there are many other noteworthy sights in the Hradčany area. Within the castle itself there is one building as yet undescribed, which requires a retracing of steps to the third courtyard and St Vitus' Cathedral. This is **Prasna vez** (the Powder Tower), located on the north side of the cathedral, just beyond the information centre.

Built as part of late 15th-century improvements to the northern fortifications of the castle, the Powder Tower was used for a variety of purposes including munitions dump and general storeroom, and was never put to the test in battle. It now serves for a variety of exhibitions. The basement display illustrates the use of the tower as a metal foundry in the 16th century, and features examples of metal casting (partly guns, but also peacetime artefacts like bells, vases and sculptures). The Ground Floor concentrates upon the original function of the Tower, demonstrating the way in which it was designed to protect the surrounding moats.

The first floor offers a reconstruction of an alchemist's laboratory. Alchemy may have been practised in the Tower, since wherever there was metalwork there were usually some pseudo-scientific hangers-on trying to turn it into gold. However, the display also examines some of more useful technologies developed in the 16th century as mining expanded in the region, which meant in turn a development of processes used to smelt and process the metals extracted. The second floor contains a fragment of Rudolf II's art, mineral and curio collection from Renaissance Europe.

From the Powder Tower it is only a short walk to the second courtyard, from which it is possible to leave the castle at the north end by the side road mentioned earlier. It is important to reiterate that all we have seen so far is **Pražský Hrad** (Prague castle), which is not so much a building as a set of buildings located within a fortified area. There is much to see in Hradčany (the name of the district) outside the castle, but everything seen so far should be considered to be inside the castle. For this reason, we do not give opening times at the end of this section for each part of the castle, because the whole area is open from 9.00 a.m. to 5.00 p.m. (except Mondays), and there is very little variation on this in the particular buildings.

Exhibitions

A short distance up the road from the side entrance to the castle, past two more stationary guards in blue uniforms, there is an exhibition of modern Czech art from the 20th century (in fact 1908-1968, the year in which the Prague Spring was put down by Soviet tanks). The exhibition is housed in **Jízdárna** (the former Riding School), and is on the left hand side as you leave the castle complex.

Only a few days after the Velvet Revolution of November 1989, a decision was made to renew an exhibition of modern Czech art which had been cancelled by the repressive regime installed by Soviet military might in the early 1970s, in a process designated by the Orwellian term "normalisation". Thereby a tradition of art which had made Prague a European centre in the early 20th century was given new life again. The exhibition begins in 1908 with the birth of Cubism in the city, and moves through a variety of styles to the new ideas of the 1960s which followed the death of Stalin. Sculpture and graphic art are included alongside paintings. Exhibitions of this sort are blossoming all over the city now, partly because of the new freedom but also because a genuinely original style which had made Prague a European centre

earlier in the century is being rediscovered. The title of the exhibition is **Český Umění 1908-1968: osobnosti a hodnoty** (Czech Art 1908-1968: Personalities and Values).

Royal Gardens

Opposite the exhibition are the best-kept gardens in Prague, to enter which you need a few crowns. Ad hoc refreshment stalls should be at hand to offer ice-cream (zmrzlina) or soft drinks if you need refreshment before going in. Apart from the usual lawns and fountains, the **Královská zahrada** (Royal Gardens) contain two interesting buildings.

The first is a 16th-century indoor sports hall designed by Rudolf II for real tennis and notable for its sgraffito walls designed by his court architect Bonifaz Wolmut in the late 1560s. Its figurative decoration was restored in the mid-20th century when the building was taken over for gatherings of communist party dignitaries. Since 1989 it has tended to function as a temporary exhibition centre, so it's worth seeing what's on. As you walk through the gardens from the only entrance the building is on your right.

The second building not to miss is the **Královské letohrádek** (Belvedere Palace) at the far end of the gardens, a Renaissance pleasure palace built in the late 16th century by Ferdinand I as a present for his wife Anna. Its arcades and its curving roof were designed to follow the style of the Italian Renaissance by an architect from Genoa, Paolo della Stella. The external colonnades depict motifs from Greek mythology and Ferdinand I presenting his wife with a flower. Presumably she preferred the palace. However, the frescoes in the Great Hall may well be out of bounds,

The Belvedere Summer House at the end of the Royal Gardens.

since extensive renovation is presently being carried out on the interior. The Belvedere Palace offers excellent views of the castle, even if it is not possible at present to look out at it from the upper balcony.

This is as far as our tour of Hradčany goes in this direction, but it is worth mentioning that the tour of Letná outlined below in the "Other Areas" section ends at this point in the Chotek Gardens on the far side of the Belvedere Palace. You can see them beyond the reconstruction works, quiet and restful in comparison with the milling throngs in the Royal Gardens, but to reach them you will have to climb over fences or walls, which is quite easy, if a little indecorous. The only formal exit to the Gardens requires you to retrace your

steps. In any case seeing the rest of Hradčany entails returning into the castle and out again by the fighting titans at the main gate.

Castle Square Area

Hradčanské náměstí (the castle square) outside the gate is a large open space full of tour groups. Like the castle itself, it is an area containing little sign of anyone living there or even of anyone Czech. What in the 16th century was a market square bustling with people shopping or working now has the air of a giant tourist theme park dominated by the former palaces of the nobility on either side. On the left as you leave the castle is the most impressive example of the sgraffito style which has just been observed in the Royal Gardens, the **Schwarzenberg-palota** (Schwarzenberg Palace), now used as a museum of military history. The rooms are worth a look even if the exhibits aren't. On the right is the **Arcibiskupský palác** (Archbishop's Palace), built in Renaissance style in the 16th century, reconstructed in Baroque style in the 17th, and then given its present Rococo style in the 18th. It is

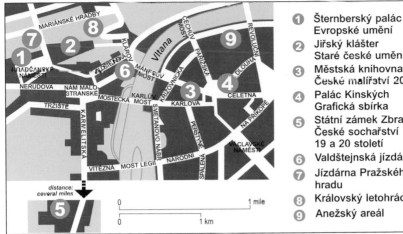

1. Šternberský palác
   Evropské umění
2. Jiřský klášter
   Staré české umění
3. Městská knihovna
   České malířství 20 století
4. Palác Kinských
   Grafická sbírka
5. Státní zámek Zbraslav
   České sochařství
   19 a 20 století
6. Valdštejnská jízdárna
7. Jízdárna Pražského hradu
8. Královský letohrádek
9. Anežský areál

*P*lan of the National Gallery.

open only once a year, on Maundy Thursday (the Thursday before Easter).

Sternberg Palace

Before exploring the square further, it is essential to slip down the passage next to the Archbishop's Palace to the 18th-century **Šternberský palác** (Sternberg Palace). This building contains a wonderful collection of art and sculpture-wonderful in that although it is not a huge collection almost every painting is worth seeing and a wide range of art is represented. It is in this palace that the **Národní Galerie** (National Gallery) has its best

exhibition. Remember that "National Gallery", like "State Jewish Museum", refers not to a single place but to a collection distributed among a number of buildings in the city—*see* the map above.

In this wonderful setting of the Sternberg Palace you can find a roomful of

*O*ne of the glories of the National Gallery Exhibition in the Sternberg Palace: Adam and Eve painted by Lucas Cranach the Elder with a very carefully placed "fig leaf".

Picasso in an excellent collection of 19th- and 20th-century French art. Dwell on Toulouse-Lautrec's *Moulin Rouge,* a smattering of Manet, Renoir, Monet, Pissarro, Chagall and Raoul Dufy, exhibited in a room dotted with Rodin sculptures which you walk around as you admire the paintings.

On the first floor there are works from the 15th to 18th centuries, including Pieter Brueghel the Elder's *The Haymaking,* a number of works by Dürer, Tintoretto, and El Greco, a Canaletto of the Thames in 1746, and a wonderful painting of Adam and Eve looking shifty with apple and serpent by Cranach. They even manage to share the same fig leaf in this particular artist's view of Eden.

Another room contains some modern art with sculpture by Henry Moore and paintings by Munch and Gustav Klimt. In all there is a little of everything and not too much of anything in this exhibition, and the palatial rooms, some of them with fine views of the area, give added atmosphere to the displays. The inner courtyard of the castle, with seats and cobbles, provides a perfect place to relax after seeing the art before moving on through the rest of Hradčany.

Palaces and Cottages

Returning to the castle square, turn right and head to the far side, passing as you go one of the many elaborate collections of gas lamps in this part of the city. At the far end opposite the castle is the 17th-century **Toscana palác** (Tuscany Palace), which was restored after the Second World War, and to the right of the Tuscany Palace, facing away from the castle, is the Renaissance Martinitz Palace.

During the reconstruction of the Martinic palác in the early 1970s, a band of sgraffito figural decoration from around 1600 was discovered on the façade of the building, depicting various biblical themes. There are other biblical and classical themes depicted in the courtyard, and a riot of ceiling decoration, in some cases with copper beam ceilings, in the great hall and other rooms inside, though these are only open for special events.

Next to the Martinitz Palace is Kanovnická, leading to a row of cottages not unlike those in the Golden Lane in appearance, but in other ways preferable to it in that people actually live and work here. Although the Golden Lane (**Zlatá ulička**) can claim that Franz Kafka lived in number 22 or that the poet J. Seifert used to live in the street, Nový Svět (which means "New World") is infinitely preferable for the fact that modern-day artists live here, their windows open to the street, through some of which it is possible to catch a glimpse of half-completed paintings and stacks of canvases. There are the familiar house signs, a disproportionate number of which are named "Golden", whether it's golden leg, star or pear. There is a wine-bar called The Golden Pear—u zlaté hrušky—which is a little tacky by Prague's high standards. This former settlement in front of the castle is particularly atmospheric because it is actually lived in—one of the few parts of Hradčany which actually conveys such an impression.

Loreto Square

Follow Nový Svět into Černínská, and you go slightly uphill to **Loretánské náměstí,** (Loreto Square) which is dominated by the 153 m (500 ft) long façade of the Černín palace on your right. Built in the 17th century for Humprecht Johann, Count of Černín, the palace was assessed by the visiting Emperor, with whom the Count had a quarrel, as little more than a huge barn. Certainly time appears to have confirmed the judgment that the building is more monumental than beautiful.

Damaged in the 18th century, it became a military hospital during the Napoleonic Wars, and then suffered the fate all fine buildings dread, becoming a barracks in 1851. At the same time the whole square became a military exercising ground. After the First World War the new Czech Republic up-graded it to the Foreign Ministry, and it was then taken over by the communist government of 1948, which continued the age-old Prague political tradition of defenestration by throwing Jan Masaryk, the last non-communist in the ruling group, out of a top-floor bathroom window. Now that the building has been restored it is likely that the decorous interior (ceiling-frescoes by V.V. Reiner), palace gardens and orangery will be open to view.

Loreto Chapel

Opposite the Palace is the **Loretánská kaple** (Loreto Chapel), a place of pilgrimage which can only be understood in the context of 17th century politics. A few years after the famous Battle of the White Mountain in 1620, when the army of the Catholic Hapsburgs defeated a rebel Protestant force whose ideas went back to the Hussites of the 14th century, an attempt was made to increase popular support for Catholicism by means of the Cult of Mary, a tradition which has always been based more on religious populism than theological reason.

In 1626 the Prague Loreto was founded as part of this endeavour to popularize Catholicism, based on the legend that a cottage in which the Virgin Mary

> **Church of the Nativity**
> This includes a painting of St Agatha offering to an angel her breasts which were cut off under torture, and what looks like Christ on the Cross but turns out instead to be St Wilgefortis who was given a beard by God to save her from marriage. More attractive are the ceiling-paintings by V.V.Reiner, but don't look too closely at the glass boxes on either side of the altar.

lived had been miraculously transferred from Nazareth to Loreto, near Ancona on the Adriatic coast of Italy. This legend grew up in Italy in the 14th century and then spread to other parts of Europe in subsequent centuries, who built their own "Loretos" in imitation of the Italian "original". The Loreto in Prague, whose population at the time was largely non-Catholic, was founded in 1626 as part of the drive to rally the peasants to Catholicism by the Blessed Catherine of Lobkowic.

The Prague Loreto, despite being patterned on the Italian, was in fact heavily influenced by Central European Baroque, and the later 18th century façade which is the traveller's first encounter with the buildings is the work of foremost Baroque architect Kilian Ignaz Dientzenhofer in the 1740s. The late 17th century early Baroque bell-tower plays Marian hymns every hour on bells cast in Amsterdam. Once inside the building the **Loretánská kaple** (Loreto chapel) itself is to be found inside the cloisters, decorated with stucco reliefs depicting scenes from the lives of Old Testament prophets. A cedarwood Madonna stands in a silver surround behind a silver grille. Elsewhere in the shrine another statue of the Virgin in Linden wood is framed in a silver plate garland of winged cherubs' heads. With

over 45 kg (100 lbs) of silver discernible in the gloom of this (from the inside) architecturally nondescript rectangular building, the impression is one of expensive kitsch, but worse is yet to come.

Moving through the cloisters, a number of chapels can be seen (not all of them on view) but it is to the **Kostel Narození Páně** (Church of the Nativity) that the visitor inevitably heads. This has a basically

The facade of the Loreto Chapel, designed in the 1740s by Kilian Ignaz Dientzenhofer.

graceful Baroque interior with excellent ceiling-frescoes by V.V. Reiner, although you have to tolerate a surfeit of cherubs, who appear to sit on or stick out of just about every item of furniture in the building. There is also an extraordinary hanging light looking like dozens of silver needles in a pin cushion.

By far the most gloriously grotesque of all Loreto's displays, however, is the "Treasury". Loretos often grew up as treasure-chambers where the wealthy made gifts to the church, and the noble victors in the Battle of the White Mountain were only too happy to encourage the means by which they hoped to become popular, or at least acceptable. Silver chalices, gilded candlesticks, gold chains and coronets all poured in, but the present Treasury on the upper floor contains only some of these items because the collection suffered from confiscations during the years of the Napoleonic Wars. Even so, this huge jewellery box has various liturgical objects and other religious exotica (most famous of which are the monstrances, in which Catholics keep the host or bread—believed to be Christ's body—for veneration at the service of Benediction). The Viennese silver monstrance with over six thousand diamonds is the star of the show, a priceless but completely tasteless piece of tat rivalled only by the Hawthorn Garland monstrance, whose 30 red corals surround the crown in a circle of berries touched off with green-enamelled leaves.

Escape from the Loreto complex leads into the pleasant environment of the restaurant/cafe **U Lorety** next door, on whose terrace it is possible to have a drink and snack opposite the Černín Palace, and relax to the gruelling chimes of a Marian hymn from the Dutch bells.

Strahov Monastery

The final stage of our tour of Hradčany is the **Strahovský klášter** (Strahov Monastery), reached by a short journey from the Loreto Square westwards along Pohořelec. Lying on the slopes of the Petřín Hill, the actual location of the monastery is on the border between Hradčany and Malá Strana, and on leaving the abbey through the orchards behind it you can join one of the routes via Úvoz and Nerudova or via Vlašská and Tržiště to the Lesser Town Square described in the section on Malá Strana. Whatever route is chosen, there is no walk down to the river from this beautiful abbey that is unrewarding.

The monastery was founded in the 12th century as a Romanesque defence of the approaches to Prague Castle, but fire and war produced the usual changes in style. After a 13th-century fire it was rebuilt in a Gothic manner, until the Hussite revolution interrupted the renewal. Two further uneventful centuries were then ended by the Swedish army, which was very powerful during the early 17th-century Thirty Years' War from 1618-1648, who raided its treasures and library. The late 17th century saw a number of Baroque adaptations which gave Strahov its present appearance, together with a framework of orchards and gardens. Further destruction was wrought by the French army, since when the abbey has been effectively preserved until the present day. The advent of a communist government in 1948 entailed the dissolution of all religious orders, and the monastery today is now a museum of national literature, with particular emphasis upon Czech work of the 19th and 20th centuries.

On entering the courtyard the first point of reference is a church on the left, the early 17th-century **Kaple sv. Rocha** (church of St Rochus). This in 1990 contained a fascinating exhibition of modern art but by 1991 had been ear-marked for a prosaic display of liturgical vestments which threatened to become permanent. Straight ahead is the 17th-century **Kostel Nanebevzetí Panny Marie** (Church of the Assumption), whose spruced-up Baroque interior looks delightful, although you may find that it cannot be entered and you have to join a queue at the entrance to look in. On the right hand side as you enter, however, is the entrance to the two most impressive sights in the monastery (viewing may be regulated to the hour and the half hour depending on numbers), the Theological and Philosophical Halls.

Unfortunately, as with the Church of the Assumption, it is only possible to see these magnificent rooms by standing at the entrance to both, and in tune with the whole atmosphere of Hradčany there is something strange about staring at an empty room, however impressive, rather than simply walking through a working library. Short information sheets are available on loan in several languages, including English.

The 18th-century **Teologický sál** (Theological Hall) is relatively low-ceilinged, its frescoes depicting true wisdom rooted in the knowledge of God framed in elaborate stucco ornamentation. It used to be possible to wander through it past the globes and lecterns, but you will probably find that it is impossible now actually to enter the rooms.

The **Filosofický sál** (Philosophical Hall) is a superb room, with a beautiful ceiling fresco showing the development of humanity through wisdom (Baroque painting allied to the philosophy of the Enlightenment with its faith in human

reason). At one end St Paul preaches at the pagan altar based on a passage in the Acts of the Apostles where St Paul finds an altar bearing the inscription "To an Unknown God" and declares that this unknown God is the God of Christianity, whilst at the other stands Moses bearing the tablets of stone given him by God on Mt. Sinai. Between them, the frescoes along the long sides of the hall feature characters from the intellectual history of the human race, many of them apparently lounging around or cavorting in true academic style.

Beneath the frescoes, heavily gold-plated walnut shelves and cabinets made by the joiner Jan Lahofer reach up to the high ceiling which is 14 m (46 ft) off the ground, a fact which shows the extraordinary dimensions of the "room". A couple of desks and a few famous busts on makeshift wooden plinths cover the floor area. They look a little incongruous, like spiked heads on a thick pole.

There are a few natural objects and curiosities on display outside the two main halls, but a more interesting collection can be found in the **Památník národního písemnictví** (Museum of Czech Literature), which is found by leaving this part of the building and going round to an entrance on the other side (although reconstruction may have changed that). Although there is little help for those who don't speak Czech, the extensive literary legacy of Czech writers here includes illustrations and displays that compensate to some extent for any lack of linguistic competence. There are also sculptures, historical maps, paintings, theatre bills, cartoons and reviews, all in the pleasant environment of the Strahov cloisters, touched up with carpets and brightly painted vaulted ceilings. There may also be particular displays around individual Czech artists and writers.

The Strahov monastery completes the tour of Hradčany. From here any one of the many routes down the Petrín Hill affords magnificent views of the city. It is not a lived-in area like the Malá Strana, but more of a permanent display whose popularity never diminishes. Places like the Nový Svět do have inhabitants, and you may feel relief in coming upon them, away from the "model town" guarded by the Toy Soldiers. Tastes vary, but it is difficult not to feel that the Czechs have been intelligent enough, even before the Velvet Revolution, to abandon this part of town as a tourist colony. An area that used to be the centre of fires, battles, or even busy markets, has now been frozen in time for the spectator sport of tourism. Characteristically, the new and very down-to-earth President of the Republic, who has his official residence in this fairyland, has elected not to live there but to remain in the family home on the riverbank in the New Town. To say this is not in any way to decry it—merely to point out that it has a very different atmosphere from those parts of this great city where local people go regularly about their daily business.

Hradčany: Opening Times

1. The opening times for all the sights in Prague Castle are the same: 9.00 a.m. to 5.00 p.m. in summer, 9.00 a.m. to 4.00 p.m. in winter (November to March), and closed Mondays. However, things will begin closing half an hour or so ahead of 5.00 p.m. (4.00 p.m. in winter). At present there is no single ticket for all the sights, and you will have to pay a few crowns for each one. Although the cathedral is free, the cathedral crypt cost 2 crowns in 1991.

2. Čcský Umění 1908–1968: osobnosti a hodnoty (Czech Art 1908–1968: Personalities and Values).
   10.00 a.m. to 6.00 p.m. Not Mondays.
3. Šternberský palác (Sternberg Palace). This is the site of the main collection of the National Gallery.
   Open 10.00 a.m. to 6.00 p.m. Not Mondays.
4. Loretánská kaple (Loreto Chapel).
   9.00 a.m. to 5.00 p.m. Closed lunchtimes 12.00 noon to 1.00 p.m. Not Mondays.
5. Strahov Monastery (including the Museum of Czech Literature—Památnik národního písemnictví).
   9.00 a.m. to 5.00 p.m. Not Mondays.

Highlights for Children

There is not much for young children on this tour. There are more interesting museums for children elsewhere, although a degree of interest might be shown by boys especially in the Museum of Military History (**Vojenské muzeum**), open 9.30 a.m. to 4.30 p.m. (not Mondays), although some might feel that there are more inspiring things to look at than collections of weaponry. The museum can be found in the castle square, in the sgraffitoed building on your left as you face away from the main gates.

For older children, apart from the exhibitions of art and architecture, the Powder Tower contains a display based on its use as a metal foundry, and some illustrations of the history of science in Prague.

However, the **Dům československých dětí** (Czechoslovakian children's house) on Jiřská in Prague Castle (that's between the cathedral and the old castle steps) provides a free creche facility, with plenty of toys, computer games and staff to look after the children.

House Signs and House Numbers

Just as many people prefer to give their homes names like "Treetops" or "The Firs", rather than be satisfied with the impersonal if efficient method of relying on a street number, so a number of houses in Prague were originally identified by signs rather than numbers. The names of houses would be represented pictorially on the outside of the buildings. The pictures might be linked to the geographical location of the building—"At the Bridge", or to the occupation of the owner—"At the Mill". Sometimes they would have a religious motif—"At the Sign of the Black Madonna", or be linked to astral bodies like stars—"At the Sign of the Two Suns".

The signs survived the introduction of street numbering in the late 18th century, and their picturesque designs In stone, metal, tin, wood or plaster contribute a great deal to the charm of many Prague streets.

Identifying a house with a sign may seem quaint, but modern identification based on number is not necessarily clearer. Most buildings in Prague have two numbers on them, one in blue and one in red. The red numbers are of no use to the visitor whatsoever—in fact they indicate the order in which the buildings entered the municipal register! It is the blue numbers which announce the normal street number so if you're seeking the right house in a street, the rule is: ignore the red numbers; look for the blue numbers.

Examples of house signs from the Malá Strana area.

Charming and Secluded, Malá Strana Keeps its Secrets for those who Seek out its Beauty

Malá Strana is the most secretive part of the city, and the best place to escape the tourist throng without losing the beauty of central Prague. Behind several of its walls are semi-public gardens reached by sneakily half-concealed entrances, whilst the air of privacy is intensified by the large number of former palaces which have been turned into foreign embassies. At the same time Malá Strana is developing into a "left bank" with artists' quarters, modish bars and, of course, the John Lennon "memorial".

(Literally "Little Side", but known as the Lesser Quarter). This is one of the best areas of Prague to explore thoroughly. For one thing, its beauties are (relatively) undiscovered. If you have found the crowds around Josefov (The Jewish Quarter) and Staré Město (The Old Town) too much to handle, or at least want a brief escape from the pressures of the tourist throng, then cross over the river to Malá Strana.

*R*iverside scene in the Malá Strana.

History

Human settlements on the left bank of the river, as on the right, go back hundreds of years. A thousand years ago the area today called the Lesser Quarter would have been an agricultural village, perhaps several villages. It acquired a new form in the 12th century, when it became integrated into the system of fortifications around Prague Castle. Originally called the New Town, it acquired its present name at the time of Charles IV, who founded the New Town on the right of the Vltava and so gave the former New Town the name Lesser Quarter. But in the context of Prague's general expansion it was not really a demotion. Rather, what were once agricultural villages outside the fortifications of Prague Castle were now protected

107

within them. Monasteries flourished and made wine on the Petřín Hill, while merchants traded beneath.

Fortunes were to change with the Hussite controversy in the early 15th century. Followers of Hus from the other side of the river challenged the imperial garrison in the Castle. The Lesser Town had the misfortune to be the battleground in the centre, and it was all but destroyed around 1420.

Rebuilding began slowly and cautiously. Further setbacks came in 1541 with a fire, and the Lesser Town continued to suffer from the religious conflicts between the Catholic Hapsburgs and the Protestant Hussites. It was the Lesser Town that saw the beginning and the end of the Thirty Years' War (1618-1648), a conflict which ended with a victory for the citizens of Prague, led by the students, as so much of Prague's political activity appears to have been, against the Swedes on the Charles Bridge.

The late 17th century saw more fortifications go up around the Lesser Town which were to remain there until the 19th century. Baroque added its mark to the fashionable Renaissance style. Well-cultivated gardens took their places beside noble palaces on and around the Petřín Hill. Unfortunately, however, the proximity of the Castle, seat of the Czech kings and the reason for the nobility to put themselves in the neighbourhood, became a much less decisive factor in raising the status of the Lesser Town when the Czech Kings, who were also Hapsburg Emperors, decided that they should reside at Vienna rather than Prague. Indeed 19th-century Prague was to suffer generally from being eclipsed by Vienna, an inferiority from which it suffered until the collapse of the Austro-Hungarian empire after the First World War.

1918 saw the birth of an independent Czech republic, and the start of a process of conversion of the noble palaces which intensified after the Second World War and the beginning of 40 years of communist rule in Prague. The state took over the palaces and converted a large number into foreign embassies, which they remain to this day. The French, American, Japanese, German and Italian embassies, to name but a few in Malá Strana, are all former palaces. Others were converted for use as state institutions of various sorts.

It is almost 400 years since the Lesser Quarter was the centre of European social and artistic life under the eccentric Emperor Rudolf II. Nowadays, in the wake of the Velvet Revolution, there are signs that Prague's "left bank" is rediscovering that status, and a large number of the city's artists and intellectuals today are choosing to live in Malá Strana.

A Tour of the Malá Strana

The best approach to Prague's "left bank" involves staying with the crowds a while longer. There are a number of bridges across the river, but by far the most spectacular is the famous **Karlův most** (Charles Bridge), renowned for the statues along its route. To start from here you can either catch the underground to Staromětská and walk down Křižovnická, take a tram along the riverbank as far as the **Smetanovo nábřeží** (Smetana embankment), or if you are coming from the Old Town merely allow yourself to be swept along by the crowds heading along Karlova.

The Charles Bridge

As with many other bridges over a river as inclined to flooding as the Vltava (at least before being tamed by dams), the Charles Bridge is a replacement of a replacement. The first bridge, dating from the 12th century or earlier, was wooden. After its destruction by floods in 1157, a second crossing, the Judith Bridge, was constructed in stone. Floods demolished this one in 1342. The third and present bridge, originally called the Prague bridge and only renamed with its present title in 1870, was begun in 1357. This sandstone bridge has survived despite persistent flood damage for over 600 years, giving rise to frequent speculation about the source of its longevity. Theories range from miraculous preservation to the mixing of eggs, wine and cheese with the mortar when it was built. Hopefully it will be equally successful in resisting the floods of tourists which are probably the main threat to its remarkable stamina today. It is closed to traffic.

At each end of the bridge is a Gothic gateway. The one on the Old Town side is one of the finest bridge towers in Europe. The western façade was badly damaged during a war with the Swedes, who in the early 17th century were a powerful military force in Europe, but the eastern façade's rich sculptural decoration has been preserved. The patron saints of Bohemia, Adalbert and Sigismund, are at the top, whilst beneath them at the centre is St Vitus, the patron of the bridge. He is flanked by two crowned figures seated on thrones, Charles IV on his right and Wenceslas IV on his left. Around and above them are various heraldic emblems of lands controlled by the Czechs when the bridge was built. The tower was designed by Peter Parler who also supervised the construction of the bridge.

By far the most outstanding feature of the bridge, however, is the set of statues which line its sides. An avenue of Baroque statues on a Gothic bridge is a remarkable combination unmatched anywhere else in the world. Since the area is extremely crowded during the summer, not only with passers-by but also with souvenir and refreshment peddlers, the best time to savour the atmosphere of the bridge is very early morning, or in winter after a light dusting

---

St John Nepomuk

A small bronze cross on the wall of the bridge marks the spot where St John Nepomuk was supposedly thrown in. If you put your hand on it and make a wish the saint will supposedly bring it to fulfilment (particularly if you then go and admire his statue).

Whatever actually caused him to suffer the watery equivalent of defenestration when he was chucked off the Charles Bridge (depontification?), St John was built up in later centuries as a Catholic martyr to rival the Protestant martyr Jan Hus. There had to be a hero to inspire the Counter-Reformation in Prague in the way that Jan Hus had obviously inspired the other side — and St John was the one for the job.

Various stories embellished the account of his death. For instance, five stars were said to have appeared above the water when he was thrown in (hence the starry halo around his head in all depictions of him). Numerous statues and monuments were erected in his honour, of which the most extraordinary is the Baroque tomb constructed for his exhumed remains in St Vitus' Cathedral. More than 2,240 lb (1,015 kg) of silver was used to display angels, saints and various heavenly hangers-on surrounding his coffin in a dangling extravaganza propped up by wall brackets.

*E*ntrance to the Charles
Bridge from the Old Town.

of snow. In summer-time you will find yourself sharing the experience with several people sleeping rough, friendly down-and-outs and small gatherings of people singing songs from the sixties assimilated to the recent overthrow of communism.

The statues were 17th-century creations, modelled after the Ponte Sant'Angelo in Rome and designed to express the new-found confidence of the Catholic Counter-Reformation. Each deserves separate attention, but three will be highlighted here. About halfway across, heading for the Malá Strana, is the figure of St John of Nepomuk, recognisable from a halo of gold-coloured stars. St John was thrown into the river Vltava (a variation on the usual Prague habit of defenestration!) on the orders of Wenceslas IV in 1393 because he refused to disclose what the King's wife said to him in the confessional. He was canonized in the early 18th century and became known as the "bridge-saint" of Catholic Europe. Near the Malá Strana end of the bridge on the

left hand side is the statue group of St Luitgard, regarded by many as the best carving of all. Christ is depicted bending down towards the blind saint from the cross and permitting her to kiss his wounds. A little nearer the Malá Strana on the right hand side is the figure of St Philip Benizi, which stands out as the only statue to be carved in marble. One other feature to look out for on the left hand side is the statue of Bruncvik, a knight who stands on an ornamental pedestal beside the bridge. In fact the column rests on one of the bridge supports on the banks of adjacent Kampa island. According to legend his original sword is walled up somewhere in the bridge. Tradition has it that this sword can be retrieved and used to defend the country should it be in peril.

There is always a good atmosphere on the bridge, even when it is very busy. There is little that is tacky about the various stalls and displays and one of the best talents is shown by those who can reproduce your profile in a few seconds using scissors and card. There is the inevitable

*M*iniature Gorbis up for
grabs on the Charles Bridge.

scaffolding around one or two of the figures, which provides a good climbing frame, a host of singers and musicians, and a common habit of sitting on or around the base of the statues, as if to update them with some contemporary equivalents. For all the pressure of numbers, this is a far more innocent and atmospheric meeting-place for the many visitors to Prague than Wenceslas Square.

That said, the avenue of statues is best experienced in the quiet of the dawn light, where its full mystic and even slightly sinister impact can be felt. The figures stand guard over the bridge as the traveller passes between them over the waters of the Vltava. They look on now as Czechs and visitors alike huddle together to talk or sleep during the summer nights of a newly-liberated city. Ironically, figures carved out of the confidence of the Counter-Reformation, which saw the rejuvenation of Catholic ideology, now serve as a traditional backcloth against which to celebrate the demise of the modern ideology of communism. Arguably many of the things which Eastern or Central Europe will have to come to terms with during the next century are reflected in this celebration of the end of a new ideology under the shadow of an older one.

Into the Lesser Quarter

Once across the bridge, which is not quite straight, since after the collapse of its stone predecessor new piers were constructed beside the old ones but the original bridge-heads were used, two bridge towers form the entrance to the Malá Strana. The smaller tower is a remnant of the Judith Bridge, whilst the other was built in the 15th century to complement the Old Town Tower. Connected by an arch, these two form the entrance to the Lesser Quarter.

Malá Strana is the perfect inner-city escape for the tourist-weary tourist. It is full of narrow, 18th-century streets at least some of which will be half-empty at any time of year. The gas-lit cobbles are most atmospheric at night, but its alleyways are enticing during the daytime too. Here you will find some of the best places to eat and drink, some of the best places to sit and think or read, such as unexpected walled gardens, and the most concentrated sense of historical Prague.

For the moment, however, the route being taken is still likely to be a busy one, especially if you are travelling in summer. If you're flagging, there is an excellent café just off the bridge on the left called the **Café de Colombia** (Mostecká 3). You may have to wait because a cord across the entrance is used to control the numbers inside, but if you do manage to find your way into its vaulted interior it is a good stop for coffee or wine, and is especially pleasant upstairs.

The Lesser Town Square

First port of call will be **Malostranské náměstí**, (the Lesser Town Square), a sloping square reached by walking straight ahead at the end of Charles Bridge (along the road called **Mostecká**, which means Bridge Lane). Malostranské náměstí is hardly recognisable as a square on first sight because it is so dominated by the **Chram svatého Mikuláše** (Church of St Nicholas) at its centre. The church and the adjacent former Jesuit seminary occupy the middle of the Square to such an extent that they virtually bisect it. Before concentrating on the church, however, it is worth looking at some of the other buildings in the Square. As you come in from Mostecká, glance first at the buildings on your right. Nearest at hand is the

Window onto the world. Facing the Lesser Quarter Square in Malá Strana.

Lesser Town Credit Bank, constructed in neo-Renaissance style at the end of the last century. Beside the bank is the **Kaiserstein Palace**, named after Helfried of Kaiserstein who reconstructed a 15th-century original in 1700. Neighbouring that is the Baroque House of the Flavins, and then completing this side of the square is one of its most noteworthy buildings, the **Malostranská radnice** (Lesser Town Hall). The Town Hall of the "district" (originally Malá Strana was not a district but one of four historic cities that make up Prague) has been on this site since the 15th century, but the present Late Renaissance Town Hall dates from the early 17th century. The building is used today for theatre, jazz and cultural displays, and may still be obscured to some extent by scaffolding. In the summer of 1991 it offered a contemporary opera based on the life of Andy Warhol.

Straight ahead of you at the top end of the square you will not be able to miss the Baroque façade of the **Sternberg palace**, but to see the large Liechtenstein Palace you will have to go around the church of St Nicholas which virtually blocks it from view. If you approach it by staying on the same side of the square that you came to from Mostecká, then you pass a number of interesting smaller buildings on your left. Note in particular the **Dům U zlatého lva** (House at the Golden Lion), a Renaissance house containing a charming small wine bar, **U mecenáše** (At the Patron of Arts) Next to this is the **Dům U tří korunek** (House at the Three Little Crowns), although its best feature, an Empire portal, has to be viewed from the back where it faces Tržiště Street behind the square. A short detour down Karmelitská, on your left as you walk towards the Liechtenstein Palace, will enable you to turn right into Tržiště and see these buildings from the other side.

The **Liechtenstein Palace** is currently being reconstructed as a centre for European musical culture, under the auspices of the Academy of Performing Arts, with a projected completion date of July 1993. It will be a worthy use for a building whose neo-classical façade stretches right across the upper end of the square.

Church of St Nicholas

The dominant feature of the square, however, is the church, a mighty Baroque building that some would see as the greatest example of Baroque in Prague. It was built on the site of an earlier Gothic church which was also dedicated to St Nicholas, and took most of the 18th century to construct. As with much else in Prague, it was a product of resurgent Catholicism. The original Gothic church had been a focus for dissent against Catholic hegemony: Jan Milíč, forerunner of Jan Hus and known as "the father of the Czech reformation", preached there in the 14th century, but after the Battle of the White Mountain in 1620 rebellion against the Hapsburg Empire and its Catholic ideology collapsed. The Emperor Ferdinand handed the church over to the Jesuit order, which built a college in the 17th century next to the building and dreamed of a new church in years to come. Ironically, soon after that dream was realized in the late 18th century, Pope Clement IV dissolved the Jesuit order and St Nicholas' was appropriated for use as a parish church instead.

Construction of the church was begun in 1702, by a Bavarian immigrant from a family of architects, Christoph Dientzenhofer, and continued after his death in 1722 by his son Kilian Ignaz. The belfry tower which completed the work was designed by Anselmo Lurago in about 1755. The whole building thus took three generations of architects about half a century to complete. It was restored in the 1950s.

Inside the church, the High Baroque interior stands in striking contrast to the relatively plain exterior, although note the sculptures of church fathers on the western façade before you go in—these were the work of J.B. Kohl. The frescoes are overwhelming. As you enter the nave, look up at the ceiling-paintings depicting the life of St Nicholas, a 4th-century bishop of Myra in Asia Minor who was regarded in medieval times as a protector of justice, particularly as patron saint of municipal administration. As spiritual defender against town hall corruption, St Nicholas is seen among other things, as saving Romans from execution during a war, dispensing oil with miraculous properties, and giving money to a man claiming that he was reduced by poverty to selling his daughter. The whole painting, at about 1,500 m² (16,140 ft²), is one of the

> ### Doctors of the Church
> The four heavies were all engaged in maintaining the orthodoxy of Christianity in the eastern part of the Roman Empire, where there were a number of challenges to the agreed statements of faith made by General Councils of the Church at Nicea and Chalcedon in the 4th and 5th centuries. To the Jesuits, these doctors of the church were stamping out heresy in the early church just as they themselves were stamping it out in 17th-century Bohemia.
>
> Yet there is an element of sham about these characters. They are not marble as they seem at first but plaster casts (technically scagliola, a mixture of plaster and glue). They are there for effect and to encourage the faithful, like any plaster saint in a kitsch window display. Whether or not it is a piece of religious trickery the whole effect is immensely powerful—something the communists, who restored this church fully in the 1950s, were to learn from.

biggest in Europe, and was the work of Johann Lukas Kracker in the early 1760s.

Move further inside, taking with you a short explanation of the church's history in English which you can obtain from the kiosk by the entrance for a few crowns, until you are standing underneath the 75 m (247 ft) high dome. Around you, underneath the dome, are four huge statues representing church teachers designed by I.F. Platzer, who was also responsible for the statue of St Nicholas on the high altar. These are quite extraordinary, and hardly an endearing reminder of what Christianity was like in the decades after it had acquired overwhelming power through the conversion of Constantine. St Basil looks as if he's swallowed his beard, whilst St Cyril of Alexandria appears to be skewering someone with his staff. On either side of St Nicholas are statues of St Francis Xavier and St Ignatius, who also appears to be using his staff as if he's just taken part in a jousting tournament.

The height of the dome is extraordinary—perhaps Kilian Ignaz was determined to outshine his father, who designed the nave! Its ceiling-paintings, by Franz Xavier Palko, depict the last judgment and the glorification of St Nicholas. If you have time to look at the paintings in the side-chapels, see the one by Palko of the death of his namesake, St Francis Xavier. Lurago's belfry shows that by the time the finishing touches were being put to the building it was going a bit rococo, a style that can also be seen in the design of the pulpit. Note, incidentally, the sculpture of the decapitation of John the Baptist on the balcony of the pulpit. He hangs over the edge in gold, whilst behind him stands a man with upraised sword, ready to send the offending head flying down among the worshippers or camera-wielding observers beneath.

On a sunny day the dome can be a welcome source of light to temper the sombre grandeur of ecclesiastical show. That said, this magnificent church is not gloomy in the way that some other Baroque churches in Prague are, and is certainly one of the most impressive sights in the city. Because of the length of time it took to construct and complete, the church is a

St Nicholas' Church dominates the Malá Strana skyline.

good illustration of the history of church architecture in the 18th century. It also has a special place in the musical life of Prague. It was in St Nicholas' church that Mozart often came to play the organ, and after his death a special commemoration of the composer, more popular in Prague than in his home city of Vienna, took place in the church, at which Mozart's own Requiem was played.

Many times while you are in Prague you will look down on the city for a "panoramic view". Make sure you pick out the dome and the belfry tower of the church of St Nicholas, standing together like Laurel and Hardy in a perfect partnership of different sizes.

Into the Lesser Quarter

On leaving the church, turn right past the stalls selling pots, puppets and postcards, and go back downhill to the edge of the square beside the **Malostranská radnice** (Lesser Town Hall), pausing for refreshment at the Malostranská kavarna, whose tables spread out into the square below the church, if you wish and space permits.

Next to the town hall you leave the square along **Letenská** and head downhill. It is a narrow road and you may have an uncomfortably close brush with a tram. This is a quieter, less "discovered" part of the Malá Strana. The high wall on the left competes with the trams on the right to provide a suitably Kafka-esque sense of being hemmed in. The ugly façade of the ministry of finance opposite completes the picture.

Waldstein Palace and Gardens

After about 180 m (200 yd), however, an entrance on your left admits you to the other side of the wall, to the **Valdštejnská zahrada** (Waldstein Gardens).

The Gardens are usually quiet, large enough to be taken for a small park, and laid out in Italian Baroque style with grottoes and an avenue of statues which are copies: the invading Swedes took the originals back to Scandinavia in the 17th century. The statues lead to a striking sala terrena. Go inside its three arches and look up at the 17th-century ceiling decorations depicting the Trojan Wars. You will also find ponds, artificial stalagmites and stalactites and a large, unused aviary in the gardens. There are occasional classical music concerts there in the summer-look out for notices at the entrance. There are always plenty of seats for a rest.

The gardens are attached to the **Valdštejn Palace** (Waldstein Palace), built for and named after Albert von Waldstein in the 1620s. He was also known as von Wallenstein, another name by which both palace and gardens are known. Von Waldstein was a man of enormous wealth and no little ruthlessness. To have his palace built where he wanted it, close to the castle, he had two dozen houses, some gardens and the town gate destroyed. At least, however, such vandalism was entered into in order to create a palace, where in the modern day it might well be undergone for nothing better than a motorway. It is not possible to go inside the palace, although its former riding school, now a centre for photographic and art exhibitions, can be visited from the courtyard immediately next to Malostranská metro station. To reach it continue down Letenská and then turn left at the junction. The metro station is a few metres up on your left hand side.

Other Gardens

There are a number of other gardens in the Malá Strana, at least as attractive if not more so than the Waldstein Gardens, but they may well be shut. On the north side of the Waldstein gardens runs the road Valdštejnská, (though to get to it you have to go out into Letenská and then make two left turns, in effect walking around the gardens). North of this street is another set of gardens, known together as the **Ledeburská zahrada**. One of them belongs to the Polish embassy and will be shut; the others may also be shut: in Prague the best things are often full or closed.

No matter if they are. There are more, and it is part of the rather secretive nature of Malá Strana to be inaccessible in places. Valdštejnská is anyway a pleasant street to walk along, according views of the Polish and Indian embassies on the way back to the Lesser Town Square. It is on this street that the entrance to the Waldstein Palace can be found, although it is currently the Ministry of Culture and visitors are liable to be chased out.

The entrance to Valdštejnská is at a busy junction of tram lines running off the Mánesův most, with traffic beginning the steep, winding climb up to the castle, and people emerging from the most attractive of Prague's tidy metro stations, Malostranská. Inside the entrance to the station copies of sculptures and pottery are exhibited, whilst outside the garden area offers a series of playful fountains made up of what appear to be little silver ladybirds spouting water. The grille in the entrance area is decorated with gold designs in the shape of musical instruments. Whilst I would not advocate a visit to the metro station as an end in itself, it is certainly a pleasant means to an end, and of course it is possible to begin your tour of Malá Strana from this station (which is on line A). Note also the small wall mural of Andy Warhol on the outside.

For those with a need of refreshment, the entrance to Valdštejnská has a take-away offering chips (which proliferated in Prague in 1991, having been virtually absent, like bananas, in 1990), usually described by the French term *pommes frites*, coffee (*káva*), soft drinks and ice-cream (*zmrzlina*).

The route along Valdštejnská leads via Tomášská back to the busy Lesser Town Square. A more interesting direction, which will convey more of the flavour of the Malá Strana, is to take the route parallel to the river. At the bottom of Letenská, instead of turning left towards the metro station, turn right into **U lužického semináře**. On the right, hidden behind high walls like much else in the intriguing Malá Strana district, is the **Vojanovy sady**, a public park disguised as a private garden. If open, it will offer a period of peace beneath weeping willows.

From the gardens keep parallel to the river. You should cross the stream of tourists moving from the Charles Bridge along Mostecká to the Lesser Town Square (tourists, like trams, tend to keep to set paths). Go a few metres with the stream towards the Square, and then turn off into one of the narrow streets on the left, either **Saská** or **Lázeňská**. The passageways around here are full of plaques commemorating visits by the famous and infamous – in this area look out for French poet Chateaubriand, the composer Beethoven and Russian Tsar Peter the Great.

Maltese Square

This route brings you out into a charming square, more village than city centre, called **Maltézké náměstí** (Maltese Square), whose centrepiece is a statue of St John the Baptist by F.M. Brokoff. Two

*S*tatue of John the Baptist in the Maltese Square, Malá Strana.

former palaces which are now embassies are other features worth noting. The Rococo façade of the Palais Turba is now the Japanese embassy, whilst the Early Baroque Palais Nostitz is now the Dutch embassy.

At the eastern end of the square is the oldest church in the Malá Strana, **Kostel Panny Marie pod řetězem** (St Mary beneath the Chain). Originally a 12th-century Romanesque basilica, the remains of which can be seen in the right off hand wall of the forecourt, it was rebuilt in the 14th century and given an attractive Baroque interior in the 17th by Carlo Lurago. Just as one bridge was built on the site of another when the first was claimed by flood, as in Charles and Judith, so one church was superimposed on another when the former was destroyed by fire (the twin ravages of an earlier period). Visiting any famous building in Prague often means going through several layers in order to find an original—even though the most recent building may be some hundreds of years old! A great deal of the city is Romanesque inside Gothic wrapped in Baroque.

Grand Priory Square

From St Mary's church go to the next small square, the **Velkopřevorské náměstí** (Grand Priory Square). The Palais Buquoy in this square is now the French embassy, but the highlight is the former palace of the Grand Prior of the Knights of Malta, a 16th-century building updated in Baroque style a couple of centuries later and now the **Muzeum hudebních nástroju** (Museum of Czech Music or Museum of Musical Instruments). Non-musicians may be surprised at how interesting the exhibition is. The **Maltézké zahrada** (Maltese Gardens) adjoining are the venue for concerts in the summer.

Kampa Island

Leave by the French embassy and you find yourself heading onto Kampa Island by means of a small bridge which takes you across the very narrow strip of water separating the island from the mainland. This narrow tributary of the Vltava is known as **Čertovka**, (Devil's Brook) tamed nowadays by dams and technology but once dangerous. Old millwheels point to the original value of this once tempestuous stream. Some very fine houses lying across the Čertovka water earned themselves the title "Venice of Prague".

Despite this, Kampa Island is usually fairly quiet. Its parkland is ex-palace garden, it has occasional displays and pottery markets, but its special feature is its views of the Old Town and the river Vltava. Time should be spent here looking across the river at the imposing sight of the National Theatre and the Old Town.

Before reaching Kampa Island, however, there is a fascinating example of more recent history in this area, a wall of graffiti begun by Czech students in the 1980s and dedicated to John Lennon. Prague nowadays is full of slogans from the sixties, and this mural of liberal idealism contrasts with the starker memorials in the Old Town, where a few candles,

> **John Lennon and Prague**
> John Lennon, like Mozart, is something of an adopted son in this city. The "John Lennon Wall" opposite the French embassy (the former Buquoy Palace) has been a battleground throughout the 1980s following Lennon's death, Prague youth decorating it with pictures and appropriate lyrics and the authorities responding (equally appropriately!) with whitewash. Since 1989, however, the murals have been able to proceed in a relatively undisturbed way. Pilgrimages to the shrine take place on the anniversary of St John's martyrdom, which is 8 December.

flowers and photographs simply register the place where a student was shot or a writer committed suicide to protest against repression.

Petřin Hill

Now is the time for some climbing in order to ascend to one of the best views of the city of Prague, with a little help from technology in the form of a funicular railway. At the end of Kampa island a set of steps take you up onto the most Legii which used to be called the **Most 1 Maye** or 1st of May Bridge until the Velvet Revolution put paid to any celebration of that particular part of the calendar. There may well be interesting stalls set out here selling books, photographs and paintings There is also a wonderful island called **Střelecký ostrov** underneath this bridge on which there are frequent open-air cultural events. For instance, a hot summer evening will often see advertisements for "zahradní divadlo" (literally "garden theatre") on this island, offering a kind of open-air cultural event with folk music, puppetry, theatre, food and drink. Watch out for the opportunity to encounter Slovakian culture here.

*I*n memoriam...
Remembering John Lennon in Malá Strana

However, don't cross the bridge. Instead head in the opposite direction up Vítězná until you reach the junction with Újezd. Turn right and after a short distance the base of the funicular railway will appear on your left. This is your means of reaching the top of the Petřín Hill—although of course fitness-conscious masochists have the option of walking.

Two other sights in Malá Strana might be worth visiting before you make the ascent. They are both to be found by continuing up Újezd until it becomes Karmelitská. The first is a church, **Panna Marie Vítzěná** (The Church of Our Lady Victorious). The interior is dark and currently propped up by scaffolding, but it contains a famous wax effigy of the infant Jesus, brought to Prague from Spain

*M*ore smothered than swaddled—the infant Jesus of Prague in one of his many costumes.

300 years ago by a Spanish noblewoman, whose daughter donated it to the church. The effigy, illuminated by strip-lights from a glass case, receives frequent changes of clothes and jewels from the Carmelite nuns into whose care it has been entrusted. The 50 or so different clothes in which the effigy is swaddled might seem to reflect some of the more unfortunate aspects of religious celibacy, but this does not appear to distract the religious enthusiasts who come to see the miraculous **Pražské Jezulátko** (Prague Jesus).

A little further on up Karmelitská is another secret garden, once again probably shut. Next to number 25 is an unmarked entrance (save for the words *Újezd Neparkovat*, or No Parking). Walk in, and you pass through two courtyards before reaching the gate of the Vrtbovská zahrada, which form a pleasant means of ascending the Petřín Hill by way of Tuscan terraces. You will probably find them closed, and it is better, if less daring, to rely on the funicular to make the ascent.

Petřín Funicular

The Petřín funicular was built in 1891, and at the time was the longest in Austro-Hungary although by today's standards it is of a relatively modest length. It was driven by a simple if ingenious method. Water was pumped into the bottom part of the upper car at the top station, whilst at the same time water escaped from the car in the lower station by means of a valve. On this principle, almost as straightforward as that of the see-saw, the cars operated until after the First World War when the system became electrical. From 1965 to 1985 track problems put the funicular out of action, but since then it has been renewed and remains an effective and popular way of climbing the Petřín Hill. An ordinary tram ticket—there are machines at either end—pays for your journey, and the Czech sign to look for is *Lanovka* (Funicular) or *Lanovka Dráha* (Funicular Railway). For those preferring to walk, a path weaves its way up the hill, snaking from side to side of the funicular, passing a statue of Jan Neruda *en route*.

There are only two stops on the funicular, but the first stop, at **Nebozízek**, has one of the finest views in the whole city. There is a restaurant which was formerly a vineyard cottage—the name Nebozízek originating from a vineyard called Nebozez—with a garden terrace for drinks, making this an ideal place for refreshment. The view of the Old Town is superb, as is the sight of the castle in the opposite direction. For those so inclined, it is an ideal photo opportunity, while the chance to pan from the Old Town right across to the castle will please those carrying around sophisticated video cameras. Others can just enjoy a drink. The café sells wonderful waffles covered in fruit and cream, guaranteed to keep children quiet.

Then it's back to the funicular and up to the top. When you leave the funicular, you will see the so-called **Hladová zed** (Hunger Wall), a 14th-century fortification designed by Charles IV to give work to the unemployed—a conception of job creation through investment in infrastructural renewal which is still beyond the understanding of many contemporary politicians! There is now a difficult choice. One route goes southwards past the nearby Rose Garden and Observatory, and then back down the hill to what used to be the Square of the Soviet Tank (painted pink in 1990 and then eventually removed in 1991!), a journey which passes a fascinating wooden church and a museum which is probably still closed for renovation. The other route goes northwards past a bizarre collection of "objects" created for the Prague Exhibition of 1891 such as a labyrinth of mirrors and a mini Eiffel Tower, eventually coming out beneath the Castle along a route which affords some of the best views of the city. Although

The Royal Observatory and gardens on the Petřín Hill.

both routes will be outlined here, time will probably permit only one, and something of the best of both worlds can be achieved by seeing the Observatory first, and then retracing your steps past the entrance to the funicular and heading north. Whilst you decide, your children might like to take advantage of the pony rides offered for a few crowns at the top of the hill.

Travelling Southwards

Taking the southward route first, a walk of no more than 180 m (200 yd) brings you to the Stefánik Observatory. Opened in 1928 on a hill away from the distorting city lights, the observatory reflects a long tradition of astronomy in Prague, which can be seen from its displays of telescopes

and astronomical clocks, including a picture of the famous one in the Old Town Square. Two of its four working telescopes are also on display, although whether you see any more through them than the top of the Eiffel Tower will depend on the weather and whether your visit is by day or night.

Finding the wooden church is not easy, since it is in the middle of the woods beside one of the winding paths that will return you to ground level. First make sure you are south of the Hunger Wall, which will start to make a steep descent towards ground level. Then take the winding path down yourself (you are in the **Kinského zahrada** or Kinsky Gardens at this point). Stagnant pools with statues ranging from a seal to the actress Hana Kvapilova accompany the descent. Then, at one of the bends in the road, a couple of hundred metres from the Empire Kinský villa, is the extraordinary sight of an 18th-century wooden church, **Kostel sv. Michala** (the church of St Michael), which was brought to Prague from the Ukraine in 1929. It is closed, neglected amidst the overgrown shrubbery around it, and probably at its best when viewed from the back where its domes can be clearly seen, which means negotiating the shrubbery. In its own way it is every bit as enchanting as St Vitus' Cathedral.

Towards the bottom of the hill the Kinský Villa appears looking like a faded sanatorium. Used as an exhibition centre since 1905, it is currently closed for improvements, and looks unlikely to re-open as a branch of the National Museum very soon. However, its seats and flowers make it a good place to sit and relax.

Emerging from the Kinský Gardens, you find yourself in the **Náměstí Sovětských Tankístů** . In the centre of the square a Soviet tank used to be mounted on a plinth to commemorate the liberation of Prague by the Red Army in May 1945. The number on the side of the tank was 23, which belonged to the division of General Lelyushenko, the first to reach Prague. Ironically, it was exactly 23 years after the liberation of Prague, in 1968, that Soviet tanks returned to crush Alexander Dubček's reforms of the so-called Prague Spring. The tank has therefore served as a reminder to the city as much of Soviet oppression as of Soviet liberation. After the Velvet Revolution in late 1989, the tank's fate was decided. Initially it was painted pink, and the words "Trojsky Kůň" (Trojan Horse) hung from it. Later it was taken away and met the same end as many other memorials of Soviet influence on Czechoslovakia. Until that too was removed in 1992 the square had at its centre a bare stone plinth with nothing on top and the odd piece of graffiti on its side.

From the square it is a short journey back along Újezd to the most Legií, a bridge which will carry you back into the Old Town beside the **Národní divadlo** (National Theatre).

Travelling Northwards

The northward route from the funicular leads to the mini Eiffel Tower, now re-opened after a long period of repair. Even the strictly socialist Olympia guide describes the construction of this 60 m (195 ft) tower as being built "on impulse". In fact a number of items in this area were formed as part of a Jubilee Exhibition in 1891 by a group called the Club of Czech Tourists, who were trying to do in the 1890s what the builders of theme parks are trying to do in the 1990s. In terms of attracting visitors to the Petřín hill they certainly succeeded.

The tower is a replica of the original built by Eiffel, though a fifth of the size, which is just as well when you're climbing it. The nearby "Labyrinth" contains a fairly simple Mirror Maze, a delightfully effective set of crooked mirrors which will turn you into a variety of different shapes and which are ideal for children, and a diorama painting of the inevitable Prague students defeating the Swedes on the Charles Bridge. Each costs a few crowns only.

The nearby **Kostel sv. Vavřinec** (Church of St Lawrence), originally a Romanesque single-naved construction but developed in Baroque style with two spires in the 18th century, is also worth a visit. The old Romanesque church was included within the new church building as its apse. The apse is the eastern end of the chancel, which in turn means the part of a church immediately about the altar, sometimes called the sanctuary. As with many churches, St Lawrence's was founded according to tradition on the site of an old pagan shrine (Christianity took over many of the customs and practices of paganism) by St Adalbert in 991. The 17th-century painting on the high altar inside the church depicts the martyrdom of St Adalbert.

Continuing in a roughly north-easterly direction, past a pleasant square area with seats, fountains and sometimes the odd caravan and campers, it is possible to make a slow descent of the Petřín Hill out of the wooded area into orchards and finally onto a path which winds its way lazily downhill, while offering some of the best views of the city. By this route you can come out at the top of **Vlašská**, and thence onto a road which eventually leads back to the main square of the **Malostranská náměstí** (Lesser Quarter).

As you descend Vlašská, you come to the **Lobkovický palác** (Lobkovick Palace) on your right, now the German Embassy. By taking a right turn and going round the back of the embassy, it is possible to glimpse the gardens, originally open to the public but closed since 1989, when they were the scene of a mass occupation by East Germans seeking West German citizenship. One feature of the gardens is a controversial statue of a car on legs (!), which spent the summer of 1990 as a feature of the Old Town Square, but which was removed to its (perhaps temporary) present home in the following year.

Continuing downhill the road meets Tržiště, and the Schönborn Palace, now the site of the American embassy, which may still be under renovation. On the right hand side of the street, it is easily recognizable from the police protection outside. From Tržiště, a left hand turn at the top of Karmelitská returns you to the main square.

One other street off the main square which should not be missed, and which can easily be incorporated into a visit to the castle, is **Nerudova**, named after the 19th-century Czech writer Jan Neruda.

Schörnborn Palace

In the early 20th century Schörnborn Palace provided temporary accommodation for Franz Kafka, who was thrilled by having an electric light (he liked to write all night), although he missed the presence of a bath. The most famous tenant since then is the current ambassador, though her success was in music rather than literature. Shirley Temple-Black is none other than the child singer who sang about the Good Ship Lollipop. Having entered the world of diplomacy, Shirley has promised for the sake of Czech-American relations never to sing again.

Once again there is the staple diet of palace-turned-embassy, this time the Thun-Hohenstien Palace which has become the Italian embassy. The steep climb becomes all the more rewarding when Nerudova gives way to Úvoz, and there are some excellent views of the city on the left, but the best feature of the street is its atmosphere, enhanced by medieval doors, cobbles and the slightly Bohemian air of an artists' quarter. It is in this area that one of the most notable features of Prague, at least in the Old Town and Lesser Quarter areas, the house sign, can be found.

Nerudova has a number of signs which use a religious motif. Look out for number 8, "At the Three Magi" (the Magi were the wise men who in Christian tradition were led by a star to bring gifts to the infant Jesus at Bethlehem) and number 35, "At the White Angel". Frequently their names were linked to astral bodies which were themselves accorded a religious significance (e.g. number 47 Nerudova, "At the Two Suns", which Jan Neruda himself lived in for twelve years, as a memorial tablet on the wall records). Signs would often retain their names after a change of ownership. Number 12, "At the Three Violins", testifies to the fact that several generations of violin-makers lived there, even though its present use is quite different.

To relieve the pressure of the climb, there is a café at number 29 which serves beer and basic food. Not a culinary delight, but enough to keep you going to the top!

This outline of ways to travel around the Malá Strana has concentrated upon streets, but much of the character of the area lies in its paths and alleyways which often open into hidden inner courtyards. Whilst this survey has been designed to avoid your getting lost in the area, in some ways getting lost is one of the best ways in which to discover and savour its atmosphere. If you have returned to the Lesser Town Square without having already found this, then set off along Tomášská for the short journey to **Valdštejnská náměstí** (Waldstein Square). Turn left off the square into the narrow **Sněmovní ulice**, and then turn right into the cul-de-sac **U Zlaté studně** (The Golden Fountain). If you haven't lost the other tourists by now, or if the garden pub at the end of the alley is full, go back to the Renaissance House at number 10 (The Golden Swan), and enter the quiet of its beautiful inner courtyard. If you have enjoyed yourself so far, don't go back to Waldstein Square, but continue along Sněmovní ulice to **Thunovská ulice,** which leads to a set of steps up to the castle. This is one of the best ways in which to make the climb up to the castle area, and to a quite different experience of the city to the secretive, self-protecting charm of the Malá Strana area.

*I*ncomparable beauty
hidden in Prague—a close-up
view of a doorway.

Malá Strana: Opening Times

1. Church of St Nicholas (Chram svatého Mikuláše).
   10.00 a.m. to 6.00 p.m.
2. Waldstein Gardens (Valdštejnská zahrada).
   9.00 a.m. to 7.00 p.m.
3. Museum of Musical Instruments (Muzeum hudebních nástroju).
   10.00 a.m. to 6.00 p.m. (Not Mondays.)
4. Stefánik Observatory.
   Weekday evenings and all day week-ends in winter. Weekday afternoons and evenings, and all day week-ends in spring and summer. Not Mondays.
5. Eiffel Tower.
   Daily 9.00 a.m. to 11.00 p.m.
6. Hall of Mirrors (Zrcadlové Bludiště).
   Daily 9.00 a.m. to 6.00 p.m.

Highlights for Children

Waffles with fruit and ice-cream at Nebozízek.

Ride on the funicular railway and on ponies at the top of the hill.

Climb up the "Eiffel Tower" with views of the city.

Change shape and get lost in the Mirror Maze.

Use telescopes and view exhibition of astronomy in the observatory.

Large and Bustling, Here is the New Centre of Prague's Daily Life

This being Prague, the long boulevard that is the Nové Město's (New Town's) most popular attraction is called a square. But there is much more here than Wenceslas Square. Founded in the 14th century for the city's poor, to keep them away from the fashionable Old Town, the irony of history has turned the New Town into the commercial and administrative heart of Prague. You have to walk further for the "sights" here, but in doing so you encounter a less touristy part of the city. The New Town shows a little of what it is like to live in Prague as opposed to merely visiting it.

This is the largest of Prague's five towns, the least pretty, the most lived-in, the most adapted to western-style consumerism, but in some ways the most interesting.

History

The New Town, like so much else in the city, was founded by Charles IV, who used it to make Prague the largest city in medieval Europe, and to relieve overcrowding in the Old Town. From its foundation in 1348 it was mainly a commercial area, particularly for the poorer communities.

*T*he crown of Wenceslas Square; a view of the National Museum.

With fortifications completed by 1350, some of which, by Vyšehrad, still exist, the area could boast town planning far ahead of its time. The streets and squares were set out in a structure which has survived demolition of the New Town's buildings, most of which were pulled down in the 19th century after the New Town lost its independence and, as the poorer area of a single city, was subjected to a radical programme of "slum clearance". Such demolition has given the New Town its present 19th-century feel, interspersed with a number of 20th-century additions, although it contains a few buildings from an earlier period.

The New Town has remained loyal to its commercial roots, since it is now the centre of Prague's best business: tourism. It is here that the visitor can find the

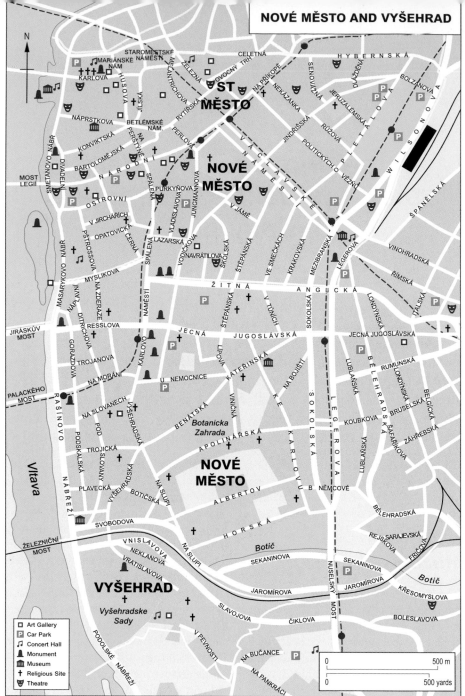

- □ Art Gallery
- P Car Park
- ♫ Concert Hall
- ▲ Monument
- 🏛 Museum
- † Religious Site
- ♨ Theatre

nightclubs (from the sophisticated to the sleazy), cafés, hotels, department stores, pizza parlours and hot dog stalls which form the inevitable "dollar area" of every emerging ex-communist city.

Nové Město and Vyšehrad areas.

A Tour of the New Town

Start with the city's most famous landmark, **Václavské náměstí** (Wenceslas Square). To call Wenceslas Square a "square" is a misnomer. It is a long sloping boulevard, at the top of which is the National Museum and the famous statue of St Wenceslas on horseback. In design it is similar to the Swedish city of Gothenburg, except that in Gothenburg a freeway was not put between the museum and the square.

National Museum

It is probably best to begin at the **Národní muzeum** (National Museum), which can be reached easily on the underground via Muzeum station. Tram catchers can get out at Vodičkova and walk up to the top (270 m or 300 yd), or catch the underground from Můstek.

The National Museum is, as museums go, dull. Its collections of minerals on the first floor, set out in endless lines and inscribed on black display cases with the appropriate names, look like the work of some pious Victorian cleric. The stuffed birds, reptiles and animals, collected in seven halls of zoology, and including one or two specimens that have become extinct, are displayed with little imagination. The only relief comes from looking out of the windows, which on one side offer one of the best views of Wenceslas Square, and the ceilings, which are a good deal more colourful than the displays.

More interesting will be the temporary features in the museum. 1991 saw a feature on the dangers of deforestation, and an exhibition of "contemporary history". There is also an up-market snack bar, the Café Museum, and a grandly designed main staircase leading to a monumental interior full of archways and balconies. For many people the highlight will be the large domed hall on the first floor which contains the "Pantheon", a memorial to great personalities of national culture and history made up of an array of statues and busts, including one of Masaryk, founder of the Czech Republic.

Constructed in grand neo-Renaissance style, the museum seen from the outside reflects a strong sense of national revival in the 19th century, and has recently been rendered more impressive still by the re-gilding of its dome. On the inside, national pride has been grafted onto the desire of "scientific socialism" to identify and tabulate the nature of humanity and its natural environment. The result is a ponderously worthy display of history and culture which is more content to list than to analyze, although already there are signs that a more vibrant approach to museums and their potential is emerging, through temporary and new displays.

Wenceslas Square

When you come out of the museum, look down Wenceslas Square from the balcony. Your reaction will possibly be mixed. On the one hand, if your image of this area was of an ancient square resonant with history and medieval charm, then you may be disappointed. Never mind, there are plenty of other areas in Prague which will conform to this image perfectly. On the other hand, there certainly *is* much about Wenceslas Square that is distinctive and resonant with history: only it is more modern history.

Wenceslas Square has been the scene of several crucial events in the recent life of Czechoslovakia. It was the site of revolutionary disturbances in 1848 and of

Wenceslas Square

Wenceslas Square was the scene of increasingly large mass demonstrations against the communist government throughout 1989. So worried did the authorities become that they constructed a cardboard copy of the entire square in Slovakia (the eastern half of the country) so that they could practise crowd control! Such "control" regularly took the form of brutal beatings, but by November 1989, when the Berlin Wall began to come down, it was clear that no amount of repression could stop the tide of popular protest. By the end of the month a million people could be found daily massing along the Square demanding that the government resign, and in the end it had to capitulate to popular pressure. Václav Havel was finally elected to the presidency on 29 December. The Velvet Revolution was over-but the work of reconstruction was just beginning.

support for Czechoslovakia's emergence as a communist state after the Second World War a century later in 1948. However, it is also remembered as the centre of unsuccessful resistance to the occupying tanks sent from the Soviet Union to crush the Prague Spring of 1968. More recently, it is remembered as the scene of unprecedented demonstrations which led, in November 1989, to the Velvet Revolution, the expression of popular protest that led to the final collapse of the regime which that earlier Soviet invasion had put into power. The events of 1968 and 1989 will still be remembered when you visit the Square, through the many flowers, candles, photographs and silent gatherings of people close to the statue of St Wenceslas. Sure to be remembered somewhere is Jan Palach, a student who burned himself alive in the Square at the age of 21 a year after the Soviet invasion in protest at the repression. The monument to St Wenceslas (sv. Václav) at the top of the Square was designed by Josef Myslbek in 1912. It features Prince Wenceslas on horseback surrounded by the statues of four saints.

More boulevard than square? Looking down Wenceslas Square with the statue of St Wenceslas in the foreground.

Wenceslas, originally Duke of Bohemia from 921 until his murder at the hands of his brother Boleslav, was fortunate enough to live a life engaged in fairly ordinary power struggles and then find himself elevated to sainthood by the church, rather like Thomas More in England. Canonized as martyr and miracle-worker, Wenceslas became the patron saint of his country, and Wenceslas remains one of the most popular boy's names in Czechoslovakia. Indeed it is the name of the current President who came to power through the Velvet Revolution Václav Havel—Václav is the correct form for Wenceslas—c.f. Václavské náměstí, Wenceslas Square.

In order to reach the monument to St Wenceslas you have to cross a large and noisy highway. Although Czechoslovakia is far less crammed with traffic than western cities, partly because of its excellent public transport provision, it's impossible not to regret the vandalism of the city planners in creating a road that effectively beheads the National Museum from the body of the square.

The square itself is also likely to engender concerns about city planning. As a rule Prague is subject to careful, indeed devoted, restoration work, which often continues for years until the scaffolding around buildings has grown old and rusty. Wenceslas Square, however, is the cosmopolitan centre of the city, full of everything transient: fast-food outlets, nightclubs advertising in neon, bars, cinemas, shops and offices. Even under communist rule the neon was present, usually advertising friendship between the socialist nations. But now market forces and consumerism have moved in their own particular ideology. Advertisements for soft-porn movies and strip shows reflect one particular "market force", the hoardings often roughly attached to the inevitable scaffolding. At the same time, however, there are some glorious buildings in the square which repay close attention and which reflect some of the finest examples of modern architecture.

One outstanding building half-way down on the right is the **Hotel Evropa**, which is a glorious example of Art Nouveau indulgence. The café terrace on the outside provides a good view of the passing crowds, but it is the interior which really impresses. A night at the Hotel

*P*rague's magnificent Grand Hotel Evropa in Wenceslas Square is a favourite venue for breakfast by day, drinking on the terrace by night, and sleeping in between the two.

Evropa is not as expensive as you might imagine, although you must book well in advance, months rather than weeks if you are travelling during the high season.

Other notable modern buildings in the "square" are more of a reaction against Art Nouveau. On the opposite side of the road to the Hotel Evropa is the Hotel Juliš, now called the Tatran, designed by Pavel Janák, who was part of the early 20th-

Wiehl's House in Wenceslas Square, a neo-Renaissance building with paintings based on cartoons by Aleš and Fanta.

century Czech Cubist movement. Two functionalist buildings face each other at the bottom of the square. One, the Palác Koruna built in 1914, was the work of Antonín Pfeiffer. The other, the **Dům obuv** (House of Shoes), is a department store built in the 1920s and designed by Kysela as a glass curtain-wall building. The Palác Koruna contains a ground floor buffet which you may come to welcome at times when it is difficult to find a place to sit and eat. If you find the "Automat" atmosphere too stifling and oppressive, pop in the entrance for a raspberry milkshake which may provide much-needed refreshment for a handful of crowns.

Two other buildings, both at the top of the square, should also be mentioned. One is the new parliament or federal assembly building, which has been built on the site of a former stock exchange. The architect, Karel Prager, was required to build the new one "over" the other without destroying it, which he did using concrete stilts. Constructed in newly communist post-war Czechoslovakia, the plate-glass and bronze tinting hovers over the little bourse whose capitalist transactions were made redundant by socialist revolution. Whatever the political significance, it hardly represents an aesthetic triumph.

Next to the parliament building is the **Smetanovo divadlo** (Smetana theatre), a neo-Renaissance building of the late 19th century designed by two Viennese, Helmer and Fellner, as a theatre for the German population of Prague: it was originally called the German Theatre. Built in 1888 as a successor to the wooden "New Town Theatre" which was itself built only 30 years earlier, its stucco decoration of the interior has hardly changed in a hundred years, despite reconstruction in the 1970s. It is now used as an opera house.

Going to the Smetana theatre will have begun to take you away from Wenceslas Square along Wilsonova, a street which used to be known as Vítězného února (Glorious February) after the date of the communist coup in 1948. It is now named after the famous American President, in whose memory a plaque was unveiled at the main station in 1990 by the current American President, George Bush.

Railway Stations

Carry on along this road for about 180 m (200 yd) in order to see Prague's main railway station (**Praha hlavní nádraží**). It was officially opened in 1909 as Franz Josefs Bahnhof, named after the Emperor of the then Austro-Hungarian Empire. As with the parliament building, different styles compete with rather than complement each other.

From the outside you can see an impressive Art Nouveau building with towers, built in the first decade of the 20th century. The signs and the traffic roaring past outside will attempt to drive you into the subterranean sections of the station. Here a three-storey departure hall designed in 1980 by J. Danda conveys the impression of being stuck between the decks of a ship. Instead, avoid the glass protrusions attempting to draw you into the plastic underworld, and enter the vestibule of the station by walking in at street level. You will find yourself standing beneath Art Nouveau decorations which you will otherwise miss: paintings by J. Frohlich and sculptures by F. Kraumann and J. Pikart. Turn left at the entrance as you face the trains, and go along to the end of the corridor to the restaurant, a visual delight even if something of a culinary nightmare, where there is more Art Nouveau decoration.

From the main station a range of options is available. There is a rather unkempt garden area outside with benches often used as emergency (or even regular) sleeping quarters by travellers and itinerants. On the far side of the "gardens" is Opletalova. If you turn right (facing away from the station) down this street, and then left into Hybernská, you come to **Masarykovo nádraží** (Prague's oldest railway station) on your right, which was opened in 1845.

Number 7 Hybernaská

Further along Hybernská, again on the right, is the former site of the V.I. Lenin museum, (number seven), formerly an early Baroque palace built in the 17th century and now home of the Social Democratic Party. In 1907 a workers' co-operative gave the former palace the name "The People's House", and in 1912 it was the scene of a meeting of the 16th All-Russian Conference of the Social Democratic Party of Russia, chaired by Lenin. It was this conference that marked the origin of the Russian Bolshevist Party which swept to power in Russia in 1917.

In the 1950s the "house" was adapted as a Lenin Museum, and bronze reliefs of events in Lenin's life were set in the building's façade like some secular equivalent of the lives of saints on the walls of churches and cathedrals. Inside were "sacred" relics of his life and work, whilst on the fourth floor the restored hall in which he chaired the Prague Conference in 1912 served as a kind of shrine.

After the Velvet Revolution of 1989 the building was closed, and then reverted to its role as headquarters of the (non-communist) Social Democratic Party. In the summer of 1991 a terse note in the window, obviously written by a long-suffering social democrat tired of being asked what had happened to the V.I. Lenin museum, advised visitors that the nearest Lenin museum was in Moscow. Events later in the year rendered this advice somewhat out of date, however, and devotees of the Soviet leader might now have to try Havana or North Korea.

Hybernská eventually leads into **Náměstí republiky**, (the Square of the Republic) which has a number of interesting sights, but the route to the Square which has been outlined here will probably only appeal to those interested in old railway stations or communists. Another route turns left rather than right along Opletalova, and then right along the narrow street Jeruzalémská. This leads into Jindřišská, next to the Gothic Church of Saints Henry and Cunigund on the edge of Maxim Gorky Square.

Turn left into Jindřišská, facing back towards Wenceslas Square. On the left hand side is the General Post Office, which six centuries ago was the site of a botanical garden, three centuries ago was a convent, and two centuries ago was a factory. The grand if functional interior was decorated with allegorical paintings depicting the postal service in 1901. Prague has very few international telephones at present, and the post office is the only place where calls can be made 24 hours a day.

Refreshment

Near to the post office are two very pleasant places for refreshment. Paris-Praha opposite is a shop with a café behind it dominated by a large picture of Paris, open until 7.00 p.m. Monday to Friday (and Saturday mornings), and usually offering a seat. There is also a café-bar next door, open until 9.00 p.m. and sporting bar stools on which the chic can perch with

their espressos and Gauloises. Then there's the Palace Hotel on the corner of Jindřišská and Panská, which has a very pleasant (non-smoking) salad bar on the ground floor. In 1991 it offered one of the best salads in Prague, and being self-service, did so with the minimum of fuss.

Return to Wenceslas Square, and head downhill away from the National Museum. However, take a detour on the way. There are many arcades leading off the street, which usually wind their way either back to Wenceslas Square or onto one of the side streets that lead off it. You'll find restaurants, snack-bars, cinemas, and shops in these arcades, together with the stairways and passages to clubs and hotels. Along one there is a garden café; along another a theatre, for instance the Semaphore Theatre at Václavské náměstí 28, whose café-bar usually has seats available. Together they provide an occasionally sleazy commentary upon the public face of Wenceslas Square outside.

Na Příkopě

At the bottom of Wenceslas Square you are at the centre of what is sometimes called "The Golden Cross". Straight ahead the road leads to the Old Town. To the left is Jungmannovo náměstí and then Národní. To the right is **Na příkopě**, a street full of ornate banks and elegant department stores. Where you are standing, at almost all times of year, there will be crowds of people, stalls selling newspapers, books, magazines and souvenirs, and money-changers enticing you to change money, usually initially in German with the word "Tauschen?", but often in English.

Look above the shop fronts at the elegant façades of the buildings along Na příkopě. This literally means "On the moat", which was once literally true, since there was a stream here between the old and new towns of Prague until it was filled in in 1760. Number 4, number 10 (the former Sylva-Taroucca Baroque Palace—head through the archway in summer and you come to a garden area with tables where you can get a seat, drink and food in descending orders of likelihood), number 12 and number 14, now a bank, are particularly attractive. On the left hand side the buildings are not so impressive, although the restaurant Moskva contains downstairs the nearest that Prague had got by 1991 to a McDonalds At the end of the street the architecture degenerates into the drab 1930s style of the Czechoslovak State Bank (compare the extraordinary interior of the bank at number 14, which could be a theatre, to the functional style here), until leading past the Powder Tower on the left into Náměstí republiky, where those who preferred the railway and Lenin can re-join the party.

*A*rt Nouveau décor on Prague's magnificent Obencí dům (Municipal House).

Municipal House

The Square of the Republic contains one of the greatest buildings in Prague for those who like Art Nouveau, the **Obecní dům** (Municipal House). Those who can't walk past the Hotel Evropa on Wenceslas Square without wandering in and admiring the decor, will have the same urge on an even grander scale here. The site has been variously occupied since the Middle Ages by houses, a seminary, a barracks and a cadet school. The present building, its yellows and greens a strong challenge to the charcoal-coloured Powder Tower next to it, dates from the first decade of the 20th century.

At the centre of the façade is a mosaic by K. Spillar, *Homage to Prague*. The rural scene of trees and trailing robes surrounds a crowned figure. To the left, a man on horseback bearing a flag appears to have disturbed two male sleepers, who look as if they are making a hasty attempt to throw blankets around themselves. On the right, a violinist entertains a stiff-looking woman in clothes with his musical skills, whilst a naked woman to his left appears to be tiring of the recital. The buildings of the city are a distant background to this strange encounter. To right and left

of the mosaic, the statues who appear like a group of climbers scaling a dangerous part of the building represent an equally grand theme, *The Humiliation and Rebirth of the Nation*. On the protruding balcony beneath the mosaic are two torch bearers, who appear like Atlases holding up transparent Rubik Cubes with the help of little cherubs. These and the other ornamental decoration of the façade are the work of K. Novak.

Inside the building two large rooms to left and right offer a wonderful environment for a snack or meal, although they are usually full in summer. The restaurant contains a painting of *Harvest Time*, folk-costumed figures and views of Prague, and on just about any busy summer's day you will get to know these very well as you wait to order. If you are keen for refreshment at all costs, it is better to seek out the cavernous basement in which a wine-bar offers drink and a table by day and dancing at night.

The Obecní dům is a treasure-trove of wonderful halls, corridors and alcoves. It does not yet seem to have organized guided tours very efficiently, and to be fair, it is very much a building in constant use for exhibitions, concerts, and so on, but the current position in 1991 was that a tour of part of the Municipal House could be undertaken with a guide on the hour. To see the wonderful Smetana Hall, however, with its many sculptures and wall paintings, all continuing with grand Art Nouveau themes of Music, Dance, Drama and Poetry, it may be necessary to attend a concert of classical music. On 12 May the Czech Symphony orchestra performs here after a pilgrimage to the grave of Smetana in Vyšehrad.

The guided tour through halls and galleries decorated with historical and allegorical paintings is not to be missed. Art Nouveau furniture is also on display, including such essential household items as a gilded aquarium encrusted with brass snails. In the violet-windowed **Sál Primátorský** (Mayorial Hall) do not miss the paintings of Alfons Mucha, doyen of French Art Nouveau in the late 19th century and designer of posters for renowned Grande Dame of the theatre, Sarah Bernhardt.

At the very top there may well be a temporary exhibition of art, which will probably be so *nouveau* that the paint is barely dry on the canvas, for which your ticket will give you free entry.

There appears to be some uncertainty about the future of this building. In 1991 some of it was open to the public, other parts were only open for special events, and one or two rumours were circulating of an "exclusive casino" there. Hopefully the effect of the Velvet Revolution will not be to replace one corrupt élite occupying buildings with another. Obecní dům, after all, means "House of the People".

Church of Our Lady of the Snows

Returning to the centre of the "Golden Cross", straight ahead lies **Jungmannovo náměstí** (Jungmann Square) and Národní. Jungmannovo náměstí is a somewhat squashed "square" with a memorial to the Czech linguist Josef Jungmann (1773–1847) who gives it its name. Do not miss—and beware, it is very easy to walk by it—the **Kostel Panny Marie Sněžné s klášterem** (Church of Our Lady of the Snows), originally conceived as a triple-naved, 100 m (109 yd) high giant to rival St Vitus Cathedral, but of which only the high presbytery (the sanctuary area around the altar at the eastern end of a church) was ever built. This presbytery became the present church, with a small courtyard outside it.

The history of the church is as complicated as that of any other Prague building. The ubiquitous Charles IV was its founder in 1347, when it was set up as part of a Carmelite monastery. In the 15th century it was a centre of Hussite preaching, and one of its most famous firebrand preachers, Jan Želivský, led a raid on the New Town Hall from here which instituted Prague's best-known contribution to violent political debate, defenestration, when a number of city councillors were "don priced" (thrown out of the windows). Their fate was not, however, as gruesome as that which befell Želivský himself, who was invited to explain his conduct to a meeting of Old Town burghers and promptly beheaded.

In fact, being on the edge of the Old and New Towns meant that the church was often the scene of clashes between the "radical" New Town Hussites and the more conservative inhabitants of the Old Town. In 1434 one of these battles brought down the church steeple. Other changes were more peaceful. In the 17th century Franciscans took the church over and gave it an overhaul, initially in Renaissance style and later with some Baroque additions. A century afterwards the present courtyard was added in neoclassical style, as a surrounding for the statues of saints outside the church entrance. If you are travelling in summer, the courtyard provides an oasis of peace where you can pull yourself out of the tide of visitors flowing from Wenceslas Square into Národní.

Inside the church, it is impossible not to be struck by the strange dimensions. Since it is an adaptation of the eastern end of what was originally intended to be a much bigger building, its 30 m (100 ft) high vaulting is hard to get used to. It is like a huge head without a body, although the big Baroque altar makes every effort to distract attention away from the height of the interior. If you can get into the gardens which lie to the south of the church, it is possible to understand its strange dimensions from the outside—and to relax away from the worldly bustle.

Jungmann Square

Back in Jungmann Square, head for Národní, passing the Adria Palace on the

*H*ot air after the revolution: balloons advertise the new Admiral Casino in front of the Adria Palace where Havel and others planned the downfall of communism in 1989.

left. The first floor of this building has a pleasant café-terrace which provides an ideal location for coffee and watching the world go by. Built in the style of a Venetian Renaissance palace for an insurance company at the beginning of the 20th century, the grimy grey and rather chunky "palace" is not perhaps a great architectural success, but it has strong recent historical associations, since its experimental Laterna Magika theatre studio in the basement was the scene of key meetings of **Občanské Fórum** (Civic Forum) during the nerve-wracking days of November 1989 as the Velvet Revolution hung in the balance.

Further down Národní itself (on Národní třída, Narodni Avenue), the Máj (May) department store on the left, built in the 1970s with glass-covered external escalators, is one of Prague's few large stores, its modern architecture chiming in with the modern Národní třída underground station outside and a ludicrous fountain which makes you long for the days when water spurted from fishes' mouths or little boys' willies.

On the right is the Albatros theatre and bookshop, which in 1990 ran a daily film show of the Velvet Revolution in several languages, but which has since widened its repertoire without forgetting those hectic days. There may well still be a photographic exhibition of the revolution in the theatre basement, and if open it is a good place for a quiet drink; quiet because unadvertised.

Národní 16, an 18th-century building known as Kanka's house after the name of its architect, acquired a new ground-floor arcade which was the scene of police violence in November 1989, when a student demonstration was attacked by police as it wound its peaceful way towards Wenceslas Square. In fact at the time of the attack the students had stopped moving, sat down in the street and offered the officers flowers, a gesture always guaranteed to bring out the Neanderthal in any riot policeman. To commemorate the event, a bronze relief of eight hands appealing for assistance hangs on the wall beneath the arches. In 1990 it was always surrounded by flowers, candles and photographs. In 1991, a lone candle was occasionally to be seen. Hopefully, there will always be something to mark the significance of times which are already moving quickly into history.

Church of St Ursula

Further down the street towards the river on the left hand side is the **Kostel svaté Voršily** (Church of St Ursula). This is one of Prague's less well-known Baroque churches, but also one of the loveliest. The interior is sumptuous but at the same time light (some of Prague's Baroque churches are rather dark and gloomy). There are beautiful ceiling-frescoes by J.J. Steinfels, stucco work by Soldati, wall-paintings by Barvitius and statues by Preiss. If not obscured by scaffolding, you can also see an excellent set of statues on the exterior of the church designed by Ignaz Platzer in 1746–47.

Next door to this 18th-century church is the former convent for which the church was built. This has been taken over in recent times as a medical institute, although a popular wine-bar (Klášterni Vinárna—literally Convent Wine-Bar) can be found on the ground floor.

Interesting Buildings

On the opposite side of the road are two examples of Art Nouveau, hidden in 1991 behind rusty scaffolding that looked well

The Topič Insurance Company—an example of Art Nouveau architecture in Národní.

on the way to becoming a monument itself, but possibly now open to view. Number 9 is the former Topič publishing house, while number 7, like the Adria Palace, was a product of the growing demand in a nervous 20th century for insurance. Both buildings were designed by Osvald Polívka in 1907-8. The one which housed the Prague Insurance Company has mosaic lettering above the windows advertising the essential ingredients of an assured financial future such as *dúchod* (pension) and *veno* (dowry).

At the bottom of the street two completely different buildings vie for attention. One is a ten-year-old glass box with a concrete courtyard outside decorated with a statue called *My Socialist Country*. Whether created to annoy Prince Charles

or as an ironic commentary upon the depressing aspects of communism, the **Nová scéna** is not easy to admire. Indeed its best characteristic is arguably the reflection of the National Theatre opposite that the glass exterior affords.

The National Theatre

Národní divadlo (the National Theatre) itself is a neo-Renaissance building with similarities to the National Museum at the top of Wenceslas Square. It was begun as an expression of Czech pride and national identity when the Austrians, who had by the 19th century absorbed much of Prague's former glory into the Austro-Hungarian empire, refused money for a national theatre and the Czechs decided to fund one from voluntary donations. The foundation stone was laid in 1868 using stones ceremoniously brought together from all over the country. For 13 years huge efforts were made to pay for and build the theatre, which was opened in June 1881 but destroyed by fire two months later. Fortunately, rebuilding only took two years and the theatre finally opened in November 1883.

The rebuilding was supervised by Josef Schulz, who also designed the National Museum. Both have the rather portentous style which comes of being self-conscious expressions of national revival. Liberally endowed with statues of figures looking victorious with wings and statues on the outside, the theatre inside is full of paintings and sculptures. If you want to examine the decor, remember that the theatre goes dark in high summer, so if you're seeking to bathe in the splendour of some operatic fantasy here come to Prague in the spring or early autumn.

Opposite the theatre on the other side of Národní is the **Café Slavia**, which before the Velvet Revolution had a partly-justified reputation as the haunt of writers and intellectuals, but which is now largely the haunt of tired tourists. The views are pleasant enough if you can obtain a window seat, but modernization and a new clientele has largely dissipated the atmosphere since then. It is suitable enough for brief refreshment.

Shooters' Island

At the bottom of Národní a bridge links the New Town and Malá Strana. It used to be called the Most 1 Máje (1st of May Bridge) after the highlight of the communist calendar, but is now known as the most Legii. Halfway across there are steps down to the leafy **Střelecký ostrov** (Shooters' island—*ostrov* = island).

The island was used from the 15th century as an army firing range, but more recently came to be the place for demonstrations of loyalty to the communist regime. It is now the venue for outdoor exhibitions and entertainments during the

summer months. Look out for posters advertising **Zahradni divadlo** (literally "garden theatre") on the island. It is often possible to fill a summer evening sitting on long wooden benches with food and drink from stalls, watching puppet displays, folk dances and plays: and for the Western visitor whose encounter with Czechoslovakia is confined to Prague it may provide the only opportunity to see something of Slovakian culture, albeit in the context of something designed to draw in the visitors.

Along the Waterfront

Continue the tour of the New Town by turning left at the bottom of Národní and follow the riverbank down **Masarykovo nábřeží** (*nábřeží* = embankment). This is

One of Prague's beautiful doorways on the Masaryk embankment.

another example of recent name-changing, since until 1990 the embankment was known as the Gottwaldovo nábřeží after the hated communist ex-president Klement Gottwald, who also had a metro station, now Vyšehrad, a museum, now closed down, and numerous streets named after him. Masaryk, on the other hand, president of the Czech Republic during the inter-war years, lost all his street signs after the communists came to power in 1948. The tables seem now to have turned once again, and Masaryk is back to his original inter-war prominence.

The high century-old buildings on the waterfront make this part of the Vltava's right bank one of the most pleasant areas in the city for a stroll. Another island soon appears, **Slovanský ostrov** (Slavonic island), which was very much a centre of social and cultural life in the last century. On the far side of the main attraction—a neo-Renaissance building used for assorted social events and as a restaurant—is a run-down garden area which in 1991 featured regular country and western concerts. Apart from retracing your steps, the only escape from these during the summer months is to hire a rowing boat and head for the opposite bank of the river.

Further down the embankment adjacent to Slovanský ostrov is the Mánes Exhibition Hall, a piece of 1930s architecture variously described as "constructivist" and "functionalist", named after a 19th-century landscape artist, Josef Mánes, who would quite possibly have excluded such a building from anything he was painting. Inside, however, there are often some very interesting exhibitions of modern art. Incongruously close to this 20th-century building is the Šitek Water-Tower (**Šitovská věž**), originally a 15th-century Renaissance tower but given an ill-fitting

hat in the form of a Baroque roof 300 years later.

Continue to walk along the waterfront, past **Jiráskovo náměstí** (Jirásek Square) with its memorial to the 19th-century Czech writer Jirásek, until you reach **Palackého náměstí** (Palacký Square). This square has a memorial to another 19th-century Czech writer, the historian František Palacký. Palacký was a strong nationalist, but one of the glories of Art Nouveau is its inability to take nationalism seriously. On a stone plinth Palacký sits like a severe giant, whilst quite incongruously various figures in copper climb over the monument like uncontrollable children who have crept up on the unassailable private den of some pompous elderly ancestor.

Churches to Visit

Just beyond the square, turn off up the hill along Resslova. Two churches are situated on the street, roughly opposite one another. On the left is the 18th-century **Kostel sv. Cyrila a Metoděje** (Church of Saints Cyril and Methodius), originally built as a Catholic church but now a centre of Orthodoxy.

A plaque on the outside wall of the church commemorates the fact that seven Czech agents were trapped here in 1942 by several hundred members of the Gestapo and SS, after having successfully carried out the assassination of Reinhard Heydrich, one of the most powerful Nazis in occupied Czechoslovakia. Indeed this was the only attempt made by the allies to assassinate a top Nazi, and it exacted a terrible revenge in the total destruction of a village outside Prague, Lidice, which was quite literally wiped off the map (*see* page 219). The assassination was organized from London (the Czech agents who

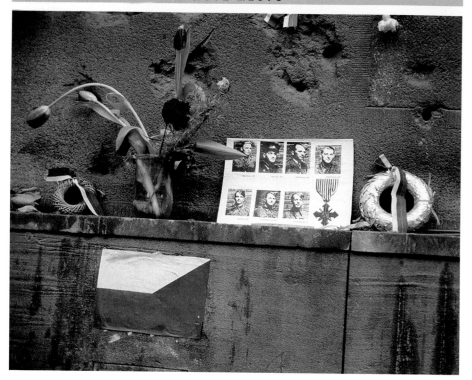

Victims of Nazism: memorial to the assassins of Heydrich who committed suicide in the crypt of the Church of Saints Cyril and Methodius.

parachuted in were sent by the Czech government-in-exile) against considerable opposition from within the country itself, where the prospect of hideous reprisals could easily be anticipated. It is impossible to weigh the complex moral questions involved; but the memorial tablet, inscribed with the names of the resistance fighters who refused to be flushed out of the crypt and eventually committed suicide, and still occasionally marked with a flower, a wreath or a photograph, shows that there is no desire to underplay the incident in Prague itself.

The other church, the **Kostel sv. Václava na Zderaze** (Church of St Wenceslas at Zderaz), tells a familiar tale of architectural history. Originally 12th-century Romanesque, but now Gothic with a Baroque choir, the church is notable for containing pews, altar and crucifix sculpted by the remarkable František Bílek, (for the František Bílek museum, see the tour of Hradčany). Finding either church open, however, is extremely difficult, and you may have to make do with the view from outside. However, there is an interesting art gallery underneath the Church of St Wenceslas.

Charles Square

Continue up the hill until you come out into **Karlovo náměstí** (Charles Square). This is Prague's largest square: in fact it is so large that it doesn't look like a square at all. It is more like a rectangle: which still makes it more of a square than Wenceslas Square! Moreover the busy road leading from Resslova to Ječná bisects the "square", eliminating any sense of unity. Even so, there are some attractive buildings in it, a park in the middle, a few interesting shops and some pleasant places to eat. With all that, who cares about geometry?

Turn left at the entrance to the square from Resslova, and you come across the Novoměstská radnice (New Town Hall) at the far (northern) end. Although it has now been hidden behind scaffolding for some years, when renovation is complete this building will be seen to rival the more famous Old Town Hall. It was here that Prague's oldest political tradition, that of defenestration, began when the radical Hussite preacher Jan Želivský and his followers stormed the building and threw several Catholic councillors out of the windows to their deaths. Those that survived the fall were impaled on pikes. Since 1960 this dubious act of popular rebellion has been marked by a sculpture of the preacher in front of the building—conceivably because of the tendency for communist historians to interpret the Hussites, and their later counterparts of the Protestant Reformation, as examples of proletarian movements, with Catholics cast in the role of ideological reactionaries defending the feudal social system.

Walk along the eastern side of Charles Square, and you come to the **Church of St Ignatius** (sv. Ignác), another building in the area which is endowed with a liberal spread of scaffolding. Its pink and grey interior is darker and gloomier than the colours suggest, but when finally cleaned up it should do some justice to the typical guide-book description of its dusty interior as "sumptuous". This 17th-century Baroque church was built as the church of a Jesuit college, which after the abolition of the Jesuit order in the country in 1773 found a more secular vocation as a hospital. Much of the eastern part of the Square is taken up by this building.

At the southern end of the square is the **Faustův dům** (Faust House), originally a late-Renaissance palace, which received its name because of an association with alchemy. In fact an English alchemist, Edward Kelly, attempted to produce gold from base metal here in the 16th century, under a commission from the Emperor Rudolf II. According to the Czech version of the Faust legend, a penniless student failed to pay his rent and was carted off by the devil to hell, although oddly enough through the ceiling, a direction in which he might have expected a happier fate! Despite this sinister past, the tradition of usage of this attractive building has been maintained with a pharmacy on the ground floor.

Edward Kelly

Promising the earth is a dangerous habit if you fail to deliver, as many an alchemist learned to his cost. Kelly was taken on by Emperor Rudolf in 1589, immediately changed a pound of lead into gold and was rewarded with a knighthood. Unfortunately he soon came to cost more in wages than he was worth as a producer of gold, and found himself in prison for "sorcery". An extraordinary career ended in death by poisoning —according to some accounts self-administered, according to others administered by the Emperor in person. Kelly's early career, which had been taken up with astrology and crystal ball gazing, turned out in retrospect to have been a lot safer than alchemy.

Returning to the west side of the square, there is an interesting bookshop at Karlovo náměstí 5, which contains a number of Art Nouveau prints and posters, and a quiet if hardly atmospheric café for refreshment next door.

Emmaus Monastery

Leave at the south-western end of the square along Vyšehradská, past the Emmaus Monastery. Founded in the 14th century for Croatian Benedictines, the monastery received its name from its completion date, Easter Monday, the date when in the words of the Christian Gospel according to St Luke the risen Christ meets his disciples on the road to Emmaus. It is also known as the **Klášter na Slovanech** (Slavonic Monastery), since it was intended as a means of renewing the Slavonic liturgy in Bohemia. Taken over by Spanish Benedictines in the 17th century, given some Baroque touches in the 18th, and Gothicized by German Benedictines in the 19th, the whole complex was badly bombed during an air raid in 1945. It was restored after the war, with two new spires looking like hare's ears created by F.M. Cerny in 1965. It is now an institute of the Czechoslovak Academy of Sciences, in places semi-derelict, and its interior treasures of stucco ceiling decorations and Gothic wall paintings are not yet on display. Walk in and try your luck!

*T*he controversial new spires of F. M. Černy on the Emmaus Church, rebuilt after damage during the Second World War, have been compared to hares' ears.

Botanical Gardens

The hill down from the monastery away from Charles Square passes Prague's Botanical Gardens (**Botanická zahrada**), which are worth a visit for a quiet respite from travels and crowds but are limited in what they have to offer. A low wall along the ulice na Slupi eventually gives way to an entrance, leading along slightly unkempt, winding paths past numerous benches, each of which appears to be semi-permanently occupied by an elderly Czech woman knitting. At least this area of town isn't swamped by tourists, just visited by a few ordinary people whiling away time in quiet.

National Security Corps Museum

From the Botanical Gardens set off along Apolinářská until you cross Ke Karlovu, where you should turn right and head southwards towards a museum which once, as the Museum of the Ministry of the Interior, documented various activities of the security forces in "defending the Czechoslovak state". In the post-Velvet Revolution days of the 1990s the **Muzeum SNB a Vojsk MV** (National Security Corps Museum) has subtly altered its nature and changed the character of its displays to fit new times.

Instead of displaying the works of "dissidents"—from the plays of Václav Havel to the songs of Bob Dylan—the museum now displays the fight against crime of a more recognisably "western" nature. A large quantity of burglar and car alarms, many of them British, occupy an upstairs room, while downstairs some vivid pictures highlight the effects of drug abuse and the means used to combat it. Examples of fraud and forgery vie with police uniforms and weaponry for attention,

145

whilst the role of the traffic police is high-lighted with a range of stop signs, cross-ings and other paraphernalia of vehicle regulation. Outside there are a few vehi-cles for children to climb in and out of, one of which offers a precarious climb to one of the best views of Vyšehrad, and a few more traffic signals. In other words the museum of police has suddenly erased all political overtones, and has substituted for the war against enemies of the state the war against crime. Like so much else in Prague, the exhibition is housed in a build-ing which formerly had a religious pur-pose: in this case a monastery of the Au-gustinian order.

Vila Amerika

Return along Ke Karlovu, past imposing if ugly faculty buildings, until you come to one of Prague's most delightful (per-haps because still relatively undiscovered) buildings, the russet red **Vila Amerika**. This early 18th-century summer palace is not in fact that grand; it is more of a coun-try house standing behind iron gates. The Villa Amerika now houses a museum de-voted to Antonin Dvořák, Czechoslo-vakia's most famous composer.

The emphasis in Prague in the summer of 1991 was upon Mozart, who had died 200 years earlier and whose "Prague con-nection" was feted all over the city be-cause he liked the place. Mozart's favourite port of call in Prague, **Bertramka**, had been turned into a major tourist venue, which meant quintupling the prices from their 1990 level, setting up a Mozart café in the street outside and fit-ting out a room at the back of the building with souvenirs such as postcards an-nouncing "Mozart loved Prague". Dvořák, on the other hand, who was actually Czech as opposed to a visiting Austrian,

hardly got a look in; which at least meant that the Vila Amerika was quiet, cost a tenth of Bertramka's price to visit, and was utterly charming.

As in Bertramka, where the music floats through every part of the house, so in the Vila Amerika strains of Dvořák fol-low you through the airy rococo rooms. Various incongruities are on display—such as a map of the seating arrangements from the university of Cambridge where Dvořák received an honorary degree, to-gether with the more predictable extracts from musical scores and concert pro-grammes. The charm of the room upstairs with its wall paintings, or even of the modest garden outside with its decorated vases, is exquisite. Occasional concerts take place here, but it is enough to savour the atmosphere on a hot summer after-noon, a couple of stray visitors wandering around, and a single devotee managing the whole building from behind a small desk downstairs.

The Vila Amerika was constructed for the Michna family as a summer retreat, and obtained its present name from being named after a 19th-century pub. Today a more famous pub exists in the vicinity of the villa, in the neighbouring street Na Bo-jiti, the **Hostinec U Kalicha** (Chalice Inn). U kalicha was made famous as the scene of the opening pages of Jaroslav Hašek's novel *The Good Soldier Švejk* (*Schweik*). "When the war's over come and visit me. You'll find me in the Chalice every evening at six," says Schweik to his friend. Hašek himself used to drink there regularly, but today the main customers are tourists, who may or may not savour the paintings and quotes on the wall, the costumed waiters and the general atmo-sphere of kitsch. From Na Bojišti it is a short distance to the underground metro

Jaroslav Hašek

Hašek's short life of forty years was mostly concentrated in the pub. He was a compulsive dabbler in both drink and ideas, unable to concentrate for long periods and unable to remain committed to a particular cause for long. He was at various times anarchist, communist, romantic Bohemian nationalist and creator of a new party committed to "gradual progress within the framework of the law".

His *The Good Soldier Švejk* presents one of many famous literary anti-heroes, the "wily warrior" whose clownish manner manages to expose the absurdities of bureaucracy and war. Hašek's own experience serving in the Austrian army during the First World War, and being taken prisoner by the Russians, was invaluable to the work, but whilst this exposé of the folly of human conflict found much favour (not least with Bertolt Brecht who read it in German translation and died with it next to his bed), it was also regarded as an immoral tarnishing of the Czech national character. As late as 1968, 50 years after the work was published and 45 years after Hašek's death, the commander of the Warsaw Pact forces that invaded Prague to quash the Prague Spring cited Švejk as a main cause of the trouble his tanks had come to deal with. A generation later it appears that the tanks were just not strong enough to cope with him!

colony. In the New Town it is possible to visit shops, cafés and restaurants, unless you spend all your time in U kalicha or in the Wenceslas Square area, which are at least as full of Czechs as of other nationalities. If you appreciate this for no other reason, you will appreciate it for the sudden drop in prices!

Nové Město: Opening Times

1. National Museum (Národní muzeum). 9.00 a.m. to 5.00 p.m. Not Mondays.
2. Mánes Gallery or Exhibition Centre. 10.00 a.m. to 6.00 p.m. Not Mondays.
3. Botanical Gardens (Botanická zahrada). 10.00 a.m. to 5.00 p.m.
4. National Security Corps Museum (Muzeum SNB a Vojsk MV). 10.00 a.m. to 5.00 p.m. Not Mondays.
5. Vila Amerika (Dvořák Museum). 10.00 a.m. to 5.00 p.m. Not Mondays.

Highlights for Children

There is a playground, though not a very good one, on Slovanský ostrov (Slavonic island). If there is a "garden theatre" (Zahradni divadlo) on nearby Shooters' island (Střelecký ostrov), then this will be ideal for children, with puppet-shows, folk dancing, music and plays.

Children would probably like a steamboat ride on the river. Embark from Palackého most (Palacký Bridge) between April and September.

The Botanical Gardens may appeal to some children.

The Albatros theatre on Národni, which is in fact a complex of theatre, cinema and bookshop, may have something entertaining for children. A surer bet would be the Magic Lantern Theatre Show at Národní třída 40.

Dětský dům, on Na příkopě 15, has a good selection of children's clothes.

station I.P. Pavolva, which is a couple of stops from the centre of town.

The New Town is perhaps the least beautiful of Prague's central areas, and it certainly requires the most walking. It would be very difficult to visit all the places described in one day, but at least it contains many areas that are predominantly full of local people going about the business of living, as opposed to areas like Hradčany which, for all their beauty, give the impression of being set out as a tourist

What is a Bohemian?

In historical terms, Bohemia was a kingdom founded in the 8th century by the Přemysl dynasty, and a Bohemian someone who comes from that area. Yet in modern parlance "Bohemian" means something else. What is it that has linked the word "Bohemian" to the image of the starving artist in the garret as seen in Puccini's famous opera *La Bohéme*, or to the suggestion of free-and-easy manners and habits?

Part of the answer may lie with the Hussite controversy. Following the burning of Hus in 1415 and the defenestration of the Catholic councillors four years later, Bohemia was virtually alone against the rest of Europe. The great one-eyed general Jan Žižka (who gave his name to the district of Žižkov, and whose statue on horseback tops the hill in that district in front of a giant granite monument) was leading an unbeatable Hussite army against all oppressors. In short, the whole of Europe, including Joan of Arc, who was going to sort the place out as soon as she'd finished with the English, was getting the wind up about Bohemia. In such circumstances, there's nothing like a scandal. The Catholic authorities, with an assurance that meant they had even managed to convince themselves, spoke of the Hussites as licentious successors to the Adamites, a movement which as their name suggested wished to return to the primitive innocence of Adam and Eve in Paradise. In effect, they wanted to take their clothes off, dance around and have a few sexual romps, as a number of other medieval sects had sought to do before them. There appears to be evidence that by the early 15th century several European languages were referring to a "Bohemian" as someone who favoured such practices, which ironically would have deeply upset the one-eyed general Jan Žižka, whilst they would have commended themselves quite well to the Popes he was opposing.

Later usage of the word, however, links a Bohemian to a gypsy, probably because of the supposition that gypsies originated from Bohemia, or at least passed through there on their way to the West. This idea probably has more validity today, when a lot of gypsies pass through Czechoslovakia fleeing persecution in Rumania, not always receiving much better treatment from the Czechs. The link with gypsies suggests the idea of a Bohemian as someone who is cut off from society, particularly through despising conventionalities. As Thackeray remarks in his famous *Vanity Fair*:

"She was of a wild, roving nature, inherited from father and mother, who were both Bohemians, by taste and circumstances."

The Westminster Review defined a "Bohemian" as a kind of "literary gypsy, no matter in what language he speaks, or what city he inhabits".

The Bohemian was a roving adventurer. Perhaps, in the words of Ralph Waldo Emerson, the Bohemian was "open to the suspicion of irregular and immoral living", but the primary sense was unconventionality and irregularity rather than immorality. "Not every Bohemian is a blackguard", as one 19th-century British magazine kindly put it.

Whatever the grounds for the term, whether the religious and sexual unconventionality of the Adamites or the social unconventionality of the gypsies, there is a question of whether there is anything "Bohemian" about Prague and its people. That must be for every visitor to judge for himself or herself. But certainly some Praguers have been very "Bohemian"—not least the famous author of *The Good Soldier Švejk*, Jaroslav

Bohemian living quarters in the Malá Strana.

Hašek. A devotee of anarchy and alcohol, Hašek began as a journalist, publishing swingeing diatribes under a false name against himself. He also invented stories, like an invasion of Prague by musk-rats, which managed to convince a sizeable section of the populace that such a horror was actually taking place. He formed a political party committed to "Gradual Progress within The Law", which despite its uninspiring moderation had a marching song which ran "To arms! To arms!" Unfortunately it did not poll very well, despite Hašek's offer of a pocket aquarium to anyone who would vote for it. However, defeat at the polls did not stop Hašek from writing the party's social and political history. Whatever his characteristics of dilettantism and practical joking, Hašek made a serious contribution to literature. He created a range of immortal characters in his novel *The Good Soldier Švejk*, mostly drawn from his experience of being mortal at the bar. Its theme is perhaps less romantic than the starving artist in the garret or the roving gypsy adventurer. Yet the resistance by means of humour to dull conformity and authoritarianism which is its anti-heroic tone does perhaps convey the best of Bohemianism in its least pretentious form. There has had to be a Bohemian spirit in that sense in Prague over the years simply for it to have been able to survive. It will be interesting to see how that spirit expresses itself towards new invasions, as the tanks go rolling out and the tourists come rolling in!

Inspiring Churches, Beautiful Buildings, and a Sense of Times Past

Prague's Old Town is beauty and history with a twist of the surreal. At one of its entrances a dark Gothic Powder Tower rubs shoulders incongruously with the mellow yellow of an Art Nouveau municipal hall. In its central square an extraordinary monument to Jan Hus looks out at Baroque façades which conceal Renaissance and Gothic remains. Spreading out from the centre are golden lanes and atmospheric alleyways with an architectural surprise at every street corner. The Old Town is a place to get lost in, with fate the only appropriate guide for your journey.

History

It is not possible to recognize the natural boundary of the Old Town nowadays. Streets like Národní třída, Na příkopě and Revoluční used to follow a line of fortifications protecting the Old Town from attack– indeed "Na příkopě" literally means "On the moat", which used to be the clear boundary between the Old Town and the New.

A *large painting by M. Aleš of St Wenceslas on horseback from a neo-Renaissance house in the Old Town Square.*

Despite the loss of these clear edges to the Old Town, however, it has retained its distinctiveness, and it is not difficult to recognize from the buildings and atmosphere around you that you are within this area of the city. The Old Town is a maze of narrow lanes and open squares, tall buildings with ornate tops and winding streets with richly decorated houses. It is full of churches, galleries, exhibitions, souvenir shops and tourists: but since the tourists, like the trams, tend to keep to set paths you will find the lanes alternately crowded and virtually empty. Sometimes it gives off the claustrophobia of a Kafka novel and feels cramped and confining; sometimes it feels intriguing and atmospheric. It is certainly unforgettable.

The familiar layering of architectural styles common to so many of Prague's bridges, churches and other buildings is true of the Old Town as a whole, which was subject to repeated flooding in the Middle Ages. As a consequence, the street level was progressively raised, and for this reason many of the houses in the Old Town have Romanesque rooms hidden in their basements. There are similar layers of Baroque in places built on Gothic originals for the same reason. Ironically, flooding has probably preserved architectural remains which would otherwise have been knocked down and replaced. Of course there are few accessible examples of this layering, but one example in the Old Town which can be visited is the House of the Lords of Kunštát and Poděbrady (*see* page 170).

This district of Prague became a town as opposed to a suburban settlement in the 13th century, when the fortifications around it were established. The more it became a distinct entity, the more its municipal government found itself increasingly at variance with the King's representative, or magistrate, who acted in the interest of the ruler. This tension existed during the period of expansion under Charles IV, when the New Town was founded, and increased under his successor Wenceslas IV, but it was in the next century that it finally boiled over.

The attitude of the Old Town burghers towards the radical Hussites was mixed. On the one hand, they welcomed a movement which appeared to challenge the authority of imperial forces that threatened their own local powers in Bohemia. On the other hand, they were worried that radical social principles in that movement might eventually challenge their own authority as well. In effect, they would use the Hussites to challenge the authority of those above them, and then crush them

before their own power could be challenged. A century later, Luther's ideas were to be exploited in the same way.

A breakdown of central government in the early 15th century, when Jan Želivský and his New Town followers threw the aldermen out of the New Town Hall windows, was used very effectively by the Old Town. They took additional power by abolishing the post of King's magistrate; additional property by confiscating land from the church and a number of unpopular German Catholic nobles; and then made sure that the radical Želivský who made such advances possible did not have so radical an effect that he undermined the position of the Old Town burghers alongside that of everyone else. They invited him to the Old Town Hall and had him executed. A number of Hussites were subsequently hanged in Old Town Square on a specially constructed gallows.

From this point the Old Town effectively controlled Prague and through Prague the rest of Bohemia. In 1458 the Czech King was elected in the Old Town Hall, now the effective seat of power. Having executed those below them, the burghers made sure that the nobility above them conformed to their will.

For several generations the centrepiece of the Old Town area, the **Staroměstské náměstí** (Old Town Square) became the focus of life, featuring processions, jousting tournaments, executions (and lesser punishments like the stocks), and street markets, which as in the modern day had to be licensed by the Town Council.

The Old Town's Gothic period, when it was relatively strong and even autonomous, gave way to a Renaissance period in which most of these powers were lost. The rise of the Catholic Hapsburg dynasty meant a new subordination of the power of the towns to that of the monarchy. For the next 300 years Prague was to play an often subordinate role in the rise and fall of the Austro-Hungarian Empire, many of whose rulers had little interest in events outside Vienna.

In the 19th century the city as a whole underwent considerable expansion. Josefov received the status of independent town to the north of the Old Town, which only opened the way to a massive programme of "slum clearance" creating streets like Pařížská, designed to provide apartments for the well-to-do.

The 20th century saw the formation of an independent Czech republic, and a number of politically significant events took place in the Old Town. In 1915 the memorial to Jan Hus, whose follower Želivský was executed by the Old Town burghers who had had indirectly made such financial and political gains from his teachings, was placed in the middle of the Square. From here it now challenges the burgher residences around it with the inscription **Pravda vitězí** (*Truth will prevail*). Thirty years later cheering crowds celebrated the arrival of the Red Army, and in 1948 the infamous Klement Gottwald announced the establishment of communist rule from the balcony of the Golz-Kinský Palace in the Old Town Square to at least half-cheering crowds.

Twenty years later the focus of historical development had moved to Wenceslas Square in the New Town, although the Soviet invasion was also resisted in the Old Town and the Jan Hus monument draped in black. Such events seem very much in the background two years after the Velvet Revolution, when the Old Town Square is packed as never before with (mostly western) visitors. The pace of change is so rapid that the inscription on the Jan Hus memorial becomes even more pertinent.

A Tour of the Old Town

Although one of the best ways of seeing this part of the city, and the same can be said of Malá Strana, is to get lost in it, this section will assume a planned route. The obvious starting-point is the **Staroměstské náměsti** (Old Town Square), arguably the best sight in Prague but make sure you see it when it's quiet in the (late!) evening as well as during the day. For most of the year you can discover it easily enough by finding a large crowd of tourists and following it. A more scientific approach is to take a metro to Můstek station. From here you will be able to look up Wenceslas Square to the National Museum at the top. Simply turn through 180° and walk in the opposite direction, moving with the general flow of human traffic. You will come to Melantrichova, a narrow lane that deposits you in the Old Town Square close to the Astronomical Clock. If you want to avoid the largest crowds, don't arrive at five minutes to the hour.

An alternative route is to take the metro to náměstí Republiky, cross over the road until you are next to the mighty Obecní dům (Municipal Hall) with its Art Nouveau decoration, and pass through the adjoining Powder Tower into Celetná. Once again, the tourist throng will carry you down to the Square like a friendly, babbling river.

Old Town Square

Once you reach the Old Town Square, wide and traffic-free, at least so far as cars are concerned, but you can very easily get tangled up with the many horse-drawn carriages offering an alternative way of seeing the Old Town, then on any spring or summer's day there will be a gathering of the nations. Tourists are often herded around in groups by an overworked guide who will try and attract a particular set of people under his or her control by holding aloft a specially agreed sign, like a red rose or a purple brolly. Many advertise their adherence to particular organizations. In August 1991, for instance, 75,000 Jehovah's Witnesses descended on the city from 39 different countries, all sporting a lapel badge with the slogan "Lovers of Freedom" in several different languages. So full of visitors is Prague in a month like August, indeed, that they become an interesting sight in themselves alongside the things that they have come to see.

The Astronomical Clock

Assuming that you have walked down Melantrichova into the Square, the first thing you will see is the astronomical clock on the side of the Old Town Hall. In the summer of 1990 the first thing you saw was an avant-garde sculpture of a car on legs, but that is now hidden in the grounds of the German embassy, presumably by popular demand.

There are three parts to this fascinating and largely 15th-century device. At the top are the moving figures which everyone comes to see when the clock strikes the hour (sometimes they are under repair and don't come out). Beneath them at the centre is the astronomical dial, and at the bottom is the calendar dial.

If we start from the bottom, the calendar dial is flanked by statues of the philosopher and the angel on the left hand side (as you look) and the astronomer and the chronicler on the right. The angel was intended to point to the current date on the external ring, but now it is a small mark at the top of the ring that does so, which is divided into 365 parts to represent each day of the year. The centre, containing the Prague coat of arms, is static; but around it are a number of turning circles. The first is that of the signs of the zodiac; the second is a set of paintings of activities appropriate to particular times of the year; and on the outside are the days of the year. These turn in harmony with one another so that it is possible at any time to see the day, the sign of the zodiac it comes under, and what people are doing!

*T*he Astronomical Clock in the Old Town Square.

The astronomical clock is even more complicated. It is flanked by figures on the left of the Miser (carrying a money-bag) and Vanity (peering into a mirror); and on the right by Death (as a skeleton) and a lute-carrying Turk. The clock itself is probably best read by concentrating on the hand which ends in the shape of a human hand. This will be pointing to one of 24 Arabic numerals on the outer ring of the clock, and will give you Old Bohemian time calculated from the moment of sunset. Inside this are more easily recognisable Roman numerals which will give you Central European time. The inner ring is marked with the signs of the zodiac, giving the position of the stars and intended (for this was the 15th century) to mark the turning of the heavens around the earth. The six-pointed golden star just outside the zodiac points to "star time". The other hands have symbols of the sun and moon. The different colours reflect the parts of the sky above (blue) and below (brown) the horizon, so that it is possible to read off from the dial whether it is day or night—something which would presumably be obvious anyway! At the very centre of the dial is a globe, the mid-point of which is Prague.

A large crowd gathers beneath the clock every hour on the hour in order to see figures of the 12 apostles emerge from the two windows above the astronomical dial. These are wood carvings by V. Sucharda made after the 18th-century originals were destroyed by fire in the last year of the war, when the Nazis deliberately set much of the Old Town Hall on fire. At the same time, the figures to right and left of the astronomical dial move. The skeleton (standing for death) pulls the rope of the bell and turns the hourglass, pointing to the fact that time has run out for Vanity,

the Miser and the Turk, whose unfortunate association with the vices was partly a product of medieval conflict between "Christian" Europe and Islam in the Near East. All three shake their head in refusal, the windows shut and then the cock crows from the window above. The mechanism is not always working, and the display is not as impressive as the two dials, but neither fact stops the crowds gathering before the hour.

The House at the Minute
Before moving into the main part of the square, it is worth noting the buildings to the left of the clock (as you face it). Immediate left is the **Staroměstská radnice** (Old Town Hall) itself: the red building is the entrance to the whole complex. Further to the left and at right angles to the rest of the Old Town Hall is the **Dům u minuty** (House at the Minute), originally a Gothic building but rebuilt during the Renaissance. The façade is decorated with 17th-century sgraffito work which was only discovered in 1919 under layers of plaster. There are various unappetising classical scenes of power, war and drunkenness, and some biblical scenes such as Jonah leaving the mouth of the whale after his three days in its belly.

Above the windows of the first floor on the south side of the building is *The Shooting of the Dead Father*. This was originally a Jewish tradition, according to which a judge decides which of three sons will inherit their father's estate by digging up the dead man's body, tying him to a tree and ordering them to shoot him. The son who shows reluctance—he is the one who refuses to hold his bow—inherits the estate! The moral value of this popular medieval tale sets off the ridiculous pictures of naked men on horseback fighting

Sgraffito decoration of the House at the Minute on the edge of the Old Town Square.

A rally beneath the Jan Hus monument in the Old Town Square. It was here that the new communist government was declared to cheering crowds in 1948. Meetings here now are very different!

or of French Kings looking uncomfortable, but very classical, in Greek and Roman costumes.

Monuments

Before going inside the Town Hall, it is worth taking in the Square as a whole, which has to be one of the greatest sights in Prague and perhaps in Europe. It is dominated by 18th-century Baroque façades, but if you climb to the top of the Town Hall tower then you can look down on steep daddle roofs which reveal the Gothic originals behind those façades. In the centre of the Square is the Jan Hus monument, dedicated on 6 July 1915 to

mark the 500th anniversary of his execution for preaching ideas very similar to those of Martin Luther which inspired the Protestant Reformation a century later.

The sculptor who produced this somewhat unsynchronized charcoal-coloured critique of Baroque extravagance was Ladislav Šaloun, and despite not finding favour with all the professional critics it has a strong emotional appeal. The saying **Pravda vítězí** (*Truth will prevail*) etched on the side, has seen Nazi and Stalinist rulers come and go already this century. Now the steps of the monument are regularly filled to over-flowing with back-

The Jan Hus Monument

Ladislav Šaloun's monument was controversial from the start, because the sculptor was deeply attracted to the techniques of Art Nouveau. The unveiling of the statue in 1915 produced the accusation of sprawling mess and a failure to produce a life-like representation (although presenting Hus as a giant might seem to be doing a favour to a man who by some accounts was very small). Compare this to the equestrian statue of St Wenceslas in Wenceslas Square, which was unveiled only three years earlier but which by comparison is very dull (or noble and serene, depending on your point of view!).

White crosses commemorate Protestant leaders publicly executed in the Old Town Square in 1621 after defeat in the Battle of the White Mountain.

packers, map readers and exhausted tour groups missing out on part of their official itinerary for the sake of a rest or a lethal Czech cigarette. Whether they will prove in their own way to be equally demanding "rulers", or at the very least the latest in a line of colonizers, remains to be seen.

Another monument against religious intolerance in the Square is the 27 white crosses set in the pavement beside the neo-Gothic wing of the Old Town Hall. The crosses mark the place where 27 Protestants were publicly executed in 1621 following the successful victory of the Hapsburgs a year earlier in the Battle of the White Mountain. The executions, on the orders of the Emperor Ferdinand II, began the process whereby largely Protestant Bohemia was wooed back to Catholicism by a combination of carrot and stick, a technique which the communists were to practise with rather less effectiveness three centuries later.

*A*nother masterpiece by Kilian Ignaz Dientzenhofer—St Nicholas' Church in the Old Town Square.

The Old Town Square
The gap created by the Nazis' destruction of part of the Old Town Hall in May 1945, a consequence of the Czechs rising up against their oppressors a week before the Soviet army arrived to liberate them (5,000 died during that week), has been a problem for various authorities ever since. Should anything be built there or not? The communist government toyed with the idea of a monument (and even a temple) to Stalin, but in the end the area was left to become a grassy site for sunbathers and visitors. There are no longer competitions to determine what should be built there, and indeed most people in Prague have come to like things the way they are.

Church of St Nicholas
Two churches stand out in the Square. To the left of the Jan Hus monument as you stand beside the Old Town Hall, just beside the top of Pařížská, is the **Kostel svatého Mikuláše** (Church of St Nicholas). This has been the site of a church since the 12th century, but the present one dates from the 18th, and was the work of the famous Kilian Ignaz Dientzenhofer, one of a famous Bavarian family of builders who moved to Prague in the 17th century. He and his father were also instrumental in the building of the other Church of St Nicholas in the Lesser Quarter.

Because of the destruction of much of the Old Town Hall by fire in May 1945, when the Nazis deliberately set it on fire before leaving, the Church stands out more than it was originally intended to do, facing what is now an open grassed area. The effect is to highlight the monumental south wing, with its white stone and rich sculptural decoration by Antonin Braun, but since the intention of the architect was to have the church viewed from a very short distance, it was meant to appear most impressive when viewed almost vertically from close by. For this reason it can appear rather "flat" when viewed from the unexpected distance created as a by-product of Nazi vandalism.

The inside of the church, on the other hand, is anything but flat. An octagonal central area is joined to oval chapels, while the light interior is topped by the cupola's curving arches.

In 1787 the church and its adjoining monastery were abolished, and it lost high altar, pews and pictures to other churches. It was a concert hall for a brief period in the 19th century, before being placed at the disposal of the Russian Orthodox

158

Church in 1871. In 1920 it was taken over by the Czechoslovak Hussite Church, which means that beside the stucco and fresco there is nothing of the rich Baroque interior that can be found in its Catholic namesake on the other side of the river. Arguably that only adds to the freshness of its bright interior, which is often used for exhibitions. In 1990 huge paper strips covered in simple shapes and other innovative designs provided a fascinating attempt to blend modern art with religious architecture. On the other hand there will be those for whom any church that isn't decked out like an opera-house full of angels, saints and cherubs is "empty".

Týn Church

The other church, the Týn Church (**Kostel Panny Marie před Týnem**—literally the Church of Our Lady before Týn), has suffered the opposite fate from that of St Nicholas. Where one has been unexpectedly opened up to view, the other has been unexpectedly boxed in by the houses around it, although it is obviously tall enough to tower over them.

This Gothic Church was built on the site of a Romanesque original in the 14th century. Its two towers dominate the east side of the Old Town Square, whilst at the centre of the west gable is a statue of the Virgin Mary with golden halo. The statue is 17th-century and an emblem of religious controversy, since the Týn Church was completed during the reign of the only Hussite King of Bohemia, George of Poděbrady.

Among his beliefs was the "Utraquist" doctrine that communion should be "in both kinds", that is to say that worshippers should not only receive the bread but also wine, which in traditional Catholic practice was reserved for the priests only. To highlight his Utraquist ideas George had a large gilded chalice put on the façade (the worshippers at communion receive wine from a large cup or chalice), together with a statue of himself. After the final defeat of Protestantism by the Hapsburgs at the Battle of the White Mountain (bílá hora) in 1620 these decorations were removed by Jesuit students at the Klementinum (the Jesuit College in the Old Town), and three years later the Virgin Mary appeared in the place of George and his chalice (*kalich*).

After the brightness of St Nicholas' Church, the interior of the Týn Church is dark and even gloomy, although it has some fascinating individual features such as the Gothic pulpit, early 15th-century font and the tombstone of the Danish 16th-century astronomer Tycho Brahe, to the right of the high altar. Brahe worked at the court of the Emperor Rudolf II until his place was filled by another famous astronomer, Johannes Kepler, after his death in 1601. He expired at an imperial banquet which had proved too much for his body to cope with; his bladder burst—although to judge from the expression on his tombstone, what he was forced to wear might have been equally to blame. A good way of seeing the church is to attend one of the many concerts held there, usually in the late afternoon.

If it is not surrounded by scaffolding, the portal of the entrance to the north side nave is particularly worth a look. Regarded as one of the most beautiful entrances in Bohemia, it has scenes from Christ's Passion (the last hours of his life after arrest in the Garden of Gethsemane) above the entrance—the beating with whips, crowning with a crown of thorns and crucifixion. To the side of the portal are sculptures of other biblical figures,

some of which have been lost, and the head of a man in a hood on the left-hand pillar who was probably the builder himself. The north portal (remember that in any church the altar is at the east end) faces Týnská street.

Around the Týn Church

The buildings that seem to crowd in front of the Týn church have their own significance. Immediately in front is the Týn school (entrance to the Týn church is through one of its arches), its white façade topped with arched gables in the style of the Venetian Renaissance. To the right of this 16th-century building is the 18th-century Baroque façade of the **Dům U bílého jednorožce** (House At The White Unicorn). As in so many other cases the process of historical layering has been at work. Originally a Romanesque building was here, but that has now been driven underground by time and the pressure to raise the level of the Old Town induced by frequent flooding. Then there was a Gothic phase, of which the Gothic rib vaulting of the arcades is evidence. In the 16th century an aristocratic family rebuilt the house in Renaissance style, and then 200 years later it was given its present late Baroque façade.

To the left of the Týn school (as you face it) is the **Dům U kamenného zvonu** (House At the Stone Bell), whose Baroque plasterwork has been stripped away to reveal its Gothic roots. Note the stone bell on the side of the house; this goes back to a plot to trap John of Lux-

*T*he Týn Church in the Old Town Square, closely shadowed by Baroque façades.

embourg and his troops when they came to Prague in 1410—a bell was rung in the Týn church to warn of his arrival. The stone bell commemorates this incident. On the first floor, windows alternate with niches for statues which have now been lost, and little of the sculptural decoration of the ground floor has been preserved, but even so the mellow stonework and simple hat of a roof make this a charming building.

Its neighbour, the late Baroque **Golz-Kinský palace**, is much grander with its rich stucco façade and attic statues of gods. Acquired in the 18th century by Prince Rudolph Kinsky, and reworked at a later stage inside and out in neo-classical style, the palace balcony of this bourgeois indulgence was found to be an appropriate place from which to announce the advent of communism in Czechoslovakia. Klement Gottwald appeared here on 21 February 1948 to announce a bloodless coup bringing the communists to power. Ironically it was from the centre of the Old Town, the traditional rich area of Prague, that communism's arrival was announced: whilst it was from the centre of the New Town, the traditional poor area of Prague, that in November 1989 a similarly bloodless coup brought about its eventual demise.

The row of houses on the southern part of the Old Town Square contains another very attractive set of Baroque façades. What will probably stand out the most is the House At the Stone Madonna, a neo-Renaissance building which was commissioned by Storch's publishing house at the end of the 19th century. Indeed before the Velvet Revolution of November 1989 it tended to be known as Storch's house, perhaps because the Stalinist authorities regarded literature as marginally less dangerous than religion. The stone Madonna herself is a small sculpture above the stone portal, but the house stands out for its painted façade, which features St Wenceslas on a white horse blessed by the hand of God which comes out of cloud above his head. St Wenceslas, incidentally, whether or not he was good was never a "good King", as the carol has it, but a prince.

Next to this building the **Dům U kamenného beránka** (House At the Stone Ram) contains one of Prague's oldest house signs and also one of its most confusing. The 16th-century sign features a young woman with an animal: but what sort of an animal? Is it a one-horned ram or a unicorn? From the 18th century the house has also been known as the House At the White (or Golden) Unicorn. It is not known which name the Stalinist authorities preferred. Unicorns being mythical beasts would not have appealed to their sense of realism, but one-horned rams would not have appealed to their sense of order.

There is a fine Renaissance portal down below, and as usual with these buildings there are Gothic traces on the ground floor in the form of rib vaults and tin-plated doors, and Romanesque remains in the basement.

The only remnant of the original architecture of the north side of the square, although it is no less attractive than the other sides, is the former monastery of the Paulines, an early Baroque building which after the abolition of the monastery became a mint.

The Old Town Hall Buildings

And so to the **Staroměstská radnice** (Old Town Hall) itself. Rather than being a single building, the Old Town Hall is a series of buildings that have been run together,

*C*lose-up of the Town Hall in the Old Town Square.

including a number whose external features we have already looked at, such as the sgraffito-decorated House at the Minute. To find your way inside, look for the red building near the astronomical clock.

There may well be a temporary art or photography exhibition in part of the buildings which will be worth seeing, and then there is the obligatory climb up the tower to a fine view of the Square from above. Save some energy—there is another fine view from the top of the Powder Tower a few hundred metres up the street.

There is a range of interesting sights in the Old Town hall complex, which you may find yourself somewhat herded around, so that each room is unlocked when you arrive and locked up again after the last grumbling visitor has been asked to leave—if you find this troublesome, tell them that you're writing a guide-book! One thing that visiting the Old Town Hall does enable you to do is to examine a number of buildings in the Square from the inside, and therefore to get a closer idea of what the architectural history of the area really means.

For instance, by going into the basement of the House At the Cockerel (part of the Old Town Hall buildings), you can at least see something, admittedly not much, of what Romanesque Prague might have looked like. On the ground floor there are a number of Gothic vaults from the various houses that make up the Hall, including one decorated with a mosaic, The Slavs' Homage to Prague. Upstairs are two ancient centres of municipal power. The Hall of the Town council has walls and ceiling dating from the late 15th century, an elaborate 17th-century coat-of-arms and an 18th-century tiled stove. The combination of dark wood and heavy furnishings is ornate but oppressive, carrying with it some of the innate pomposity of local government. A 15th-century wood-carving of the suffering Christ by an unknown artist was intended to remind councillors of the need for justice. Beneath Christ's feet an angel bears a scroll with the Latin tag *Juste iudicate filii hominis* (Judge justly, sons of men). Whether such religious admonitions had much effect is a matter for history.

Shopping

There may well be a number of concerts, temporary exhibitions, (look out for the word **Výstava** meaning exhibition) and displays in the Old Town Square which will usually repay a visit. There are also plenty of shops offering postcards, film, souvenirs and tourist information. Prague has progressed rapidly in the last two years in this respect; in 1990, for instance, good quality colour film was very difficult to obtain, whereas now it is no trouble.

More difficult to obtain is a seat in any of the cafés or restaurants in the area, but there is an excellent take-away facility facing the grassy area between the Old Town Hall and St Nicholas' Church. Called "Gyros", it offers a good, cheap fresh salad (still not easy to obtain in Prague, which is in the process of overcoming a traditional shortage of fresh fruit and vegetables), a kebab for meat-eaters (in thick slices of bread) and soft drinks. If you can find a square patch of grass there are worse places to eat a snack, and you don't have to wait an hour at the end of it to catch the eye of the waiter.

An alternative place for a more substantial snack is Vegetárka, located on Celetná ulice which joins the Old Town Square to the Powder Tower. Vegetárka is only open at lunch-times, but cannot be bettered as an unpretentious, self-service café offering plates of chips, beans, and eggs in a non-smoking environment. The queue passes the drinks first, so you can quench your thirst while waiting for food. Vegetárka, as its name suggests, has had quite a success in passing itself off as a vegetarian restaurant, which is perfectly true in that not all the dishes contain meat. But it does not specialize in vegetarian food, just a range of basic foods. Its reputation, however, does mean that it fills up with large numbers of English and American students, for whom the necessity to eat never seems to frustrate the desire to lecture the whole room on their experiences of the day.

Celetná is full of shops and shoppers, a smattering of new "western"-style cafés, a couple of traditional, and almost certainly full, restaurants (U Supa at number 22 is 14th-century), and one or two exhibitions (including in 1991 a very powerful examination of one of the less savoury of British inventions, the concentration camp). As you walk up Celetná towards the Powder Tower, look out for the **Dům U černě Matky** (House At the Black Madonna), which is number 34.

Czech Cubism

This is one example of a movement which, if it attracts you, can take you all over Prague to some of its most distant and often most interesting suburbs, namely Czech Cubism. This movement flowered in the 1910s, very much under French influence, and has a style of using strongly-defined geometric shapes. In the case of the House At The Black Madonna there is a striking combination of Cubist building and a relatively large early

Baroque house sign of the Virgin Mary behind a grille. For all that some might find such combinations strange, they are much more adaptable than the late 20th-century's offerings of pizza parlours, McDonalds and other acts of commercial vandalism threatening to destroy the city today.

The Powder Tower

The **Prašná brána** (Powder Tower) is at the top of the street. A giddy-making winding staircase admits you eventually, with the help of a rope banister and a couple of passing places, to a room with illustrations of the Old Town in history, including a large display of this area of the city in 1685. From here there is a further ascent to the top of the tower, from which you can peer through the ramparts at the town beneath, or across at the Municipal Hall in all its Art Nouveau glory.

The Powder Tower

This strange (and rather lost-looking) Gothic tower has a peculiar history. It was founded in 1475 by King Vladislav II, who received it as a coronation present. His popularity rating subsequently fell to an all-time low, his mayor fell victim to the time-honoured political tradition of defenestration, and Vladislav himself fled to the hills. It was left half-built, then turned into a gunpowder store (hence its name), and used for target practice by the invading Frederick the Great in the 18th century. By now virtually blown to bits, it was finally restored by the Czech Josef Mocker in the late 19th century, since when it has been left to look out of place next to the golden Municipal Hall and opposite the unprepossessing State Bank. It stands apologetically at the entrance to Celetná looking baffled, a perfect emblem of Prague's surreal quality as a mixture of styles.

The Powder Tower itself was one of eight 15th-century gate-towers that used to protect the Old Town from assault. Its present name derives from the 18th century, when it was used for storing gunpowder. It was reconstructed in 19th-century neo-Gothic style (hence the hat), after damage during a siege in the previous century. It is no longer, of course, a gateway to the town, but looks decidedly squashed up beside the Municipal Hall.

The Estates (Tyl) Theatre

The Powder Tower leads into náměstí Republiky and the New Town, which we have already seen. Go back a short distance to the House at The Black Madonna and turn left into **Ovocný trh**, which was originally a fruit market. At the end of this street is the unmistakable pale green of the **Tylovo divadlo** (Tyl Theatre). This lovely late 18th-century neo-Classical work is the oldest theatre building in Prague. It was originally known as the Nostitz Theatre, (it was built in 1781 by Count Anton von Nostitz-Rieneck) and served as the venue for the premiere of Mozart's *Don Giovanni*, which he completed at Bertramka in the Smíchov district of Prague. Knowing how much more receptive Czech audiences were to his music than those in most other countries, Mozart chose to have the first performance of his (arguably) greatest opera in Prague on 29 October 1787. A memorial tablet inside the theatre commemorates this event.

In 1799 the building was re-named the Estates Theatre, since it had come into the ownership of the Czech estates in that year. But this was not its last change of name. In 1945 the theatre was re-named in honour of Josef Tyl, a Czech dramatist whose comedy *Fidlovačka* contained the

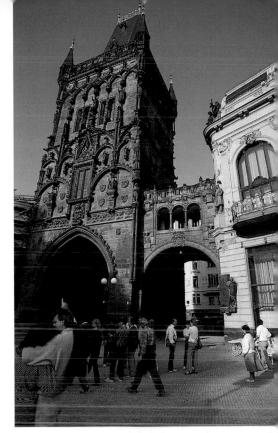

*T*he Gothic Powder Tower stands at the entrance to the Old Town, now rubbing shoulders with the mellower golden colouring of the Municipal House.

song *Where is My Home?*, which became the Czech national anthem. Whether because of his reputation for having reawakened Czech drama in the 19th century, or because of the desire to see the theatre as a symbol of national culture rather than as just another building constructed to please a rich nobleman, it is as the Tyl Theatre that the building has been known until 1992 when it was renamed the Estates Theatre again.

Whether or not you can remember the concert scenes in Miloš Forman's film about Mozart and Salieri, *Amadeus*, (scenes which are set in the Tyl or Estates Theatre), it is well worth viewing the ornate interior decoration which is based on designs by A. Wolf in the late 19th century.

Newly restored, Ovocný trh (which means fruit market) is a very attractive, if slightly quaint, cobbled area lined with houses in pastel shades between Celetná and the Estates Theatre.

Contrasting styles: the famous Oriel window of Charles University stands opposite the newly restored Estates (formerly Tyl) Theatre.

Charles University

To the right of the Tylovo divadlo (as you approach from Celetná) is the Carolinum (Latin for "Charles") or Charles University, another of the means by which Charles IV intended to put Prague on the world map. It was the first university to be established in central Europe, opening in 1348, but virtually nothing of the original remains today. All that can now be seen is a single ornate Oriel window, littered with coats-of-arms and gargoyles, whose picture is forever on display, perhaps because it is the only reminder that there has been a university here for more than six centuries.

The present-day university has buildings all over the Old Town rather than a single campus, but there is one modern building on the old site, with a central core in pink that is definitely one pastel shade too many. The words *Universitas Carolina* etched on the front hardly compensate with ancient words for the sight of the modern pile they are attached to. The university was intended to bring together scholars from all nationalities, with a constitution based upon that of the University of Paris, where Charles himself studied. His successors, however, could not maintain such an ecumenical perspective. German-speaking students fell out with Czechs, and in 1409 Wenceslas IV bowed to pressure from Jan Hus, who was the Czech Rector at the time, to remove some of the German speakers' rights. Two thousand students and many teachers thereby left and the university ceased to be an international focus of learning. The eventual triumph of Catholicism in Prague meant that the university was taken over by Jesuits, and then in more recent years it has been very much dominated by communists. Hopefully it can now return to Charles' original conception of an international centre of learning controlled by no particular ideology, religious or secular.

Changes in Prague

On the far side of the Estates Theatre are a number of streets running at right angles to what, during the tourist season, is always the main flow of human traffic in Prague, moving from Wenceslas Square to the Old Town Square and back. Head for the largest of these streets, **Rytířská**, and pause for a moment at the neo-Renaissance building with symbolic sculptures on the right as you head away from the Tylovo divadlo (it's number 29). Originally this was the Prague Savings Bank, but in the 1950s it was given an extra storey and converted into a museum. The Klement Gottwald museum was established to record, in words as recent as the 1988 Olympia Guide to the city, "the development of the workers' revolutionary movement and the building up of Czechoslovakia. It also illustrates the life and work of K.Gottwald (1896–1953), an outstanding representative of the Communist Party of Czechoslovakia and President of the Czechoslovak Republic from 1948 to 1953."

Since 1989, along with the removal of all 100-crown bank-notes bearing his image, Gottwald has lost streets, statues, embankments, an underground station and many other signs of his former omnipresence. Whatever view history takes of the man who appeared on the balcony of the Golz-Kinský Palace in February 1948 to announce the triumph of communism in Czechoslovakia, it is clear that this "outstanding representative" was generally loathed, ruthless towards his opponents and often drunk. He was reputed to have

Klement Gottwald

Like Hitler in Germany, Gottwald came to power by semi-constitutional means. The Czech communist party received nearly 40 per cent of the votes in elections after the war, and Gottwald became prime minister of a coalition government. Two years later he became president, but faced a problem with his foreign minister, Jan Masaryk, son of the venerated founder of the Czech republic, and known to have dangerous leanings towards democracy. Only one Czech political tradition could help Gottwald here, defenestration, and Jan proceeded to lean too far out of his office window late one night.

From then on it was a process of imprisonment, execution, and, of course, a surge in communist party "popularity" at subsequent communist-run polls. In 1952 several party members were condemned as "bourgeois nationalist traitors". The way to complete control was clear.

Having established himself in a state of absolute power, however, Gottwald made the mistake of Hitler and Napoleon before him, and under-estimated the power of the Russian winter. He set off to Stalin's funeral without a thick enough coat, caught pneumonia (popularly known to Czechs as "Moscow 'flu") and died. He was not missed.

died in 1953 because he could not bear to out-live Stalin.

In 1990 this building was undergoing "renovation", and indeed the new authorities tended to look with some suspicion at anyone who might seem interested in investigating it further. By 1991, ironically, it had re-opened as a bank, and instead of *Muzeum Klementa Gottwalda* on the front it bore the sign "Exchange Money". The triumph of capitalism could hardly have been more pointed!

Also very changed is the early Baroque building at number 31, once a Carmelite monastery but from 1970 the "House of Soviet Science and Culture". This building used to contain exhibitions of Soviet "achievements", which managed to fill the former refectory, looked down upon by 18th-century ceiling paintings depicting scenes from the "opium of the people". A Russian shop called "Chayka" would sell the familiar Russian souvenirs such as dolls and caviar at a price high enough to attract much touted trade from visiting western capitalists.

Continue along Rytířská, perhaps investigating some of its open-air market stalls. These have grown fuller and more enticing since the Velvet Revolution, particularly where food is concerned. In 1990 it was almost impossible to buy fresh bananas in Prague, whilst fresh fruit and vegetables generally were in short supply. Now they are much more plentiful, although the other side of the coin is that they are also more expensive. Perhaps a cynical view would be: under communism the Praguers could afford the unavailable; under capitalism they cannot afford the available.

Church of St Martin

At the end of Rytířská the **Kostel sv. Martina ve zdi** (Church of St Martin in the Walls) comes into view in Martinská street. Its name derives from the way in which its south wall was incorporated into a fortification wall of the city next to St Martin's gate. It is a Romanesque church, built in the late 12th century, many of whose characteristics have been preserved in the main nave area despite 14th-century Gothic reconstruction. Fire in the late 17th century provided the excuse for a few Baroque additions, such as the north portal, whilst the early 20th century saw the addition of a neo-Renaissance tower. As with many other churches and the cathedral in Prague, some would see evidence of different styles that do not combine well, others would be charmed by it. Unfortunately, one of the most difficult things is to get into it since repairs set in back in 1975, and it has not yet recovered.

St Martin's was at the centre of controversy in the early 15th century for offering communion in both kinds (i.e. bread and wine, whereas the laity in medieval Catholic churches of the time received only bread). Today it serves the Evangelistic Church of the Czech Brethren, who maintain the Hussite tradition that made the church famous.

Bethlehem Square

From St Martin's Church you can probably just about hear the sounds of traffic in Národní. Turn back towards Uhelný trh, and then turn left into Skořepka. At the bottom of Skořepka turn right into Husova and then almost immediately left into **Betlémské náměstí** (Bethlehem Square). The square is named after the **Betlémská kaple** (Bethlehem Chapel), another scene of Hussite activity in the early 15th century. A hundred years later one of the most radical preachers of the Protestant Reformation, the German Thomas Munzer, delivered a series of sermons here. Munzer's views were Utopian and socialist, his criticism of the church one which focussed on its wealth and uncritical relationship to the state.

Engels believed that the protest against Catholicism by the religious reform movements, like those of Wycliffe in England, Hus in Bohemia or Luther in Germany,

had to be associated with protests against the feudal hierarchy of the day. It could never be interpreted in purely religious terms. The new Communist government, following this line, tended to look sympathetically upon a building in which it saw Hus and Munzer as early exponents of socialism. It therefore decided early on (in 1949) that the chapel must be restored and in 1962 declared it a national monument. Go into the chapel with its Gothic-lined windows, extracts of tracts by Hus and others on the walls, and relatively simple wooden furnishings of oratory, choir and pulpit. Arguably its restorers could understand this sort of religion, based on the power of the word and setting out to instruct, more than they could ever fathom the mysteries and extravagances of Baroque. Next to the eastern side of the chapel the preacher's house has also been renovated. Here Jan Hus lived and wrote.

*T*he view from the castle across to the Old Town.

A number of documents relating to his life and work are displayed, not unlike the way that five centuries later rooms in which socialist and communist leaders lived and worked would be re-created.

At present the Bethlehem Chapel is under "reconstruction". It will be interesting to see whether the exhibition will be changed to represent Jan Hus rather less as proto-communist and rather more as religious reformer.

Ethnological Museum

Bethlehem Square contains an interesting museum which is quite definitely open, the **Náprstkovo muzeum** (Náprstek Museum) or, as it is usually known, the Ethnological Museum. It is housed in a complex of buildings, which in the 19th century came into the hands of patron of the arts Vojta Náprstek. A century ago Náprstek was the equivalent of today's computer buff, always buying up and displaying modern gadgets. In his case he filled the house with sewing-machines, washing-machines and refrigerators brought over from the States, and in 1862 decided to open a museum with these things, among others, on display. Other Czechs came to deposit what they had discovered on their own travels abroad, and the museum soon became a depository of items from all over the world.

The entrance is at the end of a yellow courtyard with trees that is itself a good place to rest. This museum is a welcome contrast to the National Museum, of which it is technically now a part. The Victorian classroom atmosphere of the latter's endless rows of rocks is here transformed into colourful displays from around the world, including some ornamental headgear and masks which might even be frightening enough to amuse children.

One room has an exhibition using slides and music, another (characteristic to Prague throwing off the formalism of the recent past) currently has an exhibition of modern art, and there are abundant collections of weaponry (offset, however, by a collection of peace-pipes). It does give one the slight feeling that it is more a group of knick-knacks brought back by amused Europeans than a serious attempt to present the culture of other continents, but for all that it is well worth a visit.

Along Husova

From Bethlehem Square head back the few metres to Husova and continue down its length. You may find this difficult if travelling in summer, since added to the increased numbers there is the constant rattle of hoofs as those visitors who have opted for a "romantic" tour of the Old Town negotiate the narrow lanes in a horse and cart. On the right-hand side you cannot miss the buttresses and lancet windows forming the Gothic exterior of **Kostel sv. Jiljí** (St Giles' Church). The inside of the building suffered total "Barocization" in the early 18th century. It is currently impossible to enter the main interior, which has to be viewed from behind a grille. The church was taken over in 1626 by the Dominicans, who ensured that their order was sumptuously lauded in its new Baroque decoration. The ceiling frescoes by V.V. Reiner, the famous artist who is buried in this church, are worth seeing.

House of the Lords of Kunštát and Poděbrady

Continue down Husova, to be distracted if you will by the many exhibitions and galleries on the way, and then turn left into Žetězová. Here you will find the House of the Lords of Kunštát and Poděbrady. What you will probably discover here may illustrate the principle that in Prague a museum or ancient building is a perfect excuse for an exhibition of modern art.

The "house" was originally a large Romanesque court, large parts of which have been preserved, including the whole of the Romanesque ground-floor, which is today the basement. In the 15th century the court was owned by the lords of Kunštát and Poděbrady, who reconstructed it and added a gate with access to Řetězová street. George of Poděbrady kept it as his official Prague residence until he was raised to higher things in 1458 by becoming king.

The damp cellar, decked out with dim floor-based lights, is one of the best examples in the city of Prague's original Romanesque structures. It is also used as an ideal surrounding for exhibitions. In 1991 this cellar contained carefully placed examples of modern pottery, including some outstanding items housed in metal cabins and scrutinized only through small gaps with red fluffy borders. Upstairs there were further exhibits and various pots and paintings for sale under the aegis of Galérie Ars Bohemica. A few ceramic artists hovered around to discuss their wares with anyone interested. In fact the blend of modern art and ancient setting worked very well, and will become increasingly a feature of Prague after the Revolution as people look for outlets and venues in which to exhibit long-suppressed artistic talent

Smetana Embankment Area

From Řetězová head towards Anenská and the river. **Anenské náměstí** (Anne's Square) contains the lime-green Divadlo na zábradlí, the theatre in which the

> **George of Poděbrady**
> The Hussites received wide support from the regime which preceded the Velvet Revolution because they were thought of as early communist revolutionaries fighting against a feudal system maintained in place by Catholic ideology. George of Poděbrady was similarly one of those who was regarded, despite his wealth, as ideologically pure. His efforts to establish a League of Princes to fight the Turks, at that time seen as a threat to the survival of "Christian" Europe, was interpreted as an early version of United Nations which demonstrated the Czechs' deep-seated internationalism and desire for world peace. For this reason the House of the Lords of Kunštát and Poděbrady was not allowed to deteriorate in the way that other historical monuments were left to do.

present leader of Czechoslovakia, Václav Havel, worked as a playwright for several years. A short distance further and you rejoin the traffic on Smetanovo nábřeží (the Smetana embankment). Cross over, and follow the line of houses, originally the Old Town water mills, jutting out into the Vltava river, stopping if you wish at a refreshment stall on the way. Head towards the willow at the end, which is a terrific place to relax with a coffee or beer, numbers willing. You find yourself next to a statue of the famous 19th-century composer Bedřich Smetana, sculpted by J. Malejovský as recently as 1984. Smetana's music is a background sound for any visitor who ventures outdoors in Prague.

Opposite the statue is the entrance to the Smetana museum, which has been housed since 1936 in a neo-Renaissance waterworks built at the end of the 19th century. Sgraffito decoration on the outside depicts the triumph over the Swedes on the Charles Bridge of 1648, one of the last encounters of the Thirty Years' War. Inside there is an exhibition of his life and work, including original scores, letters, musical instruments and personal effects. In the hall of the building there are frequent concerts, which are often best heard from the romantic setting of the nearby Charles Bridge. There could hardly be a more appropriate place for hearing the music from *Ma Vlast* (My Country) which describes the river Vltava's final approach to Prague, and which has become a virtual national anthem in the city itself.

Walk back to the Smetana embankment and turn left under the arches. This brings you to the edge of the Charles Bridge which joins the Old Town to the Lesser Quarter (and is described in the section on the latter). Although the narrow lanes of traffic beetling through make it hard to realize, you come out into a square, **Křižovnické náměstí** (the Square of the Knights of the Cross), whose four sides are made up by the Bridge Tower, the Church of St Francis, the Church of St Salvator on the far side of the road, and a former Renaissance building facing the Church of St Francis. In the centre of the square, which not only has traffic running through it but swarms with visitors moving onto and off the bridge, or buying drinks and knick-knacks from the new entrepreneurs of the revolution, is a cast-iron statue of Charles IV looking like a lost tourist fumbling with his wallet and keys. It was erected in 1848 to mark the 500th anniversary of the founding of the university of Prague.

Church of St Francis and St Salvator

The **kostel sv. František z Assisi** (Church of St Francis) was originally part of a monastery of the "Order of Crusader Knights with the Red Star". Despite sounding like a battalion of KGB agents, this was in fact an order of Bohemian knights at the time of the crusades, which may or may not be something completely different. The present Baroque church was the work of a French architect, Jean-Baptiste Mathey. Its most notable characteristic is a large cupola which contains a fresco of the Last Judgment, the effect of whose size is to let the light in and make this church less gloomy than most.

If you can safely negotiate Death Road outside (watch the trams especially—they're the ones that can't swerve) then **kostel sv. Salvatora** (St Salvator's Church) opposite is also a lot less gloomy than its outside suggests. The grey statues outside, which are illuminated at night, do not prepare you for the light and creamy interior. Built in Renaissance style in the late 16th century, it was soon taken over by the "Klementinum", the large Jesuit complex which is our next port of call.

Klementinum

Heading away from the river opposite the Charles Bridge is Karlova, which functions as the main artery to convey visitors from the Old Town Square (number one sight) to the Charles Bridge (number two sight). As you move (or try to) along this road, take note of what's on your left, the huge former Jesuit college known as the Klementinum. Make sure you manage to find the entrance in its massive, gloomy façade (by St Clement's church on Karlova) because its size is quite extraordinary, second only to the castle complex in area.

Where the old Jewish ghetto was razed to the ground to build Pařížská's luxurious town house apartments at the end of the last century, this part of the Old Town was razed to the ground for the sake of ideological purity. In 1556 Emperor Ferdinand summoned the Jesuits to Prague in order to re-Catholicize the Czech lands and eliminate their continuing Hussite tendencies. Initially they took over the monastery and **kostel sv. Klimenta** (Church of St Clement), which had belonged to the Dominicans for three centuries. A quarter of the then Old Town was pulled down to make way for the construction of their headquarters, the Klementinum.

The Church of St Salvator was begun at the end of the 16th century, but the construction of the Jesuit college itself was a work of the 17th and early 18th centuries. Begun in 1653, it followed the integration of Charles University into the complex in 1622, which gave the Jesuits direct control over the education system and a chance to root the principles of the Counter-Reformation firmly in the minds of Czechs.

Whether or not it was a triumph of truth over ideology, as in more recent times, the Jesuit order was abolished in 1773. The Jesuits were expelled and the Klementinum handed over to the University of Prague whose research it had previously closely controlled. Over the years it was gradually filled up with more volumes, including a great deal of material from abolished monasteries transferred under Joseph II. Today the complex is more a giant bookstore than a university, containing several million books and medieval manuscripts under the aegis of the State Library of Czechoslovakia.

To visit the place is a strange experience. Despite its location it tends to be missed out by visitors hurrying from the Charles Bridge to the Old Town Square or vice versa. You suddenly find yourself on the wrong side of high walls, in unexpectedly large, bland courtyards that are virtually empty. It is like a run-down version of the Castle without the milling crowds. Since it isn't yet officially open to visitors, the sensation of entering is like stepping off a busy Oxbridge pavement into one of the college courtyards, occupied by the odd stray student or don going about not very important business.

Apart from the inevitable statue of a student defending the Charles Bridge against the Swedes, the complex contains a library with ceiling-frescoes of the Muses (and a painting of *The Temple of Wisdom* in the centre), a Mozart Hall with rococo paintings, a Mathematical Hall with a collection of table-clocks and globes, and a Mirror Chapel, so-called because mirrors are inserted into its rich stucco interior features. In the centre of the Klementinum is the Observatorium, or observatory tower, used by the famous astronomer Johannes Kepler, the court astronomer to Rudolph II who followed Tycho Brahe in the post. There may also be temporary exhibitions of some of the huge literary and academic treasury in the compound, and there are several other

---

The Observatory In the Klementinum

The observatory was built in 1721, with frescoes depicting such early astronomical luminaries as Aristotle, Tycho Brahe, Hipparchus and Ptolemy. The extraordinary thing is that, as late as the 18th century, the earth is still depicted in these paintings as the centre of the universe. Two centuries later Prague was to be taken over by similarly unreal myths when the communists attempted to impose their secular ideology on the city. At least the Jesuits never attempted to throw Johannes Kepler out of a window!

interesting rooms and chapels. Unless things have changed recently, however, your capacity to see any of this will depend upon being able to persuade whoever is inclined to show authority in the area that you ought to be able to look around. Try saying "psam průvodce" (I am writing a guide-book).

It is difficult, inside these walls, not to feel the presence of an organization which was once as powerful and more all-embracing in its power of social and educational control than more secular creeds have been in the modern day. Whether these particular shock-troops of ideological purity operated to a better or worse effect than their modern counterparts is for each individual to judge.

If you want to visit St Clement's, rebuilt in Baroque style in the early 18th century and containing some very fine sculptures, then you should aim to be there at 5.00 p.m., the time of the liturgy (it now belongs to the Uniate church—ie Orthodox rites but in communion with Rome). At other times you're unlikely to get past the railings outside.

Other Sights in the Area

Continue along Karlova, past the many galleries, coffee-houses, exhibitions and wine-bars, many of which, like the **Dům U zlaté studné** (House at the Golden Well) are elaborately decorated. It hardly matters if you get lost in this area, since all the lanes lead somewhere interesting. The street eventually crosses Husova. To the right is St Giles' Church which we have already seen. To the left is the Clam-Gallas Palace, a magnificent Baroque building designed by Viennese court architect Fischer von Erlach. You'd expect a building like this to be standing on its own in several acres of ground, looking out onto a long driveway and facing a few ornamental fountains. Instead it is crammed into the narrow structures of the Old Town, its elaborate portal ornamentation by Matthias Braun easily missed as the stream of people flows by. Perhaps it is a characteristic feature of a city with so many treasures that, rather than flaunt them, it hardly knows where to put them.

Statues of Hercules bear up the entrance to the Clam-Gallas Palace in Husova Street.

At the end of Husova the Náměstí primátora dr Václava Vacka (formerly Dr. Vacek Square), containing the municipal library and new town hall, has been re-named **Mariánské náměstí**. In 1991 one of the best of many exhibitions of modern Czech art could be found in the municipal library in this square. It is worth pointing out once again that the National Gallery, like the State Jewish Museum, is a collective noun for several different venues, some of which may only be temporary. Tickets to the **Národni Galérie v Praze** (National Gallery of Prague) very conveniently have a list of places where art is being exhibited (including the type of art), and a map to help locate them. In 1991 20th-century Czech painters (České malířství 20. stol.) were on show in the municipal library (Městska knihovna) in this square.

From Mariánské náměstí a short journey via Linhartská and U radnice, past the

The russet red neo-Renaissance Rott Haus in Small Square (Malé náměsti).

popcorn and T-shirt ridden American Hospitality Centre, a kitsch meeting-place for the new colonizers, brings you out in Malé náměstí (the Little Square). More triangle than square, it has a Renaissance grille at the centre surrounding a now defunct fountain, and a number of striking buildings, most notably the **Rott Haus**. This neo-Renaissance house was built for a firm of ironmongers, whose name Rott is stamped on the side. It has a prominent red façade decorated with allegorical motifs and idealized figures from the world of agriculture and handicrafts, such as the sturdy worker in hat and breeches. He has

175

a scythe slung over his right shoulder and a coat draped over the left, doubtless heading for the nearest hostelry. The opposite side of the triangle has an attractive arcade lined with shops selling expensive, but very good, Bohemian glass. Squeeze past the top corner of the arcade and you are back in the Old Town Square, a short distance from the Astronomical Clock and the entrance to the Old Town Hall.

The tour so far has covered the most widely visited area of the Old Town, the part between the Old Town Square and the Charles Bridge. A less visited but equally atmospheric part of the town lies between Pařížská and Josefov on one side, and the New Town on the other. You can reach it by leaving the Old Town Square at the opposite corner to the Astronomical Clock, next to the Golz-Kinský Palace, which as part of the roving National Gallery may still have an exhibition of graphic art; if so, stop and look.

The road you should be on is **Dlouhá třída**, one of many back-streets in the Old Town that are full of atmosphere and relatively quiet. Dlouhá třída (třída means avenue) soon gives way to a street simply called **Dlouhá**, where at number 9 you can always grab a good glass of wine or *Becherovka* in the café-bar **U zlaté štiky** (The Golden Pike). Despite its nearness to the Old Town Square it is very much a locals' bar, putting a cord across the entrance and hanging up the sign *obsazeno* (full) at the slightest sign of a large troupe of visitors.

Turn off Dlouhá into Rámová, which leads to Haštalské náměstí (where the **Kostel sv. Haštala**—Church of St Castullus—is under extensive restoration) and from there set off down Anežská street to the Anežský klášter (Convent of St Agnes-Anežská means Agnes), now renovated to form an essential part of Prague's roving art collection, the National Gallery.

Convent of St Agnes

The Convent was founded in 1233 by King Václav (Wenceslas) I, and named after his sister Agnes of Bohemia. Agnes introduced the Order of the Poor Clares, a female version of the Franciscans, into Bohemia, and became abbess of the new convent in 1235. Beatified in 1874, she was officially canonized on 12 November 1989. As a mark of her pleasure at this promotion, she sent the Velvet Revolution in the following week.

The Convent has been carefully restored in a way that preserves a great deal of its Gothic character. Whatever was actually on display in the convent, it would be a pleasure simply to wander through its corridors and cloisters. In fact the Convent has a very interesting collection of Czech 19th-century painting, a number of sculptures and some fascinating photographs of the Prague Exhibition of 1891. The organizers also had the excellent idea of a "Children's Workshop", which combines a display of children's art, based on their impressions of the exhibition. There is also a collection of crayons and paper that gives visiting children the chance to produce their own work spontaneously! In effect this display is whatever the children make of it. Unfortunately there's no supervision, so you can't leave them there while you see the rest of the building.

The ground floor is largely devoted to a small number of sculptures, such as a statue of St Agnes by Myslbek, carefully placed for maximum effect in large, bare ecclesiastical rooms. You can also find a model of the original convent in the hall.

Upstairs on the first floor there is an exhibition of Czech art. Look out for the paintings of Josef Fuhrich, the landscapes and portraits of Josef Mánes, the sculptures of Peter Maixner, the extraordinary work of Hanus Schwaiger and Max Pirner, and the original of the famous poster used for the Prague Exhibition of 1891.

Designed by Vojtěch Hynais (1854-1924), the poster features two columns draped with palm leaves framing a view of the city of Prague. Wrapped around each column are banners bearing (one in German, one in Czech) single words that summarize the purpose of the century-old exhibition: Art, Science, Industry and Culture. A hundred years on from the Exhibition of 1891 there is a strong sense of the city's destiny as a centre of art, culture and successful industry in the process of being restored once more. This sense was very strongly reflected in the new exhibition of 1991 put on display in the north of the city (which is covered in OTHER DISTRICTS, *see* page 195).

Church of St James

From St Agnes' Convent, which has a good, unpretentious and usually half-empty snack bar for drinks and light meals, set off up Rybná, turn into Masná, and then go up Štupartská, a narrow lane behind the Týn Church. Alternatively take the "simple" but less interesting route up Rybná and left into Jakubská. Here you will find one of the biggest and, although it is off the major tourist trails, most attractive Baroque churches in Prague, **Kostel sv. Jakuba** (dedicated to St James). You can also find this church by turning off the heavily populated Celetná which runs between the Powder Tower and the Old Town Square, through one of

the passages in number 17 or 25, a route which almost immediately takes you from noisy bustle to relative quiet.

The church was originally part of a monastic complex, the Order of the Minorites, a kind of poor relation of the Franciscans, founded by King Wenceslas I in the 13th century. The church was completed during the reign of (who else?) Charles IV, and underwent the standard Baroque face-lift (partly inspired by fire) around 1700. Despite the introduction of Baroque, it retains the twin-steepled, triple-naved character of a large monastery church from the age of Gothic.

The size of the interior is immediately noticeable—it is the longest church after St Vitus' Cathedral. It has all the Baroque accoutrements that liven churches up to be opera houses—balconies topped with cherubs, elaborate ceiling-paintings, "stalls" along the side sporting twenty-one altars, and a large V.V. Reiner painting over the high altar commemorating the martyrdom of St James. An ornate 18th-century pulpit held up by a lion and the Baroque tombstone of Count Václav Vratislav of Mitrovice, 18th-century political bigwig, in the left-hand nave, are particularly worthy of attention.

St James' Church (sometimes called St Jacob's Church) is particularly attractive because it is large enough to absorb Baroque fancies without losing its Gothic grandeur. The former monastic buildings to the north of the church now form a music school, appropriate given the church's excellent acoustics which make it a favourite venue for organ recitals and concerts.

Take a last look at the stucco exuberance on its exterior as you leave, where figures cling to its ornate sides like confused climbers. From here you can either head back to the Old Town Square, or alternatively walk through a few more of the relatively quiet and atmospheric streets between Josefov and the New Town.

*T*he bubbling stucco facade of St Jacob's Church in the Old Town.

Shopping

If a completely different mood has taken hold of you, it is not far to náměstí

Republiky and one of Prague's three or four large department stores, **Kotva** (Anchor). In this case the site of a former Romanesque church has not developed into a bigger Gothic equivalent, later touched up by Baroque. After a few centuries of a church, a monastery, houses and fortifications on this site, it now proudly displays a six-sided concrete offering to Mammon, Prague's biggest and often bustling store. Its façade is covered with eloxal-coated aluminium panels which make it look as if it's imminently taking off back to Mars.

Here you can buy suitcases built to last, a range of wine and spirits, reams of toilet paper and, at least in 1990, dinky umbrellas in the colours of **Občanské Fórum** (Civic Forum). At the time this was appropriate enough, since Civic Forum was an "umbrella" organisation designed to bring together a wide range of opposition to the communist government before the Velvet Revolution. The umbrellas are less easy to obtain now that the political umbrella is falling apart two or three years after being exposed to the winds of office! In any case, if you've had a hard day admiring the cultural and historical sights of the Old Town, the Kotva department store could be just the place to wind down in.

Staré Město: Opening Times

1. Astronomical Clock, Old Town Square. Obviously "open" all the time—but it does exciting things on the hour every hour.
2. Old Town Hall (Staromětska radnice). 8.00 a.m. to 6.00 p.m. (9.00 a.m. to 5.00 p.m. November to February).
3. Powder Tower (Prašná Brána). 10.00 a.m. to 6.00 p.m. May to September. 10.00 a.m. to 5.00 p.m. April and October. Not Mondays, Tuesdays,

Thursdays or Fridays.
4. Bethlehem Chapel (Betlémské kaple) 9.00 a.m. to 6.00 p.m. May to September. 9.00 a.m. to 5.00 p.m. October.
5. Náprstkovo muzeum (Náprstek Museum of Asian, African and American Cultures or Ethnographical Museum). 9.00 a.m. to 12.00 noon and 12.45 p.m. to 5.00 p.m. Not Mondays.
6. House of the Lords of Kunštát and Poděbrady. 10.00 a.m. to 6.00 p.m. May to September. Not Mondays.
7. Smetana Museum. 10.00 a.m. to 2.00 p.m. Not Tuesdays.
8. St Agnes' Convent (Anežsky klášter) 10.00 a.m. to 6.00 p.m. Not Mondays.

Highlights for Children

The moving figures when the Astronomical Clock strikes on the hour every hour in the Old Town Square.

A ride through the Old Town by horse and cart, leaving from the Old Town Square.

Plays and puppet shows in the Old Town Square (sometimes).

Climbing the tower in the Old Town Hall and/or the Powder Tower.

The Ethnological Museum (Náprstek Museum of Asian, African and American Cultures) has bright and interesting displays.

St Agnes' Convent.

The Children's Workshop and Exhibition means that children can be actively involved as opposed to merely being taken around as spectators.

Puppet theatre and Marionettes. These will fascinate and enthrall some children. The Říse loutek puppet theatre at Žatecká 1, and the Divadlo Jiřího Wolkra on Dlouhá 39, are both close to the Old Town Square.

Panoramic Views and Peaceful Parks in Prague's Legendary Birthplace

Once a fortified hill of equal importance to the city as Prague Castle, Vyšehrad is not on the itinerary of many visitors. Yet it is here on the ancient crag above the River Vltava that the vision took place from which Prague was born. It is Vyšehrad that has been associated with much of the folklore and legend that was to kindle the sense of a Czech nation before it won its independence. It is here that many of the artists and writers who gave expression to that nationhood are buried. Vyšehrad is an essential part of the mythology which has formed the character of Prague.

History

The City of Prague grew up between two fortified hills, the Castle (Hrad) down stream and Vyšehrad upstream. For a time Vyšehrad was the more important of the two, when it became the permanent residence of the Czech King in the 11th century. A range of building in the area followed, including a castle and several churches. One of these, the Round Chapel of St Martin, survives to this day. This

*S*t Martin's Rotunda, a *marvellous example of Romanesque architecture and the oldest complete church in Prague.*

pre-eminence, however, proved short-lived, and after the death of Sobeslav I in 1140 the principal residence of the Bohemian Kings was transferred to Hradčany, never to return. However, it remained significant as a second residence, and the traditional coronation processions of Czech monarchs, from Vyšehrad to the Castle, was intended to symbolize the complementary importance of the two.

Charles IV, the omnipresent benefactor of the city, attempted to renovate the walls of Vyšehrad in order to link it in with the other towns of Prague. A century later, however, the area suffered devastation during the Hussite wars, when the garrison surrendered and the buildings were ransacked and destroyed by Hussites from the New Town. Its character subsequently changed. From being closely linked to the monarchy and "royal establishment", it became a "free town" of traders and craftspeople. Further upheaval came under the Catholic Hapsburgs, when the population of Vyšehrad was ejected, new brick walls built which isolated the area further, and the palace rebuilt as a barracks with St Martin's Chapel turned into a gunpowder magazine.

In the 19th century Vyšehrad changed again. The fortress was dismantled in 1866, and the area established as a public park. In this form it came into its own. A neo-Gothic church added to the romantic atmosphere, which had long been established by the rocky promontory overlooking the point where the Vltava flows down from the Bohemian forests into Prague. Having long been the centre of numerous myths and legends, most notably the story that from here the early Slav Princess Libussa (or Libuše) had a vision prophesying the future greatness of the capital, Vyšehrad became the centre for a new generation of "myth and legend makers". Romantic poets, historians, artists and others concerned to promote Czech national consciousness fastened on this area as a symbol of the country's long history and destiny. In the 1870s a special cemetery, the Slavin, was created here to honour the nation's artists, those who had given it a strong cultural identity.

Nowadays Vyšehrad is integrated into the city, but the former castle area still retains a particular character. It is much more than simply a quiet area of parkland in which to escape the crowds. Its views are outstanding, and its atmosphere, whether or not half the things that are said about it are true, is enchanting.

A cross the rooftops from Vyšehrad.

A Tour of Vyšehrad

There are a number of possible approaches. One is to come by underground to Vyšehrad (the station was formerly named Gottwaldova, after the infamous first communist president of the Republic, Klement Gottwald). The train slides along the inside of a concrete flyover and emerges into the open air, depositing you on a concrete terrace next to the Palace of Culture, a mass of steel, glass, aluminium and, of course, more concrete, built in the late 1970s. Once a centre for communist party congresses and shindigs, the building still gives the impression of not knowing quite what to do with its space. Plays, films, restaurants, exhibitions, and a nightclub with a glass floor occupy a modicum of the area required by the comrades to realize the revolution. Before you move on, take in the superb view of the New Town from the walls of the terrace, where you should have far more room to take photographs than when attempting the same thing from Prague's other original fortress, the Castle.

A second approach to Vyšehrad is to walk along the waterfront from the Charles Bridge and then make the ascent to the ancient fortress from below. For the sake of this tour, however, the less energetic option will be assumed, and you will end up going downhill to the waterfront rather than uphill from it.

Notable Sights

From outside the Palace of Culture, set off along the suburban street Na Bučance and then right into Na Pankráci, which takes you into the fortress area via the Taborite Gate, part of the 17th-century fortifications that were designed to make an armed citadel and barracks out of a medieval

castle. From here V pevnosti is the road which leads you through the more ornate Leopold's Gate, work of three Italian architects, to what is the oldest building in Prague (subject to late 19th century renovation), the Romanesque Round Chapel of St Martin (Rotunda sv. Martina), originally constructed in the late 11th century.

As can be guessed easily enough when you see the building, the word *Rotunda* comes from the Latin *rotundus* meaning circular. It has entered the English language anyway in the word rotund. These small pepper-pot-shaped churches represent a style exclusive to the Czech lands during the Romanesque period. If you manage to get inside, note the neo-Romanesque marble altar and wall painting of Christ, but bear in mind that the church is only opened at the time of services- currently Sunday at 9.00 a.m. and Monday, Wednesday and Thursday at 5.30 p.m.

St Martin's Rotunda
One feature of the Rotunda that points to the violent aspect of Vyšehrad's history can be seen by concentrating on the right hand side of the window above the right portal. A cannonball protrudes from the wall as it has done for the last two and a half centuries, since it was deposited there by the Prussians when they attempted to conquer Vyšehrad in 1757.

Unless you want to see the Baroque Chapel of Our Lady in the Fortifications (also known as Lady Mary Sancovska's Chapel, *sance* means fortifications), turn off V pevnosti into K rotundě, taking in the Plague Pillar from 1714 on the way. This is the road that leads you to the highlights of the area, the neo-Gothic Church of Saints Peter and Paul, the Slavin Cemetery and the rocky promontory from which

Libussa had her vision. If you want to you can stop off at the Deanery on your left in order to view an exhibition of the history of Vyšehrad.

Slavin Cemetery

Nothing can compare with the Jewish cemetery in Josefov, but **Vyšehradský hřbitov** (the Slavin Cemetery at Vyšehrad), full of distinguished representatives of Czech art and culture, is another reason for spending time in this city wandering through a burial-ground. Indeed after your experience of walking among the living in Prague, it may be a welcome break to be among the dead for a while.

*D*ead Poets' Society?
The tomb of 19th-century poet and writer Jan Neruda in the Slavin cemetery at Vyšehrad.

In this cemetery tombstones have become something of a decorative art, with even some very modernist styles competing with traditional memorials. For instance, look at the tombstone of Karel Hladik, which is in fact his own work called Cathedral. Most tombstones simply have the name of the dead person and his or her occupation—*sochař* (sculptor), *malíř* (painter), *umělec* (artist), *herec* (actor) often with the words *národní* (national) or *zasloužilý* (honoured) in front to mark the extent of their reputation.

The cemetery is a gallery of famous names—composers like Smetana and Dvořák, writers like Karel Čapek and Jan Neruda, who wrote stories immortalizing the Malá Strana, painters like Mikoláš Aleš and Vojtěch Hynais. Strictly speaking, the name Slavin (Pantheon) stands not for the whole cemetery but for a large common tomb inside it. Built between 1889 and 1893 and decorated with angelic statues astride an ornate sarcophagus on top of the monument, the Slavin, designed by Antonin Wiehl, contains over 50 of the most eminent Czech artists, musicians, actors and writers from the 20th century, including the violinist Jan Kubelik and the painter Alfons Mucha. No one should leave Prague without copies of Mucha's Art Nouveau posters.

Sculptor J.V. Myslbek will also be an easily recognized name, since his works are displayed all over the city—not least about 90 m (100 yd) away in the grounds alongside the church, where four monumental sculptural groups by Myslbek have found a final resting-place. They were originally destined for the **Palackého most** (Palacký Bridge), but were badly damaged during the war. When the bridge was widened it was decided that when restored they would be put somewhere else.

The park at Vyšehrad seems inappropriate for their grand style, although they might be very striking in the heart of a city. Like some unwary group of dissidents, they appear to have been marginalized to a quiet backwater for daring to challenge the irresistible needs of traffic.

The sculptural reliefs and original designs of the cemetery make it an unusually uplifting place to visit. Indeed the foresight of individuals like Hladik make parts of it a living gallery designed by the dead. It must to an extent mark a strong respect for art and literature in national life, and in defining national identity. Perhaps it also marks a respect for artistic and intellectual values as such, something which may enable Prague to resist the onslaught of the next few years as the city comes to terms with its new level of popularity after the Velvet Revolution.

Church of Saints Peter and Paul

From the cemetery it is an obvious step to visit the Church of Saints Peter and Paul, whose spires dominate the sky-line. It was reconstructed from a Gothic original (used to begin the coronation processions which ended up at the Castle) by Joseph Mocker, who reconstructed a number of Gothic buildings in Czechoslovakia including the Powder Tower elsewhere in Prague. Mocker always sought to preserve the character of his Gothic original. This can certainly be seen in the exterior of the church, but reconstruction work makes it impossible to judge the interior. On the steps of the church a few postcards and booklets are on sale. Try in particular to buy a collection of postcards in black-and-white taken from the Vyšehrad cemetery. They are quite superb.

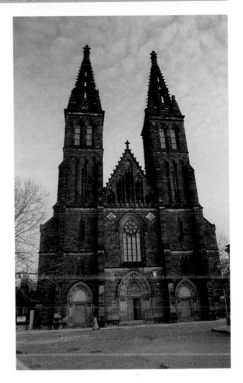

The neo-Gothic church of Saints Peter and Paul at Vyšehrad, built on the site of an 11th-century basilica.

Refreshment

At the far end of the courtyard outside the church an unpretentious café sells cheap snacks and even light meals, including, if you're missing them, chips. When you receive the bill you will realise how far prices are inflated in the centre of the city in order to milk to the full the greater purchasing power of the western tourist.

Along the Fortress Walls

The highlight of any visit to Vyšehrad is the walk along the fortress walls overlooking the Vltava river. Around this area countless myths and legends have built up over the centuries, and the walk along the edge of Vyšehrad's former fortifications makes it clear why. At the base of the fortifications, where the Vltava takes a final turn before flowing into Prague, is Libussa's (or Libuše's) Bath, where she doubtless took time off from prophesying the city's future greatness in order to have a swim. According to another legend a horse swam the river and surmounted the walls at this point in order to rescue its master Horymir. However, whatever the magical inspiration of this view, a more prosaic observation is worthy of attention.

From this point it is possible to see a great deal of southern Prague. You can look across the river at the suburbs of Smíchov and Hlubočepy, whilst on the same side of the river you can see Podolí and beyond. The view gives an instructive impression of town planning over the last 50 years. The communist policy, broadly speaking, was to maintain the historical core of Prague intact, and to ring it with high-rise blocks and worker's "estates", which could function as self-contained concrete villages. If you scan the horizon you can see these blocks overlooking the city. The tortuously detailed official

A great deal of folklore surrounds "The Devil's Pillars", the least interesting explanation of which is that this was a mediaeval attempt at telling the time.

The Devil's Pillars and Princess Libuše's Magic Powers

One view connects the magical powers of Princess Libuše, the founder of Prague, with the use of the "Devil's Pillars" as a sundial. She is supposed to have carefully read and recorded the shadows of the pillars, and then to have astonished everyone with her capacity to foretell the most suitable time for work in the fields! By such means she acquired a reputation for the power of divination, when in reality (according to this interpretation at least) her prowess was quite strictly scientific!

Olympia Guides to Prague, written during the communist era and still readily available, list large numbers of these new estates, together with the number of housing units and of inhabitants in each one.

Before leaving the area, it is worth relaxing in Karlach's Park nearby, admiring Myslbek's exiled statues and the "Devil's Pillars", probably used originally to mark the solstice or as a sundial, but according to legend the three fragments of a single pillar flung to the ground when the Devil lost a bet against a priest. The stone is not local,

186

suggesting that the pillars were originally transported here despite their considerable weight. Elsewhere in the area you can find a memorial to St Wenceslas on horseback and the remains of Charles IV's Gothic Palace, of which unfortunately very few survive.

Leave by the Brick Gate or Prague Gate, also called the Chotek Gate after the name of Prague's governor at the time, and follow the steeply descending, winding path into Vratislavova. Suddenly you are out of ancient parkland and myth-ridden fortifications, and into the ordinary life of a Prague suburb.

Prague Suburbs

For anyone interested in modern architecture, however, it is not quite ordinary. Turn right once you are on Vratislavova, and make the steep descent to Neklanova, which runs parallel to Vratislavova further down the hill. On the corner of the street, at number 30, is one of the best examples of Cubist architecture in Prague.

Cubism originated at a time in the early 20th century when the old Hapsburg (Austro-Hungarian) empire, of which Bohemia had been something of a poor relation, was in a process of dissolution. A new, independent Czechoslovak state was in the process of emerging, and there were efforts to create an independent national architecture to reflect this new independence. This style, sometimes known as "Rondocubism", combined the largely French Cubist methods with more traditional architectural shapes. Neklanova 30 is a fine example of this. The prism-shaped bulges on the outer walls of this block of flats capture light and shade at different angles, and although the dusty white building needs

cleaning it is very effective from a distance.

Further along the road towards the river, number 2 displays a similar style. On the edge of the river, on **Rasinovo nabřeží**, (a name change: this part of the waterfront used to be named after Engels!) there is another example of "Rondocubism", designed right down to the angular garden railings. If you are attracted to investigate this style further, there are a number of Cubist "villa colonies" in other parts of the city (*see* the essay on Art and Architecture).

From here a walk northwards along the waterfront, via **Masarykovo nabřeží** (formerly named after the infamous Gottwald), takes you back to the New Town. Alternatively, you can always make this the starting-point for seeing a number of the sights listed under the **Nové Město** (New Town) outlined above. Simply turn off the waterfront up the nearby Svobodova, and then continue up the flights of steps that make up Albertov, past sinister-looking buildings that nowadays mostly make up faculties of the university. You eventually reach Ke Karlovu, from which it is a short walk to the Museum of Police to the right, and the Villa Amerika commemorating Antonín Dvořák on the left. Given the fact that the New Town tour covers the largest physical area, it may be a good idea to cover some of it through a visit to Vyšehrad in this way.

Highlights for Children

Vyšehrad is a good place for children to play in. There's grass, trees, a few red squirrels and plenty of space. It has some amazing views, whether from the rock overhanging "Libuše's Bath", or from the metro station looking back at the New Town.

A typical Czech couple? Statues by J.V. Myslbek in the gardens of Vyšehrad.

Prague's Musical Background

Before the great romantic surge of Czech Nationalism with the orchestral work of Dvořák and the Grand Opera of Smetana, Prague's place in the history of music or indeed music's place in the history of Prague remains cloudy if not totally obscure. It is fitting that Gluck, the first great revolutionary of the opera, raised in the Bohemian woodlands, spent his student days in Prague without leaving the slightest record of what he studied or where it might have taken place. Not to be betrayed by a deficit of fact, Prague has developed a neat line in apocryphal incident and biographical embellishment.

Gluck for instance was said to have arrived in Prague the son of a wood-cutter. He had been wooed to the world of music at a Jesuit College in Kamnitz. Under the tutelage of the ex-church organist of Asseei, he became proficient at the violin and was said to have heard his first strains of opera in the courts of Prague whilst entertaining as a busking pauper. However unlikely the circumstances may seem the dual role of the church and the Bohemian folk culture are crucially important to all Prague's subsequent musical history.

The "impenetrable darkness" of this musical past, as described by Alfred Einstein, is inevitably illuminated by tales of the jaunty blossoming of folk music in the Bohemian countryside. Invariably termed the most musical country in Europe, we are drawn a picture of a population overburdened with viols and hurdy-gurdies in forests of wall-to-wall polka. Dvořák, Gluck and Janaček were each taught the rudiments of the ubiquitous fiddle against this rustic background before grasping keyboard skills on the church organ early in their schooling.

In 1732, when Gluck packed his viol on his back and headed for Prague, it was merely as the natural stopping-off point before the real cultural journey to Vienna. Indeed musically, Prague was seen as nothing more than a musical annex in which to tune up for the grand sounds of Vienna. Gluck himself wasn't content until he'd worked through Italy, England and France and didn't become recognized in his own country until late in life when he received an Imperial bursary.

The change in the musical fortune of the city is evident less than 60 years later, when we find Mozart galloping towards Prague scribbling furiously to finish his last opera. He had been commissioned to compose a new piece for the coronation of Leopold II, King of Bohemia. Mozart, in failing health, wrote in the carriage and through the night in the inns in which he rested so he could finish the piece before arriving. The job was completed by the skin of his teeth, with a few secco recitatives thrown in by Sussmayer, his trusty pupil, and La Clemenza di Tito was premiered to substantial acclaim in the City but left Mozart physically ruined.

Much is made of the Czech vaunting of Mozart during his lifetime, and although Mozart found a haven from the unfriendly vicissitudes of Vienna, Prague's self-congratulation may be somewhat suspicious. True, Don Giovanni was completed in a Prague summer-house and was first performed by the resident Italian Opera Company. Mozart reached the height of his talents in Prague and duly after the death of Gluck was given the accolade of Kammermusikus to Emperor Joseph II. However, instead of the thousands of florins even Gluck received, Mozart was given a paltry eight hundred, to which Mozart laconically replied: "Too much for what I do, too little for what I could do."

So if the hyperbole surrounding Prague's patronage of Herr Mozart has only scant basis in the truth at least an audience existed. From the time of Mozart's death in 1791 Prague took off as a musical centre as various orchestras and conservatoires started to appear on the scene.

Which leads us to a flourishing of indigenous composition which coincided with the rallying round the Nationalist cause. As all the histories and blurbs will tell you, after the failure of the 1848 revolutions the battlefield for the Nationalist cause was played on the fiddles of Bohemia. The two most famous and international exemplars of this "real" Czech music were Smetana and Dvořák, who seem to embody the strains of this movement rather well. Smetana was as prodigal and prodigious as Dvořák was domestic and inauspicious.

Smetana was born in 1824 to the son of a brewery manager, who was, of course, somewhat of an amateur violinist. Before young Bedřich was six he was playing in a Haydn String Quartet and was giving piano recitals at the tender age of seven. He was marketed as a greater prodigy than young Mozart and had aspirations to out-perform the virtuosity of Liszt before his teens. Smetana fell hopelessly in love with Katerina Kolar, the daughter of a family friend, with whom he'd spent many happy hours playing four-handers at the family home in Jindrichuv-Hradec. All seemed disastrous when Katrina was sent to study the piano in Prague. But with much persuasion a place was secured as resident music master in the house of Count Thun, which gave

The tomb of Dvořák in the graveyard at Vyšehrad.

Smetana a steady income and access to the delights of Prague.

Fired by the events of 1848 he gave up his post with the Thuns and wrote a patriotic march for the revolting Students Legion. But as the repression grew worse and his private school set up with Liszt's encouragement went into decline, he left for the milder climes of Sweden.

Dvořák, in the meantime, had been born in 1841, in the village inn of Nelahozeves. His father played the zither, dispensed beer and was butcher to the local cattle. Young Antonin took up the fiddle at school and although a competent musician was not encouraged to leave the village to pursue his studies. Pan Dvořák was insistent that, "You must be a butcher, and succeed to your grandfather's trade." Dvořák was duly apprenticed but used all his spare time to continue his lessons in composition and harmony with Liehmann, the lovable school-master organist who was the model for Benda in Dvořák's opera The Jacobins.

Still Pan Dvořák was intractable about Antonin's career trajectory, so the young lad sought to break down this intransigence with a display of his virtuosity that was bound to appeal to his father's natural pride. Dvořák spent many hours composing and arranging a composition of his own that was to be premiered at a village concert. He was sure that swayed by this brilliant début his father would have no other option but to send him off to Prague. Antonin, determined to keep the whole matter secret until the concert itself, wrote out all the parts and slipped them onto the arranged music stands of the village orchestra. They would play the piece unrehearsed to maximize the element of surprise. Dvořák's career hung in the balance and all went well until the band began to play. Through all his labours Antonin had been blissfully unaware that one must transpose trumpet parts to avoid a hideous cacophony.

Whether or not the amassed Dvořáks were simply hideously embarrassed by the result or mistook the piece for a prodigious work of the avant garde we will never know. However, Dvořák was promptly packed onto a peasant's hay-cart and rode the 72 km (45 miles) to Prague.

In Prague, Dvořák was swept up into the maelstrom of Wagnerian orchestration. He found lodgings with a piano in Charles Square. As a student Dvořák continued his reputation as gifted but uninspired and left to the uncertain poverty of odd jobbing with Prague's bands and orchestras. And it is here that the two heroes of Prague's musical heritage met: Smetana as founder and conductor of the Czech National Theatre Orchestra and Dvořák as a lowly violinist.

Smetana had enhanced his reputation both as a promoter of Liszt and Wagner as well as a composer of merit. His residency in Göteburg was successful but the events of 1859 when Italy's victories over Austria relaxed the iron-handed oppression of the Czech people, and the death of Katerina in the rigours of the northern winters made him turn back for Prague. It was essential that a new music should celebrate the Czech heritage, and the aggrandizement of the Czech language was an imperative. Therefore, the success of an indigenous opera was of national importance.

Smetana wrote with great seriousness. Dalibor was an opera about a semi-mythical leader—"what the Czech ought to be"—while Libuse about the foundress of Prague ended with an almost mystical vision of the city's future. But it was The Bartered Bride that caught the imagination of the country. It bore none of the bombast of the other operas and was a dollop of bumptious gaiety in the turgid stew of the mid-cen-

tury. All the more poignant as Smetana was going increasingly deaf.

For Smetana moments of levity were all too brief. By 1877 he was almost completely deaf, suffered from deep depression, loss of speech and had constant noises in his head. He carried on writing trying to repeat the astounding success of The Bartered Bride, with more racy rustic tales. He started work on an opera based on Twelfth Night but had to be admitted to an asylum as physically and mentally he was unable to cope. He died there in 1884 and was buried in the cemetery in Vyšehrad, the legendary site of Libuše's court.

All this time when Smetana was ostentatiously moulding a national identity, Dvořák was in the pit scribbling away at various pieces between shifts, most of which he would tear up as soon as they neared completion. Dvořák caught the

The tomb of Smetana in the graveyard at Vyšehrad.

opera bug but used, instead of a Czech theme, the unpromising material of Alfred the Great, and unsurprisingly the whole opera suffered the fate of the conscientious self-critic.

Gradually Dvořák dared to have his work performed publicly and by 1873 had won the respect of Smetana who began programming his work with the various ensembles with which he was connected. Dvořák in the shadow of Smetana emulated him by producing his own Dalibor. Now he was achieving recognition abroad, Brahms was quick to spot his talents, but Dvořák plodded after Smetana and remained poor.

As Dvořák's family became larger he began to teach to supplement their income. But the extra pressure did not send the composer to flights of delirium, quite the opposite. Dvořák remained resolutely mundane. He took his stimulation from the relatively new pursuit of train spotting. He would often partake vicariously by sending his pupils down to the station to give an up to the minute account. He would write in his kitchen whilst his kids ran amok and variously reported on the latest engine to arrive at the station.

By 1884, Dvořák's reputation was sufficient for him to conduct his own work in England. He was now played and published and now with the international success of his D major symphony, he could afford a cottage in the country. On his return with a £2,000 commission for a new oratorio he bought a house in Vysoká. Now that his years of poverty were behind him Dvořák indulged himself by rearing pigeons, presumably to compensate for the lack of railway stations. Dvořák was given a Professorship in Prague, was made Doctor of Music at Cambridge and toured extensively.

This connection with the "New World" confirmed him as a truly international figure. He was given a salary of £15,000 a year to run the National Conservatory of Art. This was the cultural baby of Mrs J. Thurber, the wife of a considerably wealthy wholesale grocer. Unfortunately, Dvořák was not the ideal figurehead for such an institution. He avoided all social functions, concerts and operas. Instead he went to Central Park to feed the pigeons and adopted boat watching to supplement the train spotting that so obsessed him.

Again Dvořák longed for a country retreat and found solace in Spillville which was a small town where everyone spoke Czech. It was amongst the serenity of this group of displaced Bohemians that he created some of his best known work, including the Cello Concerto in B minor and the New World Symphony. He grew increasingly interested in the music of the American "Indians" and "Negro Folksong" and did much to draw these rich traditions to the attention of the American musical fraternity.

However, Dvořák returned to Prague in 1895 and stayed there until his death in 1904. Rather than enduring anything like the histrionic last days of Smetana, he faded gradually. After catching a chill whilst train spotting at Prague's station he gradually declined over a few weeks until he expired, presumably of a stroke, whilst resting in bed.

The bedrock of a national musical tradition had been laid in Prague and the city was now an important centre for performance and composition. The seminal strands of integrating folk music and that of the church proved to be more than just a mirror of the historical trend. The work of Martinů and Janáček developed these strains to great success in the 20th century. The development of the opera as a national voice is of central importance to the music of Prague. The work of Smetana and Dvořák has given Czech music a sense of drama that has not been lost to this day.

A Zoo, an Amusement Park and a Giant Metronome—a Few Different Things to Do

There are many areas of Prague off the beaten track and yet easily accessible by public transport or within walking distance of the city centre. They will bring a blissful sense of relative peace during the high tourist season, and an individuality which is its own reward. To leave Prague without having seen the city's only château, the extraordinary "crystal palace" amusement park, or having stood on the former site of the Stalin monument, now sporting a giant metronome, would be to have missed out on seeing "something different" even in this distinctive city.

So far we have examined the main sights of Prague, but there are several other parts of this great city that are well worth visiting. Indeed, far from being "poor relations" of the main attractions, these areas are equally rewarding in different ways. Spacious parks, strange museums, eerie monuments, and, invaluable if you bring the children, visits to the zoo and a fun park are all in this section.

T he Art Nouveau Hanava Pavilion on the Letná Hill is now a night-club and restaurant.

A Day in the North

This journey will start in the northern district of **Holešovice**. Before the war this area was known as "Little Berlin", because of its concentration of German speakers, but the Second World War put paid to that form of identity. It contains a large proportion of open parkland, which compensates for the rather oppressive air of its tall, unattractive streets.

Exhibition Centre
Holešovice is best reached by tram, asking for Výstaviště (Výstava is Czech for exhibition, so you're asking for the exhibition centre). Alternatively, take the underground to Vltavská, and when you reach ground level turn right underneath the subway. You come out at Stross-

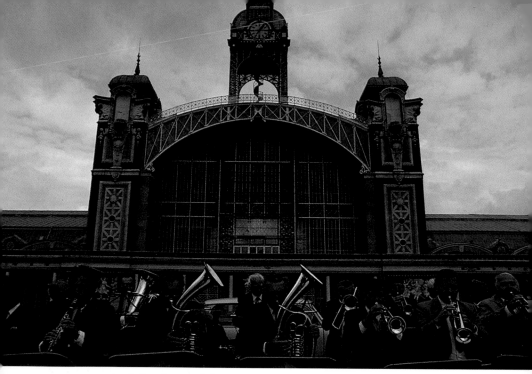

mayerovo náměstí, where a right turn up Dukelských Hrdinů street brings you out opposite the exhibition centre. It's a walk of less than one kilometre, or half a mile.

The advantage of walking there from Vltavská is that you can admire the seven-storey glass building at number 45. Originally built in the 1920s for a Trade Fair by O. Tyl and J. Fuchs, it amazed Le Corbusier so much that he felt his own ideas suddenly made redundant. Whether or not it strikes you as just another large block of soulless modern architecture, it is planned as the site of a new Museum of Modern Czech Art. It was damaged by fire in 1975 and has been in the process of restoration ever since. If open by the time you visit, it should contain an excellent collection, judging from the many peripatetic displays of modern art at present on view in different parts of the city, and desperately in need of a single home.

 Výstaviště itself is a fascinating exhibition centre cum amusement park. It has the regulation big wheel, dodgems and

*E*xhibition Park in *Výstaviště with brass band accompaniment.*

roller-coaster of a fun fair (at the far end from the entrance), but it also has serious exhibitions designed to point out the past (and future) glories of Czechoslovak art and technology. In 1991 the centenary of the Prague exhibition meant that all the stops were pulled out. Outdoor fountains danced in time to classical favourites, whilst indoors there were performances of "Laterna Magika" (Magic Lantern Theatre), films, exhibitions of photography and poster art, and a number of displays designed to show the new range of consumer choice in post-communist Prague. Large indoor spaces like aircraft hangers would contain a cross between a museum and a large department store. Everything from the postal system to the latest in space research was on display.

Výstaviště

The amusement park, which used to be named after communist journalist Julius Fučík, has developed each year into a more and more elaborate crystal palace extravaganza. Apart from the funfair at the back, it contains a "diorama" depicting the Battle of Lipany with special 3-D effects, a planetarium, a cinema complex and temporary exhibitions in areas the size of aircraft hangars. It has always been a "theme park", but since the Velvet Revolution the theme has changed, The celebration of industrial achievement remains (though not as a way of celebrating communism), but has become attached to a desire to entertain and give hard-working Praguers a means of enjoyment for its own sake.

Not all of this will remain in future years, but there will still be the wonderfully garish architecture of the Průmyslový palace, former venue for communist party congresses, a wide range of exhibitions, a number of places for food and drink and a welcome majority of Praguers out for enjoyment over the number of sightseers.

Stromovka Park

After the lively atmosphere of Výstaviště there is nothing better than a walk in Stromovka Park, formerly a game park for the royal occupants of the Castle to idle their time away hunting, but nowadays a peaceful area of semi-woodland (*strom*, predictably enough, means tree). A number of the trees look to be in poor condition, something that may well be associated with the high levels of pollution in Czechoslovakia. These have adversely affected large areas of a country one third of which is forest.

Stromovka Park covers a large area. It is not difficult to get lost, so look out for the many signs to the zoo (signed as in English or as the lengthier Zoologická zahrada—Zoological Gardens). Your route takes you under the main railway line between Prague and Berlin and then over the Vltava, until you come out in front of the Troja Palace.

Troja Palace

The landscape in front of you looks more like the Italian countryside than the middle of Prague. A hillside covered in vine leaves looks down upon the red and white of the Troja Chateau, which is surrounded by manicured gardens complete with terrace and ornamental fountains. To reach the entrance, you have to walk alongside the river and then up towards the zoo, whose entrance is directly opposite that for the château. Should you prefer to go directly to either, rather than walk from Výstaviště, then you should catch a 112 bus from Holešovice underground station.

On entering the château, visitors are required to fit large slippers over their shoes to avoid damaging the floor. Once strapped in, you can slide through a number of fascinating rooms, each with an explanatory sheet in different languages.

Troja Chateau was built in the late 17th century under Count Wenceslaus Adalbert of Sternberg, modelled on the Italian "villa" or country residence, and designed to give the noble hunters and their guests somewhere impressive to relax in after a hunt in the Stromovka game park. It is to some extent a product of the Bohemian nobility's attempt to ape the lifestyle of their wealthier Italian and French counterparts, especially after the Battle of the White Mountain had finally secured their position, and that of the Hapsburg dynasty, in their own country.

The architect of the building was Jean Baptiste Mathey, a native of Burgundy, whilst the striking murals on the interior were largely the work of Francesco Marchetti. However, Marchetti lost favour with the Count, who employed instead the services of a Dutchman, Abraham Godin, for the decoration of the Imperial Hall. The wall and ceiling murals of this room are the undoubted centrepiece of any visit to the château, and it is worth spending a few minutes on one of the chairs looking at the paintings which cover every available inch of space.

The theme of the painting is not very attractive—the triumph of Christianity, represented by the House of Hapsburg, over Islam in the form of the Ottoman Empire. It was the product of Western culture at a time when it was celebrating the defeat of an Empire which, from time to time, looked as if it might well engulf Europe as well as the Near East. Particularly in the minds of those who decorated the château was the recent liberation of Vienna from a Turkish siege in 1683.

The design of the Imperial or Great Hall is an unashamed celebration of the liberation of "Christian territories" from the Turk—and it was useful enough to the Hapsburgs to present themselves to a country with past Hussite tendencies as the only champions of the true faith against its opponents.

Whatever the ideological resonance, however, the whole design is artistically very impressive. Look, for instance, at the falling man with turban and feather, arms outstretched and hands splayed, who appears through techniques of shadow and perspective to be actually projecting from the wall. It is the wall which contains the *Allegory of the Triumph of Emperor Leopold I.*

Other highlights are the room with mural paintings showing Chinese landscapes, the formal gardens with their large collection of terracotta vases, in which the novelist Franz Kafka worked as a gardener and the monumental staircase with its battling titans. See especially the two who have fallen down inside the balustrades. Next to the château it is worth visiting the stables with more paintings by Abraham Godin, before taking some refreshment outside.

Prague Zoo

A few yards from the entrance is the city's Zoo, established in 1931 on about $40\frac{1}{2}$ hectares (100 acres) of countryside, and particularly famous for having bred the very rare Przewalski's horse, which no longer exists outside captivity. As zoos go, it is kinder towards the animals than most, and a favourite with children. To return home, if you don't fancy another walk, take the 112 bus to Holešovice and then take either the tram or the underground to the centre of the city. Alternatively, retrace your steps to the Vltava and catch the boat home—they run at roughly half-hour intervals.

The exhibition centre, park and zoo make this an ideal day out for children—who would doubtless appreciate the boat ride home into the bargain.

Letná

There is hardly enough here to fill a day's itinerary, as a consequence of which it is often missed out altogether. One way in which to see it is to tack it onto a day visiting the castle, so this particular journey ends at the František Bílek museum, from which it is possible to walk through Prague's first (and relatively quiet!) public park, the Chotkovy sady, to the Royal

Gardens and the Castle (*see* HRADČANY). As with the previous tour, this part of town is relatively free of visitors, which many would find a welcome change after fighting their way through Wenceslas Square or the Old Town Square.

Leave the tram at Strossmayerovo náměstí in Holešovice (or to be even closer alight one stop nearer to the centre of town)—currently a 12 or 17 will take you there, but the 17 is the easiest to catch. You simply stand anywhere along the river where the Masaryk and Smetana embankments form a long line beside the Old and New Towns. The 12 runs up the opposite side of the river and is only useful if you start from the Malá Strana area. The nearest underground station is once again Vltavská- besides which, the area is not far from the heart of Prague and you could always walk it!

Walk from Strossmayerovo náměstí to Kostelní, which draws you up on a fairly easy uphill climb past indifferent flats resonant with newly discovered sounds of punk. Those who've already walked some distance could always make a stop for coffee by turning off Kostelní to the left and sampling Praha Expo 58, a peculiar 1950s building established to celebrate the 1958 World Expo in Montreal. The café on the seventh floor provides an excellent view of the Vltava from an open terrace. Whatever the architecture of the building itself, it is the perfect place from which to view anything else.

National Technical Museum

Continue along Kostelní until a ugly façade to the right suggests that it might conceal a tank factory or secret police headquarters. This is the **Národní technické muzeum** (National Technical Museum), and contains a fascinating collection of technical creations. Highlight of the museum must be a huge room like an aircraft hangar. Suspended from various parts of this grand hall are a range of old planes and helicopters, while at ground level there's a collection of trains and cars. Along the sides is a display of bicycles from the penny farthing to the present models.

Another room describes the history of photography and cinematography, including examples of crude early methods of giving the impression of movement. There are plenty of knobs and buttons enabling you to try things out in this room, making it a favourite for children (and, of course, adults).

Old gramophones and clocks continue the historical theme, but there are also exhibitions of modern technology, the remnant of the former communist state's desire to show off its industrial virility. Displays of metallurgy, electronics, astronomy and nuclear power come into this category, the metallurgy exhibition giving a well-presented account of mining technology. If the onslaught of scientific achievement becomes oppressive after a while, there is always the snack bar. Being off the tourist track, the museum offers coffee and a cake for about 30 crowns.

The March of Time

Continue along Kostelní into Letenské sady, a quiet and pleasant parkland overlooking the Vltava to one side and looking towards the famous football stadium on the other, in which Sparta Prague have demolished many a foreign visitor. One of the most attractive features of this park is the presence of red squirrels, nowadays an uncommon sight in most of Europe, and a range of small dogs. Praguers tend

> **Letná Park**
>
> Night-clubbing in Letná Park is much more rewarding than in the sleazy environment of Wenceslas Square at night. The wonderful Art Nouveau Hanava Pavilion has a late-night discotheque, whilst under the former Stalin monument a rabbit warren of underground tunnels which were designed to protect the communist leadership from nuclear attack may or may not be converted into one (or even two) atmospheric night-clubs. The difficulty for the new authorities is to prevent people wandering off through the tunnels in search of Stalin's stone remains, although they will probably only find potatoes, as the tunnels were used for a while as a potato store. Trying to obtain information on this matter is to encounter surreal Prague at its finest. All that can be said at the moment is that there may or may not be a night-club under the Stalin monument (possibly called Stalin, possibly Suicide), and that it has become a favourite venue for acid-house parties.

to prefer small dogs, whose faces sometimes peer at you from the top of shopping bags. The city is almost entirely free of cats.

Eventually you come to a strategic point overlooking the Švermuv most of which used to be the site of the largest bust of Joseph Stalin in the world. From a height of $30\frac{1}{2}$ m (100 ft) and weighing a cool 14,000 tons, "Uncle Joe" used to look down on the city from this perfect "Big Brother" position, until in 1962, after a mere seven years in position, he was officially blown up. This process proved surprisingly difficult to the Prague authorities, and required a series of increasingly powerful explosions.

The head, which was removed during the Kruschev years when Stalin's reputation lay under a temporary cloud, is the subject of the film *Absurdistan*, which features it trundling around Prague on the back of a lorry looking like a grotesque stage prop.

Until 1991 nothing had replaced Stalin's head, and the area around the concrete platform on which it stood had a rather eerie feel. The walls still hold on to their dark secrets, since the rusting entrances to subterranean passages used during the communist era remain in place. This area used to be the site of mass communist rallies and more recently, in a return to older ideologies, of a rally to welcome the Pope. Now the walls are covered in graffiti and neglect, while a few locals and a smattering of tourists sit around taking in the view, although there are plans to establish a night-club here!

One change, however, is now in place—an object which, whilst ideologically preferable to Stalin's head, is not necessarily an aesthetic improvement. A giant metronome now marks the progress of time and history, providing a chiming commentary on what has taken place in the recent past. This bizarre and original "time marches on" epitaph to Stalinism is moving in its own way.

Walk further along the path beside the overhang, and you come to a game of snakes and ladders painted into the pavement. At the head of the snakes are words like *zavlivost* (jealousy), whilst the ladders are mounted by landing on more positive concepts like *společnost* (society).

Hanava Pavilion

A few metres further on is the **Hanavský pavilion** (Hanava pavilion), whose outdoor café offers more excellent views of the city. Cast from iron at the foundries of the Prince of Hanava, it was originally built for the Jubilee Exhibition of 1891, but ended up in Letná a decade later. It

A huge bust of Stalin once looked down upon Prague from the top of the Letná hill. Now a giant metronome makes the point that time passes and even the most entrenched of dictators must finally fall.

A moral Snakes and Ladders in Letná Park with Prague's bridges in the background.

Cemeteries

Prague is not only a metropolis but a necropolis, its cemeteries not only a useful reminder of history and mortality in a world liable to ignore both, but also places of quiet and rest in a bustling city. Some superb architecture (including much that is modernist) can also be found in them. One not mentioned elsewhere in this guide is the Malá Strana cemetery (Malostranský hřbitov), close to the Mozart Museum in Smíchov. It contains one of the best collections of Baroque and neo-classical architecture in Prague, particularly the cast-iron tomb of Bishop Leopold von Thun-Hohenstein, Its state of neglect at least means that in a city of changes there are places where the past is preserved, or at least allowed to decay in peace.

currently has a late-night disco on certain nights, which makes a refreshing alternative to the tourist traps of Wenceslas Square.

From the Hanava Pavilion it is a relatively short walk to the top of Chotkova, the winding road up to the castle from Malá Strana, and the František Bílek museum, at which point you can join up with the tour of Hradčany outlined above. Alternatively it is always possible to descend from the metronome to river level, and walk across the bridge to Pařížská and Josefov.

Travelling East

There are a couple of sights that will attract people for whom the bizarre is almost as attractive as the beautiful. They are to be found in the **Žižkov** area of the city, and the best start is to catch the underground to what used to be Sokolovská station but is now Florenc.

Municipal Museum

Begin by visiting the **Muzeum hlavního města Prahy** (Municipal Museum) which is close to the station. Built at the end of the last century in neo-Renaissance style, the museum illustrates the history of Prague, with examples of furniture, jewellery and sculpture from the area. Of particular interest are a collection of Prague house signs, an early 19th-century model of the city by lithographer A. Langweil, and a painting by Josef Mánes of the face of the astronomical clock in the Old Town Square. In recent years the history has been brought up to date with a fascinating display of the invasion by Soviet Tanks in 1968, with posters, photographs and handbills from the period calling for resistance. This exhibition may have been moved or taken down by now, but it is unlikely that any history of Prague in these days of free expression would omit the deeply significant events of the last generation.

National Monument

Such a display is the perfect preliminary to the next item on the agenda, a visit to the Národní památník (National Monument) This monumental granite-faced building is unmistakable as you look towards Žižkov, since it sits on the top of a hill with a statue of Jan Žižka on horseback in the foreground. This one-eyed general led the Hussites against the troops of King Sigismund and defeated them, despite being heavily outnumbered, in July 1420. The victory led to an early example of the Prague habit of name-changing. At first the hill, and then later the whole area, previously called Vítkov, was re-named after the hero of the hour.

It was in the early part of the 20th century, during the inter-war years, that the granite monstrosity behind Žižka was built as a monument to the newly independent Czech nation. After the communists came to power in 1948, it was adapted as a mausoleum for "heroes of the Czechoslovak people", like the notorious Klement Gottwald. The hill was already a commemorative place for national heroes, and was suitably sited in a working-class area of the city where support for the communists was strong. Perhaps the choice also reflected the communists' admiration for the Hussites, whose early battles against a Catholic feudal establishment they compared, not without some grounds, to their own campaign against capitalism. Indeed it was they who designed the 9 m (30 ft) equestrian statue of Jan Žižka in 1950.

At one time the building contained a Soviet Army Hall decorated with mosaics and a collection of dead dignitaries. Nowadays the bronze door with its reliefs by Malejovský remains closed, and apart from some small alterations to the external decoration, such as the removal of the communist star from the coat of arms, the area has fallen into disrepair (ie closed for reconstruction).

From Florenc station the monument can be reached via U památníku, to find which you have to negotiate a whole complex of roads and railway lines and come out on the far side of the bus station. However, since the monument itself is perched on the hill above, it acts as an insurance against losing your way.

At the top of a fairly steep climb you end up beneath Jan Žižka's statue in front of the mausoleum, looking like an emblem on the prow of an ugly concrete boat. When you've taken in the fine views of the city, it's worthwhile to walk back via the long ceremonial way which eventually leads to Pražačka and the main road Koněvova. This road used to bear the

coffins of communist leaders to their final resting-place. Now it is a half-kept park area in which you are likely to walk for a mile and pass perhaps half a dozen people with dogs.

This particular tour might not be an aesthete's delight, but it gives a sense of the recent past and a feel for a regime which, for all its corruption and repression, genuinely believed that it was introducing a new and better social order. Ironically, the mausoleum for "heroes of the Czechoslovak people" now appears more as a mausoleum to communism itself.

Among the Dead

From mausoleums to graveyards. A few metres along Koněvova is the junction with Jana Želivského, named after the

*F*lowers are sold outside the many cemeteries in Vinohrady.

famous Hussite and so far as the leaders of the time were concerned proto-communist Jan Želivský, which will take you via a fairly short walk (or a number 9 tram) to two of Prague's most interesting resting-places for the dead. The **Olšanské Hřbitovy** is a collection of cemeteries founded in 1680 when outbreaks of plague were putting pressure on the burial-grounds. It grew in subsequent years, and now forms nearly 500,000 m² of grave-yard. Fortunately at each gate there's a map. There are numerous examples of elaborate funeral sculpture and a range of famous names from the worlds of literature and art, but as with the National Monument it is the sense of history and tradition conveyed by this site, not all of it recognizable elsewhere in this fast-changing city, which comes across most strongly.

Vojenský hřbitov (The War Cemetery), is the first you come to walking from the National Monument down Jana Želivského on the left hand side. Four hundred and ninety-nine white crosses mark the bodies of 500 Soviet soldiers, with a monument sculptured by J. Bruha to the Soviet troops who fell during the (genuine) liberation of Prague from the Nazis in May 1945.

By contrast, another cemetery here once contained the body of Jan Palach, the student who burned himself to death in protest at the later "liberation" of Prague by Soviet tanks in August 1968. Concern by the authorities about his grave becoming a focus for resistance led to his re-interment in his home town 65 km (40 miles) outside Prague in 1973. Huge efforts were made to prevent a silent vigil at his graveside there in the weeks leading up to the Velvet Revolution, when the city was virtually cut off from the rest of the world in order to prevent something that

would only have had symbolic significance. But then no one valued the importance of symbols more than the communists!

The Russian cemetery contains a delightful orthodox chapel built in Old Russian style in the 1920s, whilst the best sculpture can be found on the other side of Jana Želivského in the New Jewish cemetery, founded in 1895. Among its remarkably decorated tombs is that of the famous writer Frank Kafka. Finally (although perhaps only devotees of *Harold and Maude* would go this far), there is the **Vinohradský Hřbitov** a few hundred metres away after Jana Želivského turns into Vinohradská. It contains a neo-Gothic chapel consecrated to St Wenceslas surrounded by arcades and another list of

*T*omb stone of a musician in the cemetery at Vinohrady.

The new Jewish Cemetery in Vinohrady.

notable underground (literally if not politically) figures.

It may seem bizarre to spend so much time in cemeteries, although few people have visited Prague without seeing the Old Jewish Cemetery. On the other hand, they are quiet, they contain some interesting and attractive architecture, and they reveal some of the ironies and complexities of Prague's past.

Church of the Sacred Heart

Želivského underground station is a short distance away. Take the train two stops along the line to Jiřího z Poděbrad (George of Poděbrady), a square containing a fascinating modern church built by J. Plcčnik in the late 1920s, the **Kostel Srdce Páně** (Church of the Sacred Heart). This is in some ways the most amazing piece of modern architecture in the city of Prague. Classical and Art Nouveau features combine with a large glass clock to make a definition of its style and period somewhat difficult!

Not everyone will like its mixture of traditional and modern features, and Plečnik himself was hardly renowned in his time, although views have changed since then. However, since just about every church in Prague is a mixture of styles by accident—since fire or war has required restoration in a different period—this deliberate mixture provides an interesting alternative to the Gothic, Baroque and Renaissance fusions elsewhere in the city.

Although it is easy to return to town by underground, you could walk along Slezská to **náměstí Miru**, the Square of Peace (*see* NOVÉ MESTO), and thence via the newly named **Anglická** (*Anglický*, pronounced Anglitsky, means English) to a point just behind the National Museum at the top of Wenceslas Square.

Cubism—A Tour of Dejvice

Several individual Cubist buildings, like the corner-house on Neklanova in Vyšehrad, have already been mentioned. For those who are particularly interested in this style of architecture, however, there is nothing that can compare with the Baba development in the north of Dejvice.

Baba is very much a part of the Prague suburbs, so that although a tram or the underground can get you some of the way, a bus will be unavoidable. The number 125 runs from Revoluční, the long street running down from náměstí Republiky to the river. Alternatively, you can take the metro to Hradčanská, and walk to the junction of of Buhenečská, Pod kaštany and Dejvická, from which you can catch a 131 bus.

A less complicated and more interesting approach—but one which involves a little walking!—is to take a 20 or 25 tram to the end of the line at the Hotel International in Dejvice. This 1950s pile looks positively attractive beside the ghastly glass and concrete monstrosities like the Forum and Atrium that are currently threatening to devastate the city. Its graffito decoration humanizes its rather severe shape, and the interior has interesting mosaics. The Hotel International used to be the favourite haunt of visiting Soviet dignitaries during the communist era, which means that it has effortlessly transformed itself into a venue for beer parties, nightclubs and strip-shows in the new age of capitalism. Call in for a coffee.

From just north of the hotel turn left up Pod Juliskou and Na Julisce, then right along the bus route to Na Šťáhlavce—it's a walk of less than $\frac{3}{4}$ km ($\frac{1}{2}$ mile), which draws you quickly up out of the industrial sprawl into the leafy suburbs overlooking the city.

Leave the bus at Na Šť'áhlavce. The Baba area itself is named after a hill which has had that name since the 15th century. The fine views at the top look out over the valley of the River Vltava—the best vantage point is at the 19th-century "romantic ruin" on the hill, a designer ruin made by doctoring the remains of an earlier house associated with the wine trade.

Devotees of Cubism should aim for the area made up by the streets Nad pat'ankou, Jarní, Průhledová and Matějská. There are 33 functionalist houses here, designed individually by a number of Czech architects such as Gočár, Žák, Starý and Černý, but under the overall direction of Pavel Janák. For those inclined to dismiss such architecture as "nondescript boxes" there's the compensation of the view from the hill. For those who do like the style, there's the possibility of wandering around like a cat burglar doing a preliminary reconnoitre of potential victims. You won't find many others here who aren't from the area. The detached houses, many of them left as they were when built, have sizeable gardens in the manner of suburbia, but their fascinating shapes make them exciting in a non-suburban way. The way that houses are drawn and imagined from childhood, the door in the centre, symmetrical windows of a certain size on either side and walls at equal heights, is challenged by slight modifications which have an extraordinary effect. The Baba Villa Colony is very different from the impersonal highrise blocks dominating much of the Prague sky-line as part of the former communist régime's policy of workers' villages on the edges of town.

Further Afield

What has been outlined is only a sample, and one deliberately concentrating upon the inner areas of the city. All the tours outlined above are within walking distance of the centre of Prague. There are many other sights which involve travelling to areas still within the city boundaries but a few miles from the city centre. We will not go into detail about these, but list three which are certainly worthwhile visits.

Zbraslav

This "village" within the city boundaries some distance to the south contains a former monastery. Originally 13th century it was completely re-designed in the 18th, and has been converted into an open-air Museum of Modern Czech Sculpture. Rather than being set out indoors within the confines of walls, the sculptures are "casually" laid out in the courtyards and gardens of this Baroque complex. Apart from the art, it's a good place for relaxing in the open air, though summer picnickers should beware wasps.

Star Castle-Letohrádek Hvězda

This strange six- (not five!) sided building is in the middle of a pleasant former deer park on the slopes of White Mountain (Bílá Hora), the scene of the historic victory of the Hapsburgs over the Protestant forces in 1620, an event that established Hapsburg cultural and political control in the area for centuries to come.

The park has been laid out in "English" style with broad promenades and avenues of trees since the end of the 18th century. Star Castle was built by Italian architects in the 16th century as a hunting-lodge for Ferdinand of Tyrol. After languishing for a few decades as a gunpowder store, it was later restored in the 1950s and now houses a museum devoted to the Czech writer Alois Jirásek and the painter Mikoláš Aleš, both part of the late 19th-century national revival (**národní obrození**) movement. In their determination to develop a national Czech culture which could resist the cultural hegemony of the Austro-Hungarian Empire, they both sought to raise national consciousness by re-working old Czech legends. It is therefore appropriate enough that the museum should be housed beneath the mountain on which that cultural hegemony was first established by the Hapsburgs' military success over the Protestant forces under Count Thurn.

Průhonice

On the south-eastern edge of the city in the district of Průhonice is one of Europe's biggest parks, which in the spring will be alive with azaleas and rhododendrons.

Other Areas

Other areas are certainly worth a visit, particularly if you are in search of districts like Libeň that have remained relatively unspoilt either by communist town-planning or by the later invasion of tourists. Remember that the public transport system is cheap, simple (charging per journey irrespective of distance travelled) and virtually omnipresent, so you can feel largely free to go where you like. Even late in the evening the service is regular, and selected tram lines run throughout the night. Buy a good map of the city (ask for a Plán Města), one that does not confine itself only to the centre of town (and which has up-to-date place names-an easy check is to see whether anything to do with Gottwald remains on it!). The best one, selling at 10 crowns in 1990 and doubling

to 20 crowns in 1991, is ISBN 80-7011-035-X. Its design shows a map through the frame of an ecclesiastical window shaded in blue, and it is simply headed **Praha** (Prague). It is fairly uncompromising in its detail and you may have to squint at it, but it leaves nothing out.

Other Districts—Opening Times

1. Výstaviště. Opening times vary. In the summer months this "exhibition park" will be open until late in the evening, particularly at week-ends.
2. Troja Chateau.
   9.00 a.m. to 5.00 p.m. Not Mondays.
3. Prague Zoo.
   9.00 a.m. to 6.00 p.m. daily.
4. Národní technické muzeum (National Technical Museum).
   9.00 a.m. to 5.00 p.m. Not Mondays.
5. Muzeum hlavního mešta Prahy (Municipal Museum).
   9.00 a.m. to 12.00 noon. 1.00 p.m. to 5.00 p.m. Not Mondays.
6. The New Jewish Cemetery.
   8.00 a.m. to 5.00 p.m. (4.00 p.m. in winter). Not Fridays/Saturdays.
7. Museum of Modern Czech Sculpture.
   10.00 a.m. to 6.00 p.m. Not Mondays.
8. Star Castle.
   9.00 a.m. to 4.00 p.m. Not Mondays.

Highlights for Children

Lots of rides like dodgems and roller-coaster in Výstaviště. Good exhibitions and a fountain display with musical accompaniment.

Playground in Stromovka Park, plus large expanse of parkland.

Zoo and boat ride back to centre of Prague.

National Technical Museum contains plenty of buttons to press and a very interesting display of old vehicles.

A Taste of Life and a Glimpse of Mortality, and in between Castles, Cruises and a Beer

Any stay in Czechoslovakia should include at least one day outside Prague. This section offers a range of destinations, from the chandelier made of every bone in the human body at Kutná Hora to the vineyards of Mělnik and the famous spa town of Karlovy Vary (Karlsbad), where for generations the wealthy have sought to make their ailments an opportunity for pleasure. And of course there's a fair selection of romantic Bohemian castles to choose from too.

Prague in a Day

Although a lightning tour of the city is not recommended, it has to be accepted that many people want to see the newly discovered cities of the former Eastern European bloc during a single vacation. "Doing Eastern Europe" has become a mini version of "Doing Europe". Whilst it is only marginally more desirable to try to cram Prague, Warsaw, Budapest and perhaps even St Petersburg into a one-week

V iew from the battlements of Karlstejn Castle.

holiday than to try to cover the main capitals of Western Europe in a single visit, it is as well to recognize that this is an increasingly popular itinerary for western visitors in the 1990s.

The Royal Way

If you only have one day to see Prague, then it is probably best to concentrate upon "**The Royal Way**", the route taken by monarchs on the occasion of their coronation. Since the last coronation in Prague took place over 150 years ago, in September 1836, such occurrences have long died out, initially because of the Hapsburgs' tendency to concentrate their pageantry on Vienna rather than Prague, and later because of the end of the monarchy. Royal processions are now a thing of the past. The route which they took, however,

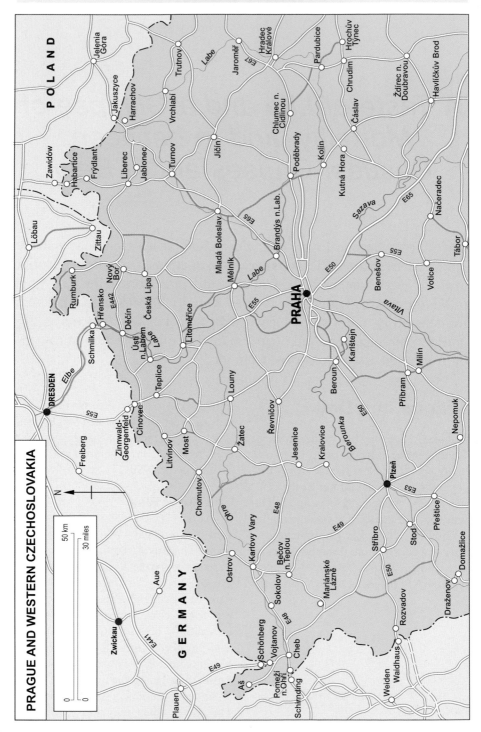

PRAGUE AND WESTERN CZECHOSLOVAKIA

which is still known as The Royal Way, is an excellent way of seeing the main sights of the city and experiencing its different charms in a single journey.

Begin at **náměstí Republiky** (which can easily be reached by underground), and start under the **Powder Tower** opposite, setting off with the flow of visitors down Celetná to the **Old Town Square**. From the **Astronomical Clock** end of the Square you then follow the narrow streets of the Old Town as far as the **Charles Bridge** (go via the **Malé náměstí**—Small Square—which is in fact shaped more like a triangle, into Karlova). Take the odd dive away from the main flow into one or two of the side-streets as you go. Cross the line of traffic at the end and come onto the statue-lined Charles Bridge. Once over the Vltava river, head along Mostecká to **Malostranské náměstí, Lesser Quarter Square**, where you should stop to see **St Nicholas' Church**, the finest example of Prague Baroque.

At this point you have to start climbing! From the top right corner of the Square as you look uphill, follow Nerudova and Uvoz until you come out close to the **Strahov Monastery** and **Loretánské náměstí, Loreta Square**. From here it is a short distance to **Prague castle** (slightly downhill this time), and **St Vitus' Cathedral** where the coronation took place.

The route is easy to follow since it is almost straight, and it does include the main sights for which Prague is renowned. The one area which it omits, the **New Town**, you could always save for the night-time (assuming that you have a day and a night in Prague). Having explored the Old Town, Malá Strana (Lesser Quarter), and Castle by day, you could go to **Wenceslas Square** in the New Town during the evening, where the main night-life is concentrated.

An older coronation procession used to run from **Vyšehrad** (once home for Czech Kings) to the more familiar castle on the opposite side of the river. However, if you have only one day and night in Prague, it is better to keep to the royal way of more recent centuries.

Day Trips from Prague

This section contains some suggestions about short journeys to places of interest within a radius of about 80 km (50 miles) from the centre of Prague. There are many fascinating places outside the capital which can easily be visited during the course of a single day, and which in most cases are easily accessible. Whether you are part of an organized coach party or choose to find your own way by car or by public transport, there is little difficulty involved. There is much more to Czechoslovakia than Prague, as a couple of trips outside the city will make clear. Such visits will also demonstrate just how much further the capital city has gone towards post-revolutionary "westernization" than other parts of the country, not to mention how much further it has gone towards western prices!

The section is organized according to two groups of headings which, despite the alliteration, offer a way of determining where to visit according to what you want to see.

*M*ap *of the areas around Prague.*

The extensively buttressed cathedral church of St Barbara at Kutná Hora.

Bones, Booze and Baths

Kutná Hora (Bones)

Less than 80 km (50 miles) east of Prague lies the town of **Kutná Hora**. Once Bohemia's second city after Prague, Kutná Hora faded in importance with the exhaustion of its nearby silver mines at the end of the 16th century. Its relatively brief period of glory (in the late Middle Ages it was equal in size to London), however, did at least allow for the construction of several very fine buildings. Some of these have survived the ravages of fire and restoration. Its present population is little more than 20,000, while silver mining has been replaced by engineering and tobacco as the town's main forms of production.

The centre of town is well-signed from the railway station, besides which the main sights are easily visible. First port of call, looking out onto the court gardens which lead down to the river Vrchlice below, is the **Vlašský dvůr** (Italian Court), a 13th-century Gothic building which has since been heavily restored. It was here that the royal mint was established, producing the Bohemian "Groschens" which made Czech Kings among the wealthiest in Europe. A small exhibition of the process of minting is worth a brief look.

Behind the Italian Court is the town's oldest church, St James (sv. Jakub). A Gothic 14th-century building, the church stands out both because of the size of its steeple and because it leans. Ironically the silver that paid for its construction was also responsible for undermining it through the subsidence created by mining.

The highlight of Kutná Hora, however, standing next to a palatial Jesuit College which perhaps sought (and failed) to eclipse it some centuries later, is the Cathedral of St Barbara (sv. Barbora), the patron saint of miners. It was built over a long period from the late 14th to the late 16th centuries, engaging generations of the finest architects of Gothic in its construction. It was intended to match the great St Vitus' Cathedral of Prague at a time when the two cities were very much rivals, but the ravages of Hussite Wars and the decline of Kutná Hora's wealth and importance in the 16th century meant that it was never quite completed. Even so it is undoubtedly a masterpiece of Gothic architecture, which you may well feel outstrips anything to be found in Prague itself. Perhaps because it reflected the brashness of a boom town, Kutná Hora's chram sv. Barbora is more extravagant in style than Gothic usually allows itself to be. From the outside it is all towers, spires and flying buttresses. Inside, where it is more restrained, note in particular the frescoes and paintings depicting miners and minters at work.

Other sights worth a glance in the city are the oldest house, known as **Kamenný dům** (the Stone House), which has a fine oriel window and is now a local museum, the 15th-century town well and the unfinished Baroque Ursuline convent, designed by Kilian Ignaz Dientzenhofer. Apart from any particular sights, however, it is worth strolling through an historic centre full of Gothic and Baroque buildings. They may not be so grand or so well restored as those in Prague, but at least

The extraordinary ossuary at Sedlec near Kutná Hora, where František Rint was commissioned to "do something creative" with the bones.

there are no crowds to fight through in order to see them. Nor are there any of the more tacky things that tourism brings with it, and which create the Czech capital's own problem of "subsidence". Like Kutná Hora in the Late Middle Ages, Prague has the problem of being threatened by the very thing that makes it (comparatively) rich.

Apart from St Barbara's Cathedral, the most fascinating sight in Kutná Hora lies in the suburb of Sedlec, about 1 km (2 miles) from the town centre and on a regular bus route. A former Cistercian monastery here is now Europe's largest tobacco factory, perhaps illustrating that opium is the religion of the people. Nearby is a 14th-century monastery church, half-destroyed during the Hussite Wars and then redesigned in Baroque by Giovanni Santini three centuries later. The most striking thing of all, however, is the underground ossuary (*kostnice*), reached by crossing the road to the monks' graveyard and heading for the ancient Gothic chapel which hangs over the entrance to this extraordinary display.

The ossuary is choc-a-bloc with human bones. The remains of at least 10,000 people are here. Inspired by the spreading of

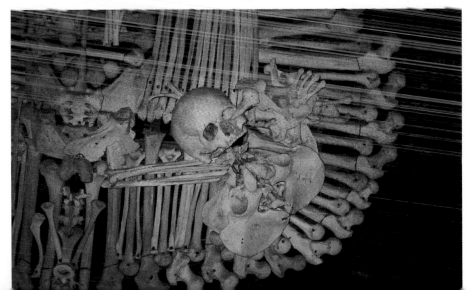

holy earth from Golgotha (literally "Place of the Skull", the site of Jesus' crucifixion in Christian tradition) over the area in the 12th century, people felt that this was an obviously appropriate place to be buried and, bearing in mind the links with Golgotha, await a future resurrection. By the end of the 19th century things were getting decidedly cramped. The solution was a bizarre one. František Rint was commissioned in 1870 to "do something" with the bones, and proceeded to design a series of skeletal decorations, including giant bells and—as the piece de resistance—a chandelier made out of every bone in the human body.

Some might view the ossuary as macabre. Others might wonder why we waste so much useful material for artistic creativity through the practice of cremation. At any rate it can be described as an unusual experience!

Kutná Hora is about an hour's journey from Prague's Masarykovo nádraží.

Bones and Mummies

Those whose taste for the macabre is not satisfied with the bones at Sedlec might like to embark on a slightly longer journey to Brno, Czechoslovakia's third-largest city after Prague and Bratislava and the political and cultural centre of Moravia. One of its most popular sights is the crypt of the Capuchin Church, erected about 1650, which contains mummies of the members and benefactors of the Capuchin cloister, displayed in caverns below the church. Five crypt rooms contain the mummified remains of about 150 monks, some of them without coffins, and decorated with an assortment of skulls and crossbones. Above the remains are useful reminders of mortality such as "What you are I was once". The crypt is open from Tuesday to Saturday and admission is a princely six crowns.

Alternatively, Čedok organize a coach trip to the city during the summer under the title "Treasures of the Czech Gothic" (G3). It is a full day excursion which, apart from Kutná Hora, also takes you after lunch to the gothic château of Český Šternberk, (see *Castles, Châteaux and Cruises*) perched romantically on the edge of a cliff about ten miles south-west of Kutná Hora. There's not much more to it than its location, however, and you may prefer to stay in Kutná Hora for the afternoon and see the bones.

Mělník and Plzeň (Booze)

No visit to the area would be complete without taking the opportunity to sample the wine. Čedok run a particularly attractive tour in this respect, under the title "In Search of Bohemian wine" (G8). It is often combined with a visit to the château at Veltrusy (*see* CASTLES, CHATEAUX AND CRUISES on page 220), but the highlight of the day is **Mělník**, a beautifully situated town placed at the meeting-point of the Vltava and Elbe rivers, and a centre of viniculture for more than a millennium. Its quiet, unspoilt (if also somewhat untended) town square is light-years away from the bustle of Prague, but the beautiful landscape looking down past sloping vineyards at the rivers below is its highlight.

Čedok will probably show you the late Gothic Church before getting down to business and providing a range of local wines along with a snack in the Château Wine Tavern which has one of the best views in town. Look out for the following (in Czech spelling):

Revovy List. Muller Thurgau.

Ryzlink. Château Mělník. Sekt Cremant Rose, which provides the rare experience of a red champagne.

Ludmila is probably the finest of the local wines. Čedok tends to offer this with cheese in the cellars of the Mělník Château, among the presses and huge decorated wine barrels. It comes in both red and white.

Although Czech wines have a growing reputation, that of Czech beer doesn't need establishing. Those whose interest in alcohol is not based on the grape might like to visit Plzeň, an industrial town with a population of 200,000, which lies about 80 km (50 miles) to the west of Prague and can easily be reached by train (the line to Nuremberg and Western Europe runs through the city and most trains stop there). The Brewery Museum at Veleslavínova 6 (slightly to the north of the main square, náměstí Republiky) contains a unique exhibition of the brewery trade and of the history of Czech brewing. As a contrast to the huge wine barrels in the cellar of the Mělník Château compare the smallest beer barrel in the world here.

The Czech beer Plzeňský Prazdroj, or in its more familiar Germanized form Pilsner Urquell, named after the city, is unsurpassable. It is of course infinitely superior to the gassy "Pils" sold in British pubs under the Pilsner name. The word Prazdroj (in German Urquell) means "source" or "original" to convey the fact that the real thing is brewed here. Real devotees may wish to head for U Prazdroje on the edge of the river where the brewery gates figured on most Pilsner labels can be found. Although there may not be an opportunity to see the brewery itself, the Restaurace Prazdroj at U Prazdroje 1 will offer a plentiful supply and food if you want it. As a medium-sized industrial town which is famous for its Skoda cars as well as for its beer—there is a Skoda museum on Korandova—Plzeň may not have the range of cultural attractions offered by other cities, but it does possess some very fine buildings and is well worth a day's visit. Note especially the **náměstí Republiky** (Square of the Republic) with its outstanding St Bartholomew's Church and the Renaissance town hall on the north side.

On 1 May 1991 a number of streets in Plzeň changed their names. Moskevská became Americká, Leninova became Husova (after the famous medieval dissident Jan Hus), Sovětská became Ruská and, perhaps as an over-egging of the pudding, Gorkého became Goethova. It seems a shame to blame Gorky for the follies of men like Klement Gottwald! Whatever the rights and wrongs of this wholesale process of obliterating the past, it doesn't make it any easier to get around, so find yourself an up-to-date street map and guide. The Čedok office on the edge of the main square should oblige. Remember that this is not Prague—there are not tourist facilities on every street corner, but at least that means there aren't tourists at every street corner either. Even in an industrial city like Plzeň the pace of post-revolutionary change has been much slower than in the capital, something that has its charms when you can find yourself in a café alone, and strike a light for cigarettes sold singly from a wine-glass behind a dusty counter.

Karlovy Vary (Baths)

About 80 km (50 miles) west of Prague is the spa town of **Karlovy Vary** (probably better known for its German name Karlsbad—literally Charles' Bath! —which was named after its founder the Emperor Charles IV). For over 600 years Karlovy Vary's thermal springs (the Czech word Vary means boiling or cooking) have been

Taking the waters at Karlovy Vary (Karlsbad).

exploited for relaxation or the treatment of chronic illnesses. Since those who went there expected to be treated in style, the various springs are surrounded by baroque colonnades and smooth marble floors, all of which can easily be traced by following the only main thoroughfare in the town which winds alongside the River Teplá.

The 12 springs in use (there are about 60 in all) are at various temperatures ranging from about 40°C (104°F) to about 70°C (158°F). You can taste the water either from a plastic cup or by the traditional vessels which require you to drink from a long spout, as if taking tea directly from the pot. The hottest spring, at 72° C (162°F), takes the form of a fountain in the Yuri Gagarin colonnade, designed to cement Soviet-Czech friendship and

therefore probably in line for a name change when a new generation of planners gets to work.

Few people like the taste of the water, which has absorbed dissolved minerals from up to 2 km (1 mile) below the earth's surface. Nevertheless it has been regarded for centuries as a restorative, particularly where the alimentary tract and metabolic disorders are concerned. At one time people drank it like Plzeňský Prazdroj, but nowadays it is taken in greater moderation and probably proves more beneficial.

Karlovy Vary has an atmosphere of wealth and cosmopolitanism not often found in Western Czechoslovakia. It has the air of a resort, set in a valley among thickly wooded hills and catering to the rich on retreat, its curative potential a convenient excuse for a holiday (this is no health farm). Not so long ago it was a favourite retreat for high-ranking Eastern bloc communist officials doubtless following in the footsteps of Karl Marx, who came here "for the waters" several times in his later years. Though its clientele may now be changing, its function of providing stylish enjoyment has not. Even the casino survived 40 years of communist rule.

Karlovy Vary is a town dedicated to the pleasure principles. Its monumental high-sided 19th-century buildings include some of the grandest hotels in the world. One such is the exotic Hotel Pupp founded at the turn of the 18th century on the Alte Wiese, conveniently situated next to a funicular railway which can carry the weary up the hillside at no cost to their frail health. Its shops are full of delicacies ranging from coffee and cakes to intricate and beautiful china and glassware. And naturally enough for such a place, even though it lacks the sea or the weather at Cannes, it hosts a biennial film festival in the August of even-numbered years.

Karlovy Vary is located in a part of Czechoslovakia which used to be known as the Sudetenland, which was annexed by Hitler in 1938 on the grounds that its substantial German-speaking minority was being oppressed. This excuse was enough to satisfy Neville Chamberlain, who brought back the "Peace in Our Time" agreement from a meeting with Hitler in Munich, which effectively dismembered Czechoslovakia. It is noticeable how many more people here than in Prague speak in German although some of them, of course, are German tourists on a day trip across the border, and the influence of the German-speaking minority is recognizable in what is a far more "Germanic" town than others further east.

For those wishing to walk off the effect of rich cakes or other pleasures, there are a range of walks in the hills through dense layers of beech and oak, occasionally opening out to yield spectacular views.

Head for the wooden crucifix above the Alte Wiese (taking the lanovka or funicular if you wish for part of the way), and then make your way up to the Peter the Great Memorial where the best views are on offer. In several other parts of the wood there are observation towers from the top of which you can see the surrounding landscape and escape the slightly claustrophobic air of walking through a valley surrounded by tall buildings and thick, pressing woods on every side.

Karlovy Vary can be reached by both bus and train, which arrive on the north side of the city about $1/2$ km ($1/4$ mile) from the main spa area. Alternatively, Čedok offer a day trip which encompasses both Karlovy Vary and the village of Lidice a few kilometres outside Prague. It is a somewhat incongruous combination, since the contrast could hardly be greater between the pleasure resort on the one hand and a village razed to the ground and (literally!) obliterated from the map by the Nazis on the other.

Lidice

Lidice was a former mining village that the Nazis destroyed in revenge for the murder of one of their top officials, "Reich Protector" Heydrich, by the Czech resistance (see page 141 NOVÉ MĚSTO). The men of the village were killed along with some of the women and children, the rest of whom were sent away to concentration camps. The village was then flattened and removed from sight. A green hillside marks the place where the village stood, and a small museum contains photographs of those who died and a few possessions like identity cards. A Garden of Friendship nearby contains roses sent from all over the world. It is a poignant monument and symbol of resis-

*R*emembering the victims of Nazi oppression: one of the few survivors from a village literally wiped off the face of the earth guards its memory.

tance to fascism. Many villages around the world changed their name to Lidice after Hitler's action, a symbol of determination that it should not be "removed from the map" as he intended. The display is all the more effective for its simplicity and for the small reminders in the fields outside of what the village once was, like the foundations of the school. There is a short film about the history of Lidice, including footage taken by the Nazis themselves of the village being destroyed.

If you wish to visit Lidice on its own there is no difficulty since it is barely 19 km (12 miles) out of Prague and you can get there by bus.

Castles, Châteaux and Cruises
Karlštejn, Křivoklát, Orlík, Zvíkov, Veltrusy, Konopiště and the River Vltava

Karlštejn, Křivoklát, Orlík (Castles)

The castles of Bohemia are an obvious favourite for any visitor, and there are many to choose from. By far the most well-known in the vicinity of Prague is **Karlštejn**, the most visited castle in Czechoslovakia, situated about 32 km (20 miles) south-west of the capital. You will probably find as many visitors here during the summer months as at any of the main sights in Prague itself.

The castle dominates the skyline of a small wine-producing town, Karlštejn, which has barely 1,000 inhabitants. It was built in the mid-14th century by the omnipresent Emperor Charles IV as a safe haven for the crown jewels and a few relics of the saints. Karlštejn is the stereotypical romantic castle, perched on a rocky hill high above deep forests. Indeed it is

220

arguable that it is at its best viewed from a distance as part of a breathtaking Bohemian landscape.

In the 15th century King Sigismund removed the jewels from Karlštejn Castle (they are currently in St Vitus' Cathedral, Prague) and it lost its importance until achieving its present role as a popular destination for trippers in the early 19th century. Arguably this was also its original role since Charles IV used it as a retreat from Prague. Restored in the late 19th century, the castle contains former imperial apartments, a Chapel of the Holy Rood (medieval term for the Cross), whose walls are inlaid with semi-precious stones, and a massive Great Tower over 30 m (100 ft) high. These and other rooms may not all be on display (attempts are currently under way to open up more of the castle to visitors), but enough will be open to reveal some of the fine panelling, paintings, including wall-paintings, and ceilings of the interior.

Karlštejn Castle is on the Čedok itinerary (G5), which includes in the price lunch at the restaurant next door. Alternatively, trains from Smíchov station in Prague run hourly and take the best part of an hour to reach their destination.

Křivoklát is a little further than Karlštejn, perhaps 48 km (30 miles) west of the capital. Originally a wooden hunting castle of Bohemian royals dating from as far back as the 12th century, Křivoklát Castle was rebuilt in Gothic stone and eventually taken over in the 19th century by romantic novelists and artists seeking inspiration. Its Great Hall and Chapel contain a range of Gothic sculptures and paintings. There are a number of woodland walks that can be combined with a visit to the castle. Křivoklát can either be combined with Karlštejn in a Čedok tour

(G5), or else visited independently by train (change at Beroun) or bus (from Dejvice station in Prague). Both journeys take the best part of two hours.

Orlík Castle also originates from the desire to hunt. Perched on the edge of the Vltava river, the castle is aptly named after the eagle's nest, representing both its position and the "eagle eye" of the hunter. If you are a devotee of Empire furniture, trophies and paintings from hunts gone by and collections of weaponry then this is the place for you, although as with other Bohemian castles the reality is rather less impressive than the appearance. It can be reached in impressive enough style by boat from the River Vltava, but once arrived you are confronted, apart from the hunting memorabilia, with a mock-Gothic pile. **Zvíkov** is 5 km (3 miles) further upstream (although since the whole area has been taken over by the construction of the Orlík Dam, "upstream" has lost some of its meaning), and contains some fine early Gothic art in its chapel.

Both castles are contained within a single Čedok outing (G4) by coach and boat, but the highlight of the tour may be more the river and the sight of the castles in the distance than the tour of their interiors. This part of Bohemia gave particular inspiration to the Czech composer Smetana, whose symphonic poem *Ma Vlast* (My country) is a great national favourite. The most famous part of his musical poem describes the course of the Vltava river from this part of Bohemia into Prague, although in the 19th century it was a rather more dangerous and exciting waterway than modern technology has made it nowadays. If you go independently, remember that the whole journey by boat takes several hours, so you may prefer to go by bus and reach your destination within about ninety minutes.

Konopiště, Veltrusy (Châteaux)

The only château in Prague itself, Troja Palace, is described above (*see* OTHER AREAS). Some very fine châteaux, however, are within a few miles of the city. Konopiště, (once again the subject of a popular Čedok tour G6) is about 48 km (30 miles) south-east of Prague. Once

The Gothic Castle of Konopište, one of the most visited haunts in Bohemia.

again its collection of hunting trophies may grate with, or at least bore, those whose capacity for enjoying the sight of stuffed animals and the weapons used to dispose of them is limited. However, it does have an interesting collection of furniture and tapestries, and significant historical associations. It was here that the Archduke Ferdinand lived until his assassination in 1914 sparked off the First World War. Its distinctive towers give it a striking appearance, while the English park and garden outside, dotted with Italian sculptures, make for an enjoyable stroll.

More charming is the château at **Veltrusy**, an 18th-century Baroque building designed for the counts of Chotek with a distinctive green dome and a collection of interesting period furniture. At least the urge to hunt is not dominant in this building, although the grounds outside were clearly used for this purpose. Veltrusy is included in the Čedok tour of Mělnik (G8), but it can easily be visited by train to Nehalozeves. If you get off at the previous station, Nehalozeves zastávka, then you can also visit the château of Nehalozeves, a plain building which was originally a late 16th-century Renaissance construction and is now enlivened by sgraffito decoration.

Cruises

If you have time enough, it is well worth your while to spend some of your time in Prague on a boat. A number of cruises on the Vltava are on offer, of which the most comfortable is probably Čedok's cruise by "historical steamer" (G7). This trip by paddle steamer takes in many of the most imposing sights in the city and on its outskirts. Dinner and musical entertainment on board is thrown in with the price, and

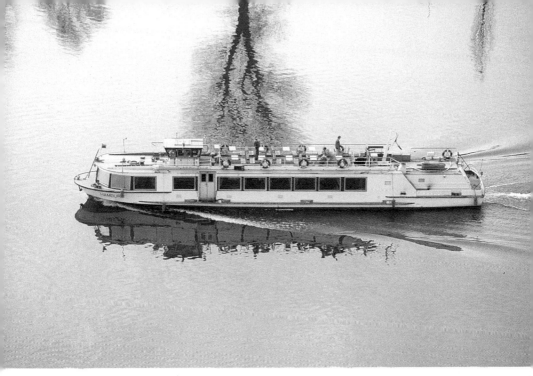

One of the best trips out of the city is by boat on the Vltava.

the trip will take you past some sights which will probably not be included even in the most comprehensive of city tours.

Particularly impressive is the view "from below" of Vyšehrad, originally a rival to Prague Castle in importance, and the limestone rocks of Barrandov further upstream, full of prehistoric fossils. This is currently the area in which Prague's film and TV studios are located, although with the present fluctuating economic climate they are liable to become fossils themselves.

The trip eventually takes you past many of the newer housing estates on the edge of the city, indicating the general policy of the communist town planners in the mid-20th century. Their approach was to leave the historical heart of the city largely untouched and to build large housing and living complexes away from the centre. Such methods certainly filled several potentially fine landscapes with dull concrete tenements, and undoubtedly relied upon a comprehensive public transport network to succeed. However, it did preserve the heart of Prague from the ravaging that other cities received when the planners took over where the bombers of the Second World War left off. Such an approach had its disadvantages, but present post-revolutionary tendencies to construct hideous modern edifices like the Hotel Atrium right in the heart of the city paint it in a rather better light.

Other Ideas

There are many other trips that can be made through western Czechoslovakia on a day's outing. Many Czechs (and of course all Slovaks!) are keen to point out that there is much more to their country than Prague, which is all that a substantial number of visitors to this nation ever see. If you are able to spend some time away from the capital this can only add to the breadth of your experience.

Czechoslovakia has a rich and interesting natural landscape. Something like a third of the country is made up of forest. It is an ideal place for ramblers, hikers or those interested in caving. An enterprising new group based in Prague, Enex, organizes "environmental walks" in summer or winter (in winter, skiing can be inserted into the programme) according to an itinerary planned by the visitor himself or herself. They arrange the "walking safaris", which can include canoeing, rafting and horse-riding, according to an itinerary planned by yourself according to

*T*he forests of Bohemia. Over a third of Czechoslovakia is forest, much of it is threatened by pollution.

your own time and interests. Alternatively you may want to take part in a tour arranged around a particular environmental issue such as deforestation. Such tours can be combined with a visit to Prague itself and offer an alternative way of experiencing the country to that of making trips to well-known "sights". You simply set off to explore the wonderful Czech countryside according to your own programme.

Day Trips: How to do Them and Opening Times

All the trips outlined above can be made by means of a coach journey organized by Čedok. The cost ranges from about 500 to 1,000 crowns per person, which is more expensive than independent travel, but which has the advantage of comfort,

knowing that you will reach your destination and free refreshments (a full meal on the longer tours).

The coaches tend to leave early in the morning (about 8.00 a.m. or 9.00 a.m.) from outside Čedok offices in the city centre (particularly the main office at 24 Wenceslas Square). You can book the trip from any Čedok office and although you may be unlucky they are rarely sold out. With tinted windows and comfortable seats, the coaches are of good standard.

You will also be given a guided tour, usually in three languages (English, French and German). Since the Revolution, the guides have tended to concentrate rather more on historic buildings and rather less on the latest housing estate or factory in their descriptions. They are extremely helpful and informative, and this is one of the most pleasant ways to see Bohemia. Those who wish to travel further afield with Čedok can take tours involving overnight stays.

If you wish to travel independently there is little problem with bus or train for most destinations, and the cost is very cheap (50-100 crowns for most places). Both are slow, but since the journeys outlined above are all within 80-95 km (50-60 miles) of Prague you never have to travel for more than two hours, and the views are always scenic.

Those travelling by car can obviously reach their destination quickest of all-assuming they don't get lost! There are few stretches of dual carriageway, let alone motorway, but at the same time there are as yet few cars either. Road signs are not as plentiful as one would like, so take a map.

Not all the trips take place on a year-round basis, and not all the sights are open throughout the year. Čedok tend to operate from May to October, although June to September are the only four months when all of the trips are operating. Karlštejn is open all year (as is the brewery museum at Plzeň). Křivoklát, Konopiště, Orlík and Nehalozeves are open from April till October. Veltrusy, the Mělník Château and the museum at Lidice are open from March to October, and the castle at Zvíkov from March to September. All these sights are closed on Mondays.

Useful Addresses

1. Čedok Tour Operators: (a) Václavské náměstí (Wenceslas Square) No. 24. Tel. 2356356 or 2359249. (b) Bílkova Street 6 (opposite the Inter-Continental Hotel in Josefov). Tel. 2318255 or 2316619. (c) Čedok Intertravel, Na příkopě 18. Tel. 2127111 You can also book through the hotel you are staying at.

2. ENEX (Environmental Walks and "Walking Safaris"). Kopeckého 8, 169 00 Prague 6. This is some way from the centre behind the Spartakiádní stadium in Strahov, although the trams that run past the castle take you to Bělohorská nearby. Tel. 352202.

Similar things are organized by Heart Adventures, based at náměstí Míru (Square of Peace) 18, 120 00 Prague 2. Tel. 251151. Since Metro Line A runs to náměstí Míru this is easy to find.

The numbers of such "entrepreneurs" is rapidly increasing, so look out for new information when you arrive. You will not be able to walk around the city during the summer months without having leaflets pressed into your hand offering ways of seeing the capital and region by boat, balloon, aeroplane, hired minibus or car-to name but a few! Some of the offers may be expensive, and don't pay in advance!

As the Sun Sinks Slowly Over the Yard Arm . . .

Since the Velvet Revolution of 1989 Prague has come to life. Every week a new jazz or rock venue opens, a new exhibition of formerly banned art appears, or a new theatre group tries its luck under the financial constraints of capitalism. Whatever your cultural interests, there is enough to do and more in this city, whilst the night-life is also a lot freer than before the Revolution. The disco beat keeps sounding, and the wheel of the casino keeps turning, well beyond the midnight hour, whilst deep in the Romanesque bowels of Prague some smoky club will be open where you can disapprove of all the changes or discuss Tolkien.

Culture, Nightlife and Entertainment

Prague has a range of cultural activities worthy of a European capital. Whether it's grand opera, ballet, classical music and theatre, folk, jazz or the particularly strong theatrical traditions of the city in areas like mime and "laterna magica" (Magic Lantern theatre), the repertoire is wide and of a very high quality.

The impact of the Velvet Revolution on the range of cultural provision in Prague

*T*he Municipal House (Obenci dům)—perhaps Prague's finest Art Nouveau building.

has been mixed. On the one hand, new and formerly banned cultural expressions, such as rock music, have the opportunity to develop freely; on the other hand, the constraints of the new financial restrictions on the arts put a real question mark against some forms of artistic expression which received generous subsidies under the former regime. It remains to be seen how this will develop for the 21st century.

Listed below is a wide range of cultural offerings from Mozart operas to Allen Ginsberg poems. Obviously English-language newspapers like *The Prague Post*, and even the posters and fly sheets that the visitor encounters on the day, will provide the most up-to-date listings of what's on, but the selection here shows what a comprehensive selection is available.

The plush interior of the Smetana Theatre.

Opera and Ballet

The former Týlovo divadlo (Týl theatre), closed for major restoration, has now re-opened for 1992. Looking resplendent in pastel shades, it featured in Miloš Forman's film about the life of Mozart,

Amadeus. It has now been re-named The Theatre of Estates (Stavovské divadlo), and is located at Ovocný trh 6 (Tel. 22 72 82-8). It is a favourite venue for Mozart concerts—it was here that the first performance of Mozart's *Don Giovanni* took place in 1787, the composer preferring a Prague venue where his music was far better appreciated than elsewhere.

The National Theatre (Národní divadlo), one of Prague's finest neo-Renaissance buildings and worthy of a visit for the decor alone, let alone the music, is located beside the River Vltava at 2, Národní (Tel. 20 53 64).

The Smetana Theatre (Smetanovo divadlo) is in the New Town, close to the main railway station off the top of Wenceslas Square on Wilsonova (Tel. 26 97 48).

Performances at all three venues usually commence at 7.00 p.m.

A pot-pourri of classical tit-bits, easy on the ear and out to catch the tourists, can be heard at Opera Mozart, located next to the Old Town end of the Charles Bridge at Novotného lávka 1. It's pretty insipid stuff, but sounds very impressive when you catch the strains of Smetana's *Ma Vlast* standing on the Charles Bridge on a hot summer's evening overhearing the performance.

Outside the city centre, but worth a visit, is the Karlin Music Theatre, (Hudebni divadlo v Karlině), at Křižikova 10, Praha 8 (Tel. 22 08 95). This theatre often produces operetta and musicals, for those whose tastes lie in that direction.

Classical Music

Classical music is performed at many venues, including a number of open-air venues during the summer months.

Look out for performances at the Palace of Culture (next to Vyšehrad underground

station), which has a number of classical concerts and plays in The Congress Hall. The Smetana Hall of the Municipal House (Obecní dům), in náměstí Republiky, hosts many concerts. A range of smaller, chamber music performances can be enjoyed in venues like The Convent of St Agnes of Bohemia (17 U milosrdných ulice), the Adria Palace near the bottom of Wenceslas Square at 31 Jungmannova St, St Nicholas' Church in the Old Town Square, St Giles Church in the Old Town at 8, Husova ul., at Bertramka (The Mozart Museum, located in Smíchov at 169 Mozartova ulice) and at the Dvořák Museum at 20 Ke Karlovu ulice.

This is only a selection of what is on offer. During the summer months classical music can be heard at open-air venues like the Waldstein Gardens in Malá Strana (Valdštejnske náměstí 10) or in the garden adjoining the Museum of Musical Instruments at Lázeňská 2.

A particularly good time to hear classical music in Prague is during the Prague Spring festival, an annual international music festival which is held in the second half of May and very beginning of June. The festival opens with a performance of Smetana's *Ma Vlast* in the Smetana Hall of the Municipal House, and continues with a wide range of international composers and performers. This is undoubtedly the best time of year for concerts. The repertoire stays faithful to Czech composers like Dvořák, Smetana, Janaček and Martinů, whilst at the same time performing a large number of works by major and minor composers from around the world—with a heavy emphasis on Mozart, whom Prague appears to have adopted as a kind of honourary Czech on account of his preference for having his works performed in the city.

Art and Architecture in Prague

Few cities anywhere in the world can have such a rich abundance of architectural styles as Prague. Take, for example, what is probably the most well-known sight in the city , the Old Town Square. In its centre the famous Art Nouveau statue of Jan Hus, a controversial product of the early 20th century, looks out upon a set of 18th-century Baroque façades. Climb up to the roof of the Old Town Hall, however, and you can look down on the steep daddle rooves of the Gothic originals which lie behind these façades. Then again, closer inspection at ground level reveals examples of Gothic rib vaulting and later examples of Renaissance styles, for instance the gables of the Týn school. To cap it all, beneath the ground level, which was raised in medieval times to resist frequent flooding, are examples of the Romanesque style in which the first buildings in the area were fashioned.

There are numerous areas of the city like the Old Town Square. They represent not just fine examples of a particular architectural style, but of the history of architecture through all its most notable phases. Sometimes the consequence is an almost incongruous partnership, as where the Gothic Powder Tower stands next door to the Art Nouveau of the Municipal Hall. Sometimes historical accident rather than deliberate design seems to have generated a perfect fusion of styles, as in the Old Town Square itself. Often the various styles are brought together in a single building, as in the case of St Vitus' Cathedral. The result is a richness and individuality which must be difficult to match anywhere else in the world. Although much can and has been written on the Gothic and Baroque glories of Prague, it is worth paying attention to two important movements which have appeared only in the last century, both of which are well represented in the city, namely Art Nouveau and Cubism. The influence of these two movements tends to be lost in the blur of their more famous antecedents, and yet they have contributed a great deal to making Prague what it is today. This section will focus on the nature of these styles and will also suggest where in Prague the best examples of Art Nouveau and Cubism can be found. A final paragraph will remind you of where the main art exhibitions in the city are to be found.

Art Nouveau

Art Nouveau laid the foundation for modern art and design. It sprang out of neo-Baroque and neo-Gothic movements, and rapidly spread throughout Europe during the generation or so before the First World War. It exploited new design concepts in cast iron, steel and glass which had been released by the industrial revolution. In Prague, which at the time was part of the most advanced manufacturing centre in the Austro-Hungarian empire, Art Nouveau had a particular impact.

The earliest of Prague's Art Nouveau structures were built for the Jubilee Exhibition of the Kingdom of Bohemia in 1891. Influenced by the Eiffel Tower in Paris, architect Bedřich Munzberger built the Průmyslový palác (Industrial Palace) largely of metal and glass. It is still part of the Exhibition grounds located at Výsttaviště in the Holešovice district. The miniature Eiffel Tower on the Petřin Hill, now open to the public after recent closure, and the decorative Havanský Pavilion on Letná Hill (not far from the metronome which has replaced Stalin's head, and now with a café/restaurant by day and discotheque by night), were also built for the Jubilee.

After these early constructions, Art Nouveau in the city gained momentum. Although the movement in Prague never achieved the originality of Spain's extraordinary Antonio Gaudi, it produced a wide range of wonderful styles across the arts—in painting, sculpture, architecture, photography and the applied arts (ceramics, jewellery, furniture, fashion, printing and in particular the developing forms of poster art). Art Nouveau used the tools of the industrial revolution-iron, steel and glass-in order to criticize the drabness and inhumanity of human life in industrial society.

You can see examples of Art Nouveau architecture and painting in the Obecní dům (Municipal House) in the Square of the Republic, whilst the Umělecko průmyslové muzeum v Praze (Museum of Applied or Decorative Arts), in 17 listopadu 2, contains numerous examples of Art Nouveau styles in the applied arts. The best place to see Art Nouveau sculpture is the Bílek villa, located just outside the Castle area at Mieckiewiczova 1, which contains a wonderful collection (including some furniture) of the work of František Bílek, an outstanding

Idyllic rural scenes were common in Art Nouveau's challenge to the grimy smoke stacks of the industrial revolution. This scene graces the Novák department store in Vodičkova Street.

sculptor, graphic artist and designer, whose superb Crucifixion hangs in St Vitus' Cathedral.

Other buildings in Prague which should not be missed are the main railway station (whose Art Nouveau glories are easily lost when most of the signs steer you down to the space age lower storeys), the Hotel Evropa in Wenceslas Square, and a number of buildings in Národní (for instance the Topic publishing house) and along the Masaryk embankment. Away from the centre of town you should try to visit House Helenka, No. 1078 Na Václavce in the Smíchov district of Prague.

Perhaps the best representative of Art Nouveau style in Prague is Alfons Mucha, who achieved international recognition for his posters of the actress Sarah Bernhardt. He is most well-known for his poster art promoting theatre productions, cigarettes and even baby oil, but he was also responsible for fine murals and work in stained glass (for instance inside the Obecní dům or Municipal House). Mucha employed those symbols and motifs with which Art Nouveau sought to look away from the smoke stacks and blackened chimneys of the industrial revolution to a rural idyll steeped in folklore and ancient traditions. Swans, peacocks, lilies, poppies, tulips, and the phoenix surround peasant costumes and rural landscapes. It is a movement that sought to turn its back upon the claustrophobic conditions and ugliness of uncontrolled industrial expansion, and has left an enduring legacy of beauty in the architecture (and perhaps to some extent the attitudes) of Prague.

The Cubist house of the Black Madonna in Celetná. The caged Madonna is Baroque, but seems strangely in place on the side of the building.

Cubism

For many people Cubism means Pablo Picasso's paintings. In reality the movement found expression, like Art Nouveau, in a variety of art forms, including sculptures, ceramics, glasswork, architecture and furniture. In the early 20th century it made its way rapidly from Paris to Prague and was soon highly influential upon artistic movements here.

In early 1992 a wonderful exhibition of Czech Cubism from 1909 to 1925 (Český Cubismus 1909–1925) located near the entrance to Prague Castle (not the main entrance but the one beside the royal gardens at U Prašného mostu 55, near to where tram 22 drops you) displayed some of the range of Cubist work in Prague, with a video presentation of some of the most well-known Cubist buildings in the city. A superb illustrated book on Czech Cubism was available in Czech for just 300 crowns, and in German for a rather more costly 1,000 crowns! It is very much to be hoped that the National Gallery (of which this exhibition was a part) can find a means of putting Cubist work on

permanent display. Look out for the work of Otto Gutfreund, Bohumil Kubišta, Antonin Procházka and Joseph Gočár. The most well-known Cubist buildings in the city are the House of the Black Madonna at Celetná 34 (a perfect example of ways in which traditional and modern styles can blend together, the Baroque house sign an ideal partner for the Cubist house), and some of the buildings below Vyšehrad near the river on the New Town side (namely Nezlanova 2, a corner house which is very striking indeed, Neklanova 34 and the house with the zig-zag garden railings facing the river on the Rašínovo embankment).

The best examples of Cubism, however, can be found by visiting the Baba Villa colony in Dejvice, a group of 33 functionalist houses with wonderful views of the city, all individually commissioned and built under the guidance of Pavel Janák.

The area is not on any metro or tram line (although it's not far from the Hotel International which has a regular tram

service, and you could walk from there within fifteen minutes), and you should catch the 125 from Revoluční or 131 from metro Hradčanská unless times have changed. Viewing the houses is a bit like snooping around other people's homes, but they do provide a wonderful

Blood and guts in the National Gallery. Pink cherubs overlook a typically violent scene painted by Rubens.

example of what can be done when even the smallest challenge is made to the presumptions of symmetry and design which inform most house-building. It is as if someone were to re-arrange a face a little, perhaps by swapping the position of nose and mouth. A small alteration in design makes for a huge difference in perception.

Experiencing these obviously Cubist buildings and what makes them so distinctive will enable you to notice the careful geographical asymmetry of so many of Prague's other buildings, which you might not otherwise have noticed. That said, even though for this writer Cubism is one more glorious example of the way in which Prague teeters between the real and the surreal, there are those for whom the Baba Villa colony may seem like "a bunch of boxes on a hillside". To them I can certainly recommend the invigorating walk from the Hotel International!

Art Exhibitions in Prague

The National Gallery of Prague (Národní Galerie v Praze), like the State Jewish Museum, is a collective noun for nine separate exhibitions, eight of them in the centre of town (the ninth is the Museum of Modern Czech Sculpture at Zbraslav, about 16 km (10 miles) from the centre but well worth a visit on a fine day, since the sculptures are laid out "naturally" in the open-air gardens of this Baroque complex). The nine locations are:

1. The Sternberg Palace next to the main entrance to Prague Castle, which has a wide range of paintings from several periods.

2. Czech Gothic and Baroque Art in St George's Convent within Prague Castle.

3. 20th-century Czech painters in the Municipal Library in what is now Mariánské náměstí.

4. Graphic Art in the Golz-Kinský Palace in the Old Town Square.

5. The Museum of Modern Sculpture at Zbraslav.

6. The former Riding School opposite the Waldstein Gardens in Malá Strana which contains an exhibition of fine art and photography.

7. The Picture Gallery inside Prague Castle, which contains a relatively small collection of art from Renaissance to Rococo and tends to be shut.

8. The Belvedere summer house in the Royal Gardens beside the castle. This has only recently been renovated and at present the exhibition of Cubist art is in the Riding School opposite the entrance to the Royal Gardens. Try there first!

9. 18th-and 19th-century Czech art in the wonderful surroundings of St Agnes' Convent in the Old Town.

When you buy a ticket to any of these exhibitions you will find a map on the reverse side of it, which currently identifies where each of these nine venues is located (they are in Czech, but in the order given above, which therefore provides a translation unless they have changed since 1992). The three largest collections, however, are the Sternberg Palace and St George's Convent in the Castle area, and St Agnes' Convent in the Old Town area (1, 2 and 9 on the map on the back of your ticket). You should find them open on any day except Monday.

There are numerous art galleries in Prague which hold temporary exhibitions and promote the work of contemporary painters (some of whose paintings will be for sale). It is worthwhile browsing through some of these as well as visiting the formal galleries outlined above. It is also important to recognise that there is something of a travelling circus of modern art exhibitions since the Velvet Revolution liberalized artistic expression, and you should follow the advice given by up-to-date news-sheets when you arrive.

Theatre, Mime and Puppets

The controversially designed Nová scéna next to the National Theatre on Národní produces a range of modern plays (Tel. 20 62 60), whilst examples of the Magic Lantern technique can be found at Laterna Magika, Národní třída 40. Divadlo Semafor along one of the many alleyways off Wenceslas Square (number 28) has good performances of musical comedy and mime– and the café in the foyer is a fine place for a drink. Some of the performances spawned by Magic Lantern techniques are of poor quality and designed simply to please tourists with a few dancing girls and tricks. The All Colours Theatre at Celetná 17 (near the Old Town Square) would seem to fall into this category, and there will doubtless be many other examples in the 1990s. Much more effective are the performances at Klub Obchodu in the heart of Josefov (at Pařížská 4). If the superb Odysseus is still playing at the Palace of Culture, don't miss it. It is a fantastic example of Magic Lantern techniques.

There are performances of mime at the Braník Theatre at Branická 63, Praha 4 (Tel. 46 05 07), and at the studio of mime artist Boris Hybner at Národní třída 25. The entrance hall, bar and theatre are set out, like Beau Geste, with dummies as well as live patrons! The repertoire ranges from Concerto Grosso, a "catastrophic soirée", to Gagman, a slapstick story of the pioneer beginnings of Hollywood film work. Not to be missed.

There are over fifteen permanent puppet theatres in Czechoslovakia. Two examples in Prague are Spejbl and Hurvinek at Řimská 45, Praha 2 (tel. 25 16 66) and Říše loutek (Puppet Kingdom) at Žatecká 1, Praha 1 (tel. 232 34 29). And see what's on at the centrally placed Albatros at Na Perštýně 1.

The combination of play and film in Laterna Magika (Magic Lantern Theatre) should not be missed).

*P*uppetry is very popular in Prague, and there are many puppet shows for children and adults in the city.

There are several places which offer a range of arts activities, including jazz, poetry readings, contemporary opera, exhibitions and so on. Two to mention are Malostranská Beseda on the corner of Lesser Quarter Square (Malostranské náměstí), which has several rooms, often devoted to a variety of activities, and the smaller Viola at Národní 7.

This is only a small selection of what is available. For full listings, consult *The Prague Post* or *Prognosis*, which contains a very useful Visitors' Guide.

Film

Wenceslas Square is full of dubbed American blockbusters that many people will doubtless have gone to Prague to get away from. This is unfortunate, because Prague's Barrandov studios (now under threat of closure) produced a fine set of films in the 1960s, known as the Czech New Wave, and produced directors like Miloš Forman who went on to achieve international recognition. There are superb Czech animation films too, but you may find it difficult to see them in Prague.

If you do go to a film, watch out for those marked with a small square. They're the ones that have been dubbed into Czech.

Jazz and Folk

The Reduta Jazz Club (Národní 20, Tel. 20 38 25) is reputed to be Prague's best. It is certainly the most expensive, with an entrance fee of around 100 crowns. But its plush furniture and pictures (including the unmissable one in the bar of Duke Ellington with camels coming out of his head), make for a very pleasant atmosphere.

The Press Jazz Club (Pařížská 9), situated on the first floor of the Union of Journalists building, is like a huge barn. In fact it's a wonderful place—reached by a spiral staircase, not too much to get in (about 50 crowns), and the lofty walls sporting jazz photos and superb avant-garde French magazine posters. Because of its size you are likely to have little difficulty finding a table, and the place is open until 2.00 a.m. To top it all, the jazz, though more avant-garde than the Reduta, is wonderful. Don't miss it.

The Agharta Jazz Centrum (Krakovská 5), near the top right hand corner as you

*O*ne form of modern art? This is on a wall in the Malá Strana.

look up Wenceslas Square, has a record shop which never closes selling a range of jazz records and CDs, a coffee shop, cocktails and jazz from about 8.00 p.m. to midnight.

There is frequently jazz at the Supraclub (Opletalova 5), which is also close to Wenceslas Square, this time on the left hand side as you look up. The Jazz Art Club (Radiopalác, Vinohradská 40, Praha 2), is a bit further out from the centre but often has very good music.

Concerts of folk music from different regions are held at the *Municipal Library* (Mariánské náměstí 1), and in the summer there are often open-air performances, together with exhibitions of folk art, on Střelecký ostrov, one of the small islands in the middle of the River Vltava. The other island, Slovanský ostrov, has country and western music at week-ends.

The "Alternative Scene"

Prague has a few venues that have a wonderful "sixties" feel about them. One of the best is the Mamma Club (Elišky Krásnohorské 7) in Josefov. Started by a bunch of student journalists, it is locked into an R.E.M. time-warp, but if you don't mind it being a bit crowded at times there's a range of performances ranging from Allen Ginsberg poems with electrical guitar accompaniment to death-rock art

Equally sound, and usually rather quieter, is Borát at 18, Ujezd, just across the river on the Malá Strana side of the most Legii. Three floors of graffiti, posters, sound and drinks make for a relaxing time, and you will meet quite a few Czech people here. They don't play so much R.E.M. either.

If you fancy somewhere away from the centre, why not walk up the hill to Strahov and the student campus, where you'll find Strahov 007. The accent here is very much on punk music, and there's the odd live rock band. Nearer to home is the Rock Café at Národní 22, next to the Reduta Jazz Club.

Open till 5.00 a.m. is the Rock Club Bunkr spol., at Lodecká 2, near to the Square of the Republic. You can get in for under 50 crowns, and the music runs from about 9.00 p.m. through the night.

Nightclubs

Prague since the Velvet Revolution has developed its fair share of seediness to attract western businessmen with more money than sense. There are now strip-clubs and floor-shows along Wenceslas Square, inheritors of the time when seedy communist dignatories used to go along to the… strip-shows and floor-shows. The clubs are often loosely connected to various hotels along the Wenceslas Square boulevard where the businessmen are probably staying. The only saving grace is that the decor in one or two of these places has a certain charming decadence.

Having said that, there are a number of genuine night-clubs as well, although they tend to be tacky imitations of tackier western originals, and you sometimes have virtually to bribe the bouncers in order to get in.

The best night-club for a relaxed drink and dance, a mixed clientele of locals and visitors and a reasonable entrance fee is the F-Club. Like much else on Wenceslas Square it's semi-hidden. Look for the sign on the right hand side as you walk up the square-you pass along an alleyway and then downstairs to a cavernous basement in which an extraordinary stone alligator hangs pendulously from a wall, whilst low lights and mock stalactites give the impression of dancing in a cave. Open till 2.00 a.m.—and expect a lot of yesterday's hits (possibly including R.E.M.).

Buying Tickets

A number of Čedok offices will sell tickets for the main theatre and concert venues. The main office is at Na příkopě 18.

A new service for tourists is the Bohemia Ticket International, which provides tickets for a wide range of cultural events. There are three central addresses:

Na příkopě 16 (just off the bottom of Wenceslas Square).

25, Václavské náměstí (obviously on Wenceslas Square).

8, Karlova ulice (this is the main street in the Old Town running between the Charles Bridge and the Old Town Square).

Some hotels will also provide you with tickets.

Language Guide

The Slav languages are commonly regarded as very difficult, at least for those whose background lies in the traditions of Western Europe and America. Many visitors will prefer not to bother with learning Czech at all, but there are three good reasons for picking some up:

1. It will be appreciated by the people who live in Prague. Until the Velvet Revolution Russian was the second language (and many signs remain in the Cyrillic script of Russian), whilst a number of the older people speak German (a product partly of wartime invasion, and partly of the historical presence of a large German-speaking minority, particularly in the west of Czechoslovakia). Since 1989 there has been a rush to learn English, and many Czechs will welcome the chance offered by a large influx of English-speaking visitors to improve it. At the same time, however, a reciprocal effort to learn some Czech will be appreciated.

2. It's not that difficult. The sight of several cohabiting consonants without a vowel between them and the hordes of accents may be off-putting, but once the pronunciation has been mastered the grammatical structure is no more difficult than that of many more familiar languages.

3. There is no harm in being able to speak an attractive language, the language of much fine contemporary literature, and one which has sufficient similarities to Russian to make it easier in turn to learn that language too.

On a short trip it will only be possible to pick up a few key words and phrases. sections in which they would occur.

What is given here is a short summary of the most useful general words and phrases, plus a guide to pronunciation.

Pronouncing Czech

Vowels and Dipthongs

a (short a) like u in cut.
á (long a) like a in father

Practise with the Czech word for coffee-káva.

au pronounced like ou in out.

Practise with the Czech word *Automat*, a kind of snack-bar, eg Automat Koruna at the bottom of Wenceslas Square.

e (short e) like e in vet.
é (long e) like ai in pair.

Practise with *déle* meaning longer.

ě is pronounced ye as in yesterday.

It is common to see an e with a *háček* (pronounced Hah-Check), as the sign is called (it literally means "little hook"). For instance, "Thank you" in Czech is *Děkuji*, which is pronounced Dyeh-koo-yi. The common verb *dělat* (meaning "to do") is pronounced Dyeh-lat.

ie is pronounced as ě is pronounced.

i (short i) like i in slit.
í (long i) like ea in feat.
ý is pronounced as í.

Practise with the words *bílý* (meaning white) and *biftek* (meaning steak).

o (short o) like o in pot.
ó (long o) like o in lord.

Practise with *maso* (meaning meat) and *folklór* (folklore).

u (short u) like oo in book.
ů (long u) like oo in pool.

Practise with *ruka* (meaning hand) and *dům* (meaning house). Sometimes long u is written ú, as in *úloha* meaning task or role.

Consonants

A number have the same sound as in English. Those that don't are as follows:

c is pronounced "ts" as in "its". For instance *moc*, pronounced "mots", which means "very" or "too much" (a useful word if you want to say that you find something too expensive).

č is pronounced "ch" as in "cherub". For instance *klíč*, meaning "key", is pronounced "kleech".

ch is pronounced as in the Scottish "loch". For instance *chápat* meaning to understand. In Czech dictionaries, "ch" comes after "h".

d' is pronounced as in the English word "duped". For instance *d'ábel*, meaning devil, is effectively pronounced "Dyah bel".

g is always a hard sound, as in "get", never soft as in "gesture". Hence *galerie* and *gramofon* are pronounced with a hard "g" as in their English equivalents.

"j" is pronounced as the "y" in "yellow". Hence *jeden* meaning "one" (with a masculine noun) is pronounced "yeden". But note that before a consonant (e.g. *jsem* meaning "I am", or *nejsem* meaning "I am not") it is weakened or silent.

ň is pronounced like the "ni" in "onion". For example, *Číňan*, "Chinaman".

š is pronounced "sh" as in "shop". For example, *šest* (six), *šesty* (sixty) and *špatný* (bad, awful).

t' is pronounced like the "t" in "stew". For example *t'uk* meaning "clink". It is weakened at the end of a word—e.g. the Czech equivalent of Bon Appetit, *Dobrou chut'*.

ž is pronounced like the "s" in "pleasure", such as *žena* (woman), *držet* (to hold).

ř is hard to describe! Most people have at some time tried to pronounce the name of the composer Dvořák. Make the *ž* sound, then flatten the tip of the tongue as you do when making the *r* sound. Now try to combine the *r* and the *ž*! Examples are *řada* meaning "line" or "queue", *řeka* meaning "river" and *říjen* meaning "October".

Tips on stress

Always stress the first syllable of a word. Beware stressing the second syllable simply because it has a long vowel and the first syllable has a short one. For instance, don't pronounce *malý* (meaning small) as if the emphasis lay on the second syllable.

Basic Czech Vocabulary

A key thing to learn is that *ano*, sometimes pronounced jo or no, means yes! *Ne* means no.

Please	**Prosím**
Thank you	**Děkuji**
Thank you very much.	**Děkuji moc**
Man	**Muž**
Woman	**Žena**
Chlapec/Kluk	**Boy**
Dívka	**Girl**
Good day	**Dobrý den**

(a more friendly and informal equivalent of Hello is *Ahoj*).

Goodbye	**Na shledanou**
Good morning	**Dobré ráno**
Good evening	**Dobrý večer**
Goodnight	**Dobrou noc**
I understand	**Rozumím**
I don't understand	**Nerozumím**

Many words can be turned into the negative using ne- in this way (*eg jsem* and *nejsem*, I am and I am not).

Where?	**Kde?**
When?	**Kdy?**
Who?	**Kdo?**
What?	**Co?**
Why?	**Proč?**
Where is?	**Kde je?**

similarly *Kdy je, Kdo je* etc.

Excuse me	**Prosím/Promiňte**
Sorry	**Pardon**
How are you?	**Jak se máte?**

(*Jak se maš* is a more familiar way of asking, equivalent of occasions when you use

240

the German "du" or French "tu". Literally the sentence means How do you have yourself?).

Today	**Dnes**
Yesterday	**Včera**
Tomorrow	**Zítra**
At once, now	**Hned**
Later	**Později**
Never	**Nikdy**
Here	**Tady**
There	**Tam**
Everywhere	**Všude**

"This" and "that" depend on whether they describe a masculine, feminine or neuter noun. Use the masculine form "*ten*" or "*tento*" to say "this one" ("that one" is the same). But "*to*" will be used when the word "that" is used to refer in general rather than to a particular noun. For instance "that is good" will be "t*o je dobré*". "*To je*", meaning "That is" or "It is", is common. Eg "*To je pravda*" (It is true).

With	**S**
Without	**Bez**
How?	**Jak?**
But	**Ale**
And	**A**
Also	**Také**
A little	**Trocha**
A lot, very much	**Velice**
Large	**Velký**
Small	**Malý**
More	**Víc**
Less	**Méně**
Good	**Dobrý**
Bad	**Špatný**
Hot	**Horký**
Cold	**Studený**
To the left	**Nalevo/vlevo**
To the right	**Napravo/vpravo**
Near	**Blízko**
Far	**Daleko**
Push	**Tam**
Pull	**Sem**

Silly	**Hloupý**
Clever	**Chytrý**
Old	**Starý**
Young	**Mladý**
New	**Nový**
New Town	**Nové Město**
Old Town	**Staré Město**
Happy	**Šťastný**
Sad	**Smutný**
Heavy, difficult	**Těžký**
Light, easy	**Lehký**
Vacant	**Volný**
Reserved/Occupied	**Obsazený**
No entrance	**Vstup zakažan**
Entrance	**Vchod**
Exit	**Východ**
Emergency exit	**Nouzový východ**
Help!	**Pomoc!**
Stop!	**Zastavte!**
Sunday	**Neděle**
Monday	**Pondělí**
Tuesday	**Úterý**
Wednesday	**Středa**
Thursday	**Čtvrtek**
Friday	**Pátek**
Saturday	**Sobota**

Numbers—one is *jeden, jedna* or *jedno* depending on whether the noun it is attached to is masculine, feminine or neuter. Thus *jeden večer* means one evening, *jedna tužka* means one pencil, and *jedno divadlo* means one theatre.

Two is *dva* in the masculine, but *dvě* in the feminine and neuter.

Other numbers have the same form whatever the gender of the noun they are attached to.

Nought	**Nula**
One	**jeden/jedna/jedno**
Two	**dva/dvě**
Three	**tři**
Four	**čtyři**
Five	**pět**
Six	**šest**

Seven	**sedm**
Eight	**osm**
Nine	**devět**
Ten	**deset**
Twenty	**dvacet**
Fifty	**padesát**
A hundred	**sto**
A thousand	**tisíc**
January	**Leden**
February	**Únor**
March	**Březen**
April	**Duben**
May	**Květen**
June	**Červen**
July	**Červenec**
August	**Srpen**
September	**Zaří**
October	**Říjen**
November	**Lístopad**
December	**Prosinec**

Tools for Sentences

All that can be provided in a guide-book is help on basic words and phrases, with advice on pronunciation. To develop sentences you will have to learn some verbs and the way in which they decline. You should buy an introduction to the language for this—the best guide (which comes with a tape) is *Colloquial Czech* by James Naughton (published by Routledge).

To put your first sentences together, you need to know the declension of what in most languages is always the most irregular verb, the verb "to be". In Czech to be is "*být*", which declines *jsem* (I am), *jsi* (you are), *je* (he/she/it is), *jsme* (we are), *jste* (you are), and *jsou* (they are).

The subject pronouns are *já* (I), *ty* (you), *on* (he), *ona* (she), *to* (it, that), *my* (we), *vy* (you-plural), *oni* (they).

Já jsem Angličan: I am an Englishman.
Já jsem Angličanka: I am an English-woman.

Já jsem Čech/ Česka: I am a Czech man/woman.
Já jsem Američan/Američanka: I am an American man/woman.
Kde je Václavské náměstí? Where is Wenceslas Square?
Jste student? Are you a student?

Basic verbs like to have (*mít*), to do (*dělat*), and to see (*vidět*) are necessary for simple sentence construction. Here are a few sentences based on the verbs *mít* and *mluvit* (to speak):

Do you speak English?	**Mluvíte anglicky?**
Are there any rooms free?	**Máte volné pokoje?**
I understand a little, but I speak (the language) badly.	**Trochu rozumím, ale mluvím špatně**
I love you	**Mám tě rad**

(literally I have gladness in you).

It is useful to have a small, dictionary (*slovník*). Look out for "*Česko Anglický a Anglicko Český Slovník* (Czech English and English Czech Dictionary).

Useful Words and Phrases

Cheers!	**Na zdraví**
Can I have the bill, please	**Platit, prosím**
Is that seat free?	**Je to volno?**
cinema	**kino**
concert	**koncert**
theatre	**divadlo**
Could you get me tickets for...	**Můžete mi obstarat vstupenky na...**
I'd like to go to a concert.	**Chtěl bych navštívit koncert.**
closed	**zavženo**
open daily	**otevřeno denně**

General Food

boiled	**varený**

242

fried	**smažený**	*potato*	**brambory**
grilled	**na roštu**	*raspberry*	**maliny**
pickled	**nakládaný**	*salad*	**salát**
raw	**syrový**	*strawberry*	**jahody**
roast/baked	**(za)pečený**		
smoked	**udený**	***Favourite Courses***	
stuffed	**plněný**	*apple cake*	**jablkový koláč**
beef	**hovězí maso**	*apricot dumplings*	**merunkové**
bread	**chléb**		**knedlíkem**
butter	**máslo**	*fried carp with...*	**smažený kapr s...**

(don't confuse with *maso* meaning meat; and look out for *M.m* on menus meaning with butter)

		goulash	**guláš**
		mixed salad	**míchaným salátem**
		omelettes	**omeleta**
cheese	**sýr**	*potato soup with*	**bramborová**
chicken	**kuře**	*mushrooms*	**polévka s**
dumplings	**knedliky**		**houbami**
eggs	**vajíčka**	*pancakes*	**palačinky**
fish	**ryba**	*Prague ham*	**pražská šunka š**

(usually *kapr*, carp, or *pstruh*, trout)

ham	**šunka**	*roast ham with*	**zapačené šunka s**
mustard	**hořčice**	*asparagus*	**chřestem**
pasta	**těstoviny**	*roast pork with*	**vepřové se zelím**
pepper	**pepř**	*sauerkraut*	
pork	**vepřové maso**	*steak and eggs*	**biftck s vejcem**
salt	**sůl**	*trout in*	**pstruh na másle**
soup	**polévka**	*melted butter*	
sugar	**cukr**	*wiener schnitzel*	**vídeňský řízek s**
apple	**jabiko**	*with potato salad*	**bramborovym**
apricot	**meruňka**		**salátem**
		(with horseradish)	**(s křenem)**
banana	**banán**	*(with pickle)*	**(se okurkou)**
beans	**fazole**		
cabbage	**kapusta, zelí**	***Drink***	
carrot	**mrkev, karotka**	*beer*	**pivo**
cauliflower	**květák**	*brandy*	**koňak**
celery	**celer**	*coffee*	**káva**
grape	**hrozni**	*milk*	**mléko**
grapefruit	**druh citrusu**	*mineral water*	**minerální voda**
lemon	**citrón**	*tea*	**čaj**
mushroom	**houba, žampión**	*tap water*	**čistá voda**
orange	**pomeranč**	*wine*	**víno**
peach	**broskev**	*(white bílé; red černé)*	
pear	**hruška**	*dry wine*	**suché víno**
pea	**hrách**	*mulled wine*	**svařené víno**
plum	**švestky**	*wine and soda*	**vinný střik**

The Right Place at the Right Price

Hotels

Since the Velvet Revolution, Prague has seen a sudden increase in foreign visitors, and accommodation can be difficult to find at some times of the year, although it is getting easier as new hotels are being built. Listed below is a selection of hotels in three price bands. The first covers accommodation up to 2,500 crowns. In the second, prices will vary from about 1,250 to 3,000 crowns per double room per night. The third covers accommodation in luxury hotels with excellent facilities and will cost not less than 5,000 crowns per night for a double room. Cheaper accommodation, costing between 750 and 1,000 crowns per night can be found through one of the agencies listed on page 19, and

will involve self-catering in your own apartment. Another alternative listed on page 19 is to camp.

■ up to 2,500 crowns per double per night;
■■ 1,250 to 3,000 crowns per double per night;
■■■ about 5,000 crowns per double per night;

Hotel Adria ■
Václavské náměstí 26
Praha 1
Tel. 236 04 72
In the heart of Wenceslas Square.

Hotel Alcron ■■■
Štěpánská 40
Praha 1
Tel. 235 92 16
143 rooms. A luxury hotel just round the corner from Wenceslas Square. Plzeň regional cuisine is served in the restaurant.

Hotel Ambassador ■■■
Václavské náměstí 5
Praha 1
Tel. 22 13 51
114 rooms. Expensive hotel which overlooks Wenceslas Square. Good facilities and large entertainment centre within hotel.

Hotel Atlantic ■■
Na poříčí 9
Praha 1
Tel. 231 85 12
Fax. 232 60 77
60 rooms, 2 restaurants. Winter garden, Bar. Social hall Conveniently located close to shops and sights.

Hotel Atrium ■■■
1 Pobřežní St
Prague 8
Tel. 231 11 37
786 rooms, each equipped with mini bar, telephone and colour TV. Controversial new metal and glass construction. Biggest hotel in Czechoslovakia, built in 1991. About ¹/₂ km (1 mile) from the city centre. Restaurants, Swimming pool with bar and fitness centre.

Hotel Central ■■
Rybná 8
Praha 1
Tel. 6 40 54
Close to the centre of town.

Club Hotel Praha ■■■
Průhonice 400
Praha, 252 43
Tel. 72 32 41-9

*P*rague offers a range of choices, from the ultra-modern Hotel Forum to the more traditional Hotel Central shown opposite, and not forgetting the "botels" like the Albatros.

Very fine converted building in attractive parkland. Sports centre offering tennis (specialist coaching available), squash, swimming, bowling, sauna and massage. Two rooms for disabled visitors.

Motel Club ∎∎
252 Průhonice
Tel. 75 95 13
Located on main Prague–Brno road, 15 km (12 miles) from city centre. Swimming pool, sauna, nightclub.

Hotel Diplomat ∎∎∎
Evropská 15 (until recently Leninova)
160 000 Praha 6
Tel. (02) 3314 111
Fax. (02) 341 731
Business hotel, but tourists will also enjoy all comforts available. Car and limousine hire, fine food and fitness centre, night club. Disabled access and 5 rooms for disabled people. About 3 km (1¹/₂ miles) from centre.

Hotel Družba ∎
Václavské náměstí 16
Praha 1
Tel. 24 06 07 or 235 12 32
Small, central hotel.

Hotel Esplanade ∎∎∎
Washingtonova 19
Praha 1
Tel. 22 25 52
Fax. 26 58 97
Telex. 12 10 67
63 rooms. Secluded location not far from the National Museum and close enough to Wenceslas Square to give easy access to the beauties of Prague. One of Prague's best hotels.

Hotel Evropa ∎∎
Václavské náměstí 25
110 00 Praha 1
Tel. 236 52 74
104 rooms. Built in 1889 by Bělský. Original panelling, light fittings, glass and tiles. Art Nouveau gem. Charm and atmosphere.

Hotel Forum Praha ∎∎∎
Kongresová 1
140 69 Praha 4
Tel. 410 111
Fax. 42 06 84
Telex. 122 100
Glass and concrete space-age outfit, with all mod cons and a Peugeot 605 for limousine service. Beer-cellar, four-lane bowling, fitness centre, beauty parlour, hairdressing salon.

Hotel Hybernia ∎∎
Hybernská 24
Praha 1
Tel. 22 04 31
In the centre of town.

Hotel Inter-Continental ∎∎∎
Curieových náměstí
Praha 1
Tel. 28 00 111
394 rooms. Luxury hotel in heart of Josefov, overlooking the Vltava, a short distance from the Old Town Square. Very convenient. Excellent restaurant. Sauna. Fitness Centre.

Hotel International ∎∎∎
15, Koulova Street
160 45 Praha 6
Tel. 311 82 01 or 331 98 17
Fax. 311 60 31
Once the meeting place for visiting Soviet communist dignitaries. This marble and granite 1950s hotel now specializes in beer parties, folk music and brass band music. Czech cuisine. Unusual and very comfortable hotel. Situated about 3 ¹/₄ km (2 miles) from the city centre.

Hotel Jalta ∎∎∎
Václavské náměstí 45
Praha 1
Tel. 26 55 41
Fax. 26 53 47
Telex. 121 580
84 rooms. Small luxury hotel in the heart of Wenceslas Square. Excellent accommodation. International cuisine, Moravian wines. Renowned casino which plays in Austrian schillings with exchange office open all night.

Juniorhotel ∎
Zitna 12
Praha 2
Tel 29 99 49
Anyone under 30 can stay at this hotel, which offers very basic facilities and is often full of students.

Hotel Meteor ∎∎
Hybernská 6
Praha 1
Tel. 22 42 02
Central location near Republic Square. Standard accommodation. Restaurant.

Hotel Olympik ∎∎∎
Sokolovská 138
Praha 8
Tel. 82 85 41
317 rooms. Modern hotel near to the city centre. Fine international cuisine restaurant.

Hotel Opera ∎∎
Těšnov 13
Praha 1
Tel. 231 56 09
Basic facilities. Restaurant.

Hotel Palace ∎∎∎
Panská 12
Praha 1
Tel. 26 83 41
Exceptional hotel located just behind Wenceslas Square. Recently restored prestigious establishment. Once patronized by the European aristocracy. Superb dining. Buffet bar.

Interhotel Panorama ∎∎∎
Milevská 7
140 00 Praha 4
Tel. 416 111
Fax. 42 62 63
Telex. 123 576
432 rooms. French and Czech restaurants. Sauna and solarium. Swimming pool. Bars and restaurants. Night club.

Park Hotel ∎∎∎
Veletržní 20
Praha 7
Tel. 380 71 11
234 rooms. This is a modern hotel on the left bank. Conveniently located and very popular.

Hotel Paříž ∎∎
U Obecního domu
Praha 1
Tel. 236 08 20
Fax. 236 59 48
86 rooms. Recently renovated Art Nouveau gem. Very popular. Large restaurant. Situated near the Powder Tower.

Hotel Praga ∎∎
Smíchov
Plzeňská 29
Praha 5
Tel. 54 87 41 - 3
Within easy reach of Vila Bertramka. 47 rooms, 120 beds. Restaurant with Czech and international cuisine. Bar.

Hotel Praha ∎∎∎
Sušická 20
166 35 Praha 6
Tel. 333 8111/3306
Fax. 312 17 57
80 rooms, apartments and suites. Fifteen minutes' drive from city centre. Luxurious hotel in beautiful garden. Views of city. Grand Restaurant. Old Prague Beer Club. Sauna. Swimming pool. Tennis. Bowling.

Hotel Splendid ▮▮
Ovenecká 33
Praha 1
Tel. 37 54 51
Very good basic hotel situated on the left bank.

Motel Stop ▮▮
Plzeňská 215a
Praha 5
Tel. 52 11 98
Bar. Restaurant.

Hotel Tatran ▮▮
Václavské náměstí 22
Praha 1
Tel. 235 28 85
In the heart of Wenceslas Square.

Hotel Zlatá Husa ▮▮
Václavské náměstí 7
Praha 1
Tel. 214 31 11
72 rooms. Popular, busy hotel with entertainment complex.

Botels

If you fancy sleeping on the river, then you may be attracted to the idea of a "botel", although these "hotel barges" are not particularly cheap.

Botel Admirál ▮▮
Hořejší nábřeží
Praha 5
Tel. 54 74 45-9
Telex. 123 568
Bar and restaurant. Terrace, exchange office, souvenir shop.

Hotel Albatros ▮▮
Nábřeží Ludvíka Svobody
Praha 1
Tel. 231 36 00
Fax. 23 19 /84
Telex. 121 721
Bar and restaurant. Summer terrace, exchange office, souvenir shop. Close to city centre.

Botel Racek ▮▮
Na Dvorecké louce
Praha 4
Tel. 42 60 51-5
Telex. 122 202
Bar and restaurant. Terrace, exchange office, souvenir shop.

Karlovy Vary

Bristol Láseňské Sanatorium ▮▮▮
Sadová 19
360 98 Karlovy Vary
Tel. (017) 213 111/213 514
Luxurious accommodation. Spa and rehabilitation services, medical treatments and dental services in hotel. Wonderful cuisine, special diets. Fitness centre, tennis, sauna. Swimming pool. Helicopter sightseeing.

Hotel Dvořák ▮▮
Nová Louka 11
360 21 Karlovy Vary
Tel (017) 24 145
Fax. (017) 22 814
High standard accommodation with comfortable rooms. Excellent restaurant. Swimming pool, sauna, spa centre, fitness centre.

Grandhotel Pupp ▮▮▮
Mírové náměstí 2
360 91 Karlovy Vary
Tel. (017) 22121
Fax. (017) 24032
Established in 1701. Once patronized by the crowned heads of Europe. Beautiful setting. Large, luxurious hotel offering stylish accommodation and good facilities. Spa services available.

Restaurants

Expensive

The following restaurants are rather expensive. A good meal will cost more than 250 crowns per head. Remember to reserve a table as demand is high for the popular establishments.

Čínská Restaurace
Vodičkova 19
Tel 26 26 97
Open 12 noon to 3p.m., 6p.m. to 11p.m. Specializing in Cantonese and Szechuan cuisine, this restaurant is both fashionable and expensive.

Nebozízek
Petřinské sady
Tel. 53 79 05
Open 11a.m.–midnight. Beautifully located halfway up Petřín Hill. Astounding views of the Old Town and the Castle.

Parnas
Národní 1
Tel. 26 50 17
Open 7p.m.–1a.m. Candle-lit restaurant on the river's edge near the National Theatre.

U Malířů
Maltézské náměstí 11
Tel. 53 18 83
Open 11a.m.–3p.m. and 6p.m.–11p.m. Expensive. Recently taken over for French haute cuisine. Food and setting wonderful. Recommended for a "special occasion".

Vinárna U Sixtů
Celetná 2
Tel. 236 79 80
Open 12 noon–1a.m. Open late and conveniently situated near Old Town Square. Specializes in Moravian wines.

Vinárna u Zátiší
Liliova 1
Betlémské náměstí
Praha 1
Tel. 26 51 07
Open 11a.m.–3p.m. and 6p.m.–11p.m. Very fine range of international food

Moderately Priced

Good food and atmosphere without great expense. None of the below will cost you more than 250 crowns per head.

Berjozka
Rytířská 31
Praha 1
Tel. 22 38 22
Open 11a.m.–11p.m. The best place in Prague for Russian food.

Crazy Daisy
Vodičkova 9
Tel. 233 13 10
Open 10a.m.–11p.m. American restaurant featuring a very British red telephone box. Good relaxed atmosphere. Scores well on vegetarian dishes and salads.

Kalypso
Slezká 134
Praha 3
Greek cuisine. Closed Sunday and Monday.

Kosher Restaurant
Maiselova 18
Tel. 231 09 09
Open only for lunch, 11.30a.m. to 1.30p.m. Located in the heart of the Jewish Quarter.

Mayur
Štépánská 61
Praha 1
Tel. 23 69 92 2
Indian food available between 12 noon and 4p.m. and in the evening between 8p.m. and 11p.m. Closed on Sunday.

Myslivna
Jagellonská 21
Tel. 27 74 16
Popular restaurant specializing in venison and pheasant.

Palace Hotel Cafeteria
Panska 12
Open from 12 noon–9p.m. Good for vegetarians. Best salad bar in town. Self-service, non-smoking establishment with high standards.

Panorama
Part of the Palace of Culture, next to Vyšehrad metro
Tel. 417 21 19
Open 11.30a.m.–4p.m. and 5p.m.–11p.m. Located in modern functionalist building. Offers good views of Prague.

Rybárna
Rybárna *means fish restaurant, but may be limited to the favourites carp (*kapr*) and trout (*pstruh*).*
43, Wenceslas Square
Fish restaurant with snack-bar at entrance, Baltic Grill inside on the right, more expensive restaurant on the left.
On Gorazdova near the Rasinovo embankment there is a very atmospheric little fish restaurant, occasionally patronized by President Havel who lives in a nearby flat.

U Golema
Maiselova 8
Tel. 232 81 65
Open 11a.m.–10p.m. Cosy and intimate restaurant in the Jewish Quarter, with a range of Jewish specialities. Closed Sunday.

U Mecenáše
Malostranské námĕstí 10
Tel. 53 38 81
In the heart of the main square in the Lesser Quarter (Malá Strana), it offers a reasonable meal in medieval surroundings.

U Rudolfa
Maiselova 5
Praha 1
Tel. 232 26 71
Open 10a.m.–10p.m. Small but pleasant restaurant situated in the Jewish quarter .

U Šuterů
Palackého 4
Praha 1
Tel. 26 10 74
Open 11a.m.–midnight. Restaurant, "hunter's lounge", bistro, snack bar and wineroom in a stylistic setting.

U svatého Tomáše
Letenská 12
Located in the Malá Strana (Lesser Quarter). Former monastery serving dark beer (Braník 12). Traditional if not outstanding, Czech food.

Valdstejnska Hospoda
Valdstejnska námĕstí
Tel. 53 61 95
Open 11a.m.–3p.m. and 6p.m.–11p.m. Elegant and at the top end of this price range. The Prague Post *insists that it is recommended by the British ambassador.*

Vegetárka
Celetná 3
Tel. 232 46 05
Not strictly a vegetarian restaurant, but an easy-going cafe which specializes in beans, eggs, sausages and chips. Close to the Old Town Square.

Vikárka
Vikárská 6
Tel. 53 51 58
Very popular restaurant inside Prague Castle, opposite St Vitus' Cathedral.

Viola Trattoria
Národní 7
Tel. 235 87 79
Italian restaurant in the heart of the Old Town, not far from the National Theatre.

Vlatvaská Rybí Restaurace
Podolská 2
Tel. 43 11 90
Fish restaurant in the Vyšehrad district of town.

Vltava
Rašínovo nábřeží
Tel. 29 49 64
Open 11a.m.–10p.m. Situated right on the edge of the river.

Bar Que Huong
Havelska 29
Tel. 22 55 84
Specializes in Vietnamese food.

"Chicago's Famous Pizza"
Malé námĕstí 14 and
Jose Martiho 376
Praha 6
Fresh pizzas. Open from 11a.m.–10p.m., and if you want a home delivery ring 316 42 42.

Downstairs in Moskva
Na příkopĕ 29
Upstairs serves Georgian and Russian middle cuisine, whilst underneath "Arbat" delivers Russian fast food, including shashliks and kebabs from the southern republics.

Dům Potravin
(House of Food)
57 Wenceslas Square
(close to St Wenceslas' statue)
Open from 8a.m. to 8p.m. and offers a good, quick sit-down meal.

Globus
Dejvická 27
(in the Dejvice area)
Prague 6
Chinese restaurant open from 11a.m. to 11p.m.

Indian Snack Bar
Štĕpánská 63
(just off Wenceslas Square)
Open from 11 a.m. to 11 p.m. Vegetarians beware because bits of diced chicken get into every dish.

Mikulkás Pizzeria
Benediktská 16
Tel. 231 57 27
Wine bottles decorate the stucco walls to give the "Italian Bistro" feel. The spaghetti bolognese is particularly good, and so are the salads.

Sate Grill
Pohořelec
Praha 1
Good, cheap Indonesian fare can be consumed fast-food style between 10.30a.m. and 8p.m.

Cafés

Prague is a city which loves cafés. If your idea of a good day is to linger over a cup of coffee and perhaps a liqueur, discuss the changes, and watch the rest of the world pass by, here is a selection of places which should suit you.

Café de Colombia
Mostecká 3
Malá Strana
Open noon–midnight. Just off Charles Bridge in the Lesser Quarter Café with Gothic vaults provides refreshing Colombian coffee and a range of wines. A thick red cord across the entrance to regulate numbers may mean a short wait.

Café Slavia
Národní 1
Open daily 8a.m.–midnight. Selection of coffees, sandwiches and snacks, and alcoholic drinks. Ice-cream sundaes (pohár) are good in summer, mulled wine (svařené vino) is warming in winter. Popular meeting-place since it opened in 1863.

Evropa
25, Wenceslas Square
Open till 11p.m. The summer terrace is the "in" place to be seen on a summer night. Coffee and liqueurs. Interesting Art Nouveau interior. Breakfast from 10.30a.m.

Paris-Praha
Jindřišská (right opposite the main post-office close to Wenceslas Square)
A French delicatessen, at the back of which there's a small café. Good spot for morning coffee and French snacks. Next door is a chic little café selling coffee and alcohol until 9p.m., also part of Paris-Praha complex.

U Fleků
Křemencova 11
Praha 1
Tel. 29 24 36
Open until 11p.m. Seating (wooden benches) for over a thousand. Thoroughly kitsch, totally chaotic, but enormously popular. The famous dark Flek 14° beer is one source of attraction.

U Malvaze
(The Jug)
Open 10a.m.–9p.m. daily. A large wooden keg hanging above the door makes it instantly recognizable. A cosy haunt.

U Medvídků
(The Little Bears)
Na perštýně 7
Staré Město
Open 11a.m.–11p.m. Beer has been brewed here since the 13th century; the building dates from the 14th. Try the Budvar beer.

U Městské Knihovny
Valentinská 11
Staré Město
Open 10a.m.–11p.m. daily. Rough pine panelling and un-fussy chandeliers. It offers two light and one dark beer (Holešovice, Gambrinus and Smíchov). Pleasant atmosphere; cosmopolitan mixture of visitors and locals.

U Šumavy
Štěpánská 3
Open 9a.m.–10p.m. Relax underneath the wicker-shaded lamps in this locals bar, with "pub grub", smoky atmosphere and Budvar beer, the strongest in town, brewed in České Budějovice

U Vejvodů
Jilská 4
Staré Město
Open 10a.m.–10p.m. Arched windows, marble floors and pillars, wrought-iron chandeliers, domed ceilings and a slightly decayed air. Vegetarians should try the breaded cauliflower (květák). Local beer is Smíchov 12°.

U Zlatého Tygra
(The Golden Tiger)
Husova 17
Staré Město
Open 3p.m.–11p.m. weekdays. 13th-century cellars and a long history of artistic patronage, opened in the last century. Reputedly a favourite haunt of the President. Smoky, atmospheric place, full of locals.

Index

INDEX

INDEX

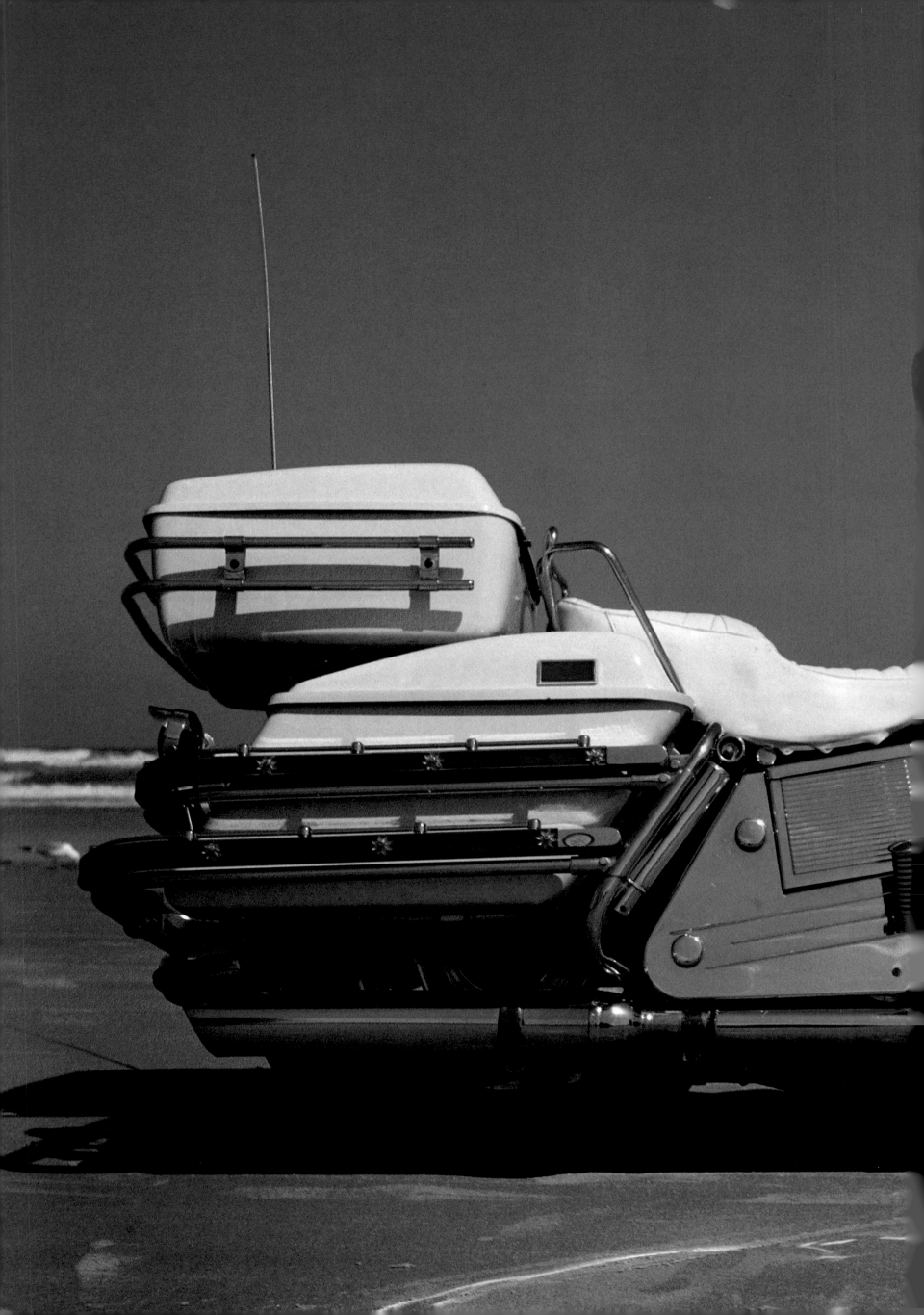

HARLEY-DAVIDSON

TONY MIDDLEHURST

MAGNA BOOKS

Published by Magna Books
Magna Road
Wigston
Leicester LE8 2ZH

Produced by Bison Books Ltd
Kimbolton House
117A Fulham Road
London SW3 6RL
England

ISBN 1-85422-014-4

Printed in Spain by Cayfosa Barcelona

Reprinted 1992

Page 1: Power and beauty...Rivera-carbed Evolution Low Rider ticks at rest after a leisurely cruise in the sun.

Pages 2-3: Archetypal Harley: the gold, chrome and white leather excess of a '76 Electra Glide in a classic setting – Daytona Beach.

Below: Everyone's dad knows at least one story about a guy who took despatches to the front line on one of these – the ever-dependable WLA45 (1942).

Contents

Introduction

I'll never forget my first ride on a Harley.

It was the back end of the 1970's, when the summers seemed so much hotter and the roads so much more open. I was a callow youth then, still buzzing with the adrenalin – and the disbelief – that came from having landed a job as assistant road tester on a motorcycle magazine. I'd been 'broken in' on a succession of mind-numbingly quick Japanese superbikes, until finally I was ready to be trusted with my first 'hog' – a cherry red 1000cc Sportster.

Nothing that I had sampled before could have prepared me for the other-worldliness of that Sportster. Crimson peanut tank set off by acres of chrome, crude V-twin motor leaping about (rather alarmingly, it seemed) inside an impossibly spindly frame, freeway forks plunging and heaving in protest at the English A-roads, rock-hard seat and suspension pummelling my spine . . . Right then, the Sportster seemed about as inaccurately named as any motorcycle could be. Agricultural, noisy, thirsty, uncomfortable – it was the ultimate in excess. And I loved it.

I loved it even when, less than two miles into what was supposed to be an uplifting ride down to the Sussex coast (shared by an at first reluctant lady passenger), the clip holding the exhaust pipes together fell off. One piece of bent wire and several burned fingers later, the bike sounded disturbingly like an ailing World War II bomber, but at least we were rolling again. The lady was less than impressed, so I cut my losses and headed home. Just as well, since the clutch lever was so unbelievably heavy that I had been in some serious doubt about the long-term health of my left wrist.

Before the Evolution motor came along in the early 1980s. it had never been an easy job defending Harleys against their many detractors. Things are different now, of course. Now H-Ds can stand comparison with a surprisingly wide cross-section of competitors. But in nearly ninety years of continuous manufacture, the world's most famous and charismatic motorcycle company has always had a devout following among motorcyclists who recognise (and can afford to pay for) that certain indefinable quality which sets the Milwaukee machines apart from the rest.

In my time on *SuperBike* magazine, I lost count of the number of times photographic sessions involving test Harley-Davidsons were interrupted by members of the public. Misty-eyed men seemed to appear from out of nowhere, each of them with an H-D anecdote to retell. No other test bikes ever aroused anywhere near the same level of awed curiosity as Harleys did.

I always listened to those fellows, on the basis that I'll end up the same way when I'm an old man . . . and then I'll need someone to listen to *my* anecdotes.

Did I ever tell you about the time I was riding an '84 Low Rider across the Arizona desert, for example? Now, *that* was an adventure . . .

Whether you're a racer or an antique collector, a loner or a club rider, there is a motorcycle with the words 'Harley-Davidson' written on the tank just waiting for you. Pictured here are the storming XR750 dirt trackers, the classic '30s knuckehead and the buddy seat and tank emblem which set all Harleys apart in a crowd.

Three Men and a Shed

History abounds with stirring 'rags to riches' tales of successes achieved through adversity, of triumphs snatched from the jaws of disaster, of fulfilments forged on the unlikeliest of anvils.

The Harley-Davidson story is a classic example of this genre. Despite two world wars and several economic depressions, both global and local, the world's most charismatic motorcycle manufacturer has survived intact, right through to the present day. In truth, to regard it as merely survival is to understate the magnitude of H-D's achievement over some ninety years of existence. The extraordinarily humble nature of the company's beginnings in the first decade of the twentieth century only serves to add extra poignancy to the robustly healthy situation in which Harley-Davidson now finds itself.

Despite the best efforts of ever more aggressive opposition, Harley-Davidson have flourished. Ironically, the springboard for the present prosperity – which could not have been predicted by the most optimistic of observers as recently as the 1960s – did not result from slavish pursuit of the 'if you can't beat 'em, join 'em' philosophy resignedly adopted in the 70s and 80s by other, non-Japanese motorcycle manufacturers. Rather, it has been secured through a dogged determination – at times perceived by industry pundits as bordering on the suicidal – to stick with the original values of strength and simplicity embraced by the factory founders all those years ago. Now, Harley-Davidson are well placed to move confidently towards the next century, building on their curiously traditional (some would say old-fashioned) range of motorcycles – and on one of the most potent product images in history.

This image, a particular quality exclusive to Harley-Davidson which is as hard to define as it is easy to recognise, has in the past formed the basis of countless treatises and dissertations by writers, academics, psychologists and even theologians. It is a quality spread over a wide canvas, defying categorisation and transcending all barriers. Old or young, enthusiast or antago-

nist, advertising copywriter or abbatoir cleaner – not matter what your social class or upbringing might be, the name of Harley-Davidson is almost certain to evoke some kind of response.

Like Band-Aids, Harleys have gradually assumed a near-generic identity in the public's mass consciousness. Even the frailest of grandmothers knows that a Harley-Davidson is a motorcycle; how many would know the same of a Kawasaki? At the other extreme, there are groups of diehards who refuse to acknowledge the existence of any other make of motorcycle, such is their blind allegiance to the Harley creed. And creed is not too strong a word in the opinion of those whose entire lifestyle is based on the near-religious experience of riding in a pack of thundering H-Ds. When it bites, the Harley bug bites deep.

It is unlikely that William S Harley or his ex-schoolchum Arthur Davidson anticipated such a degree of reverence being accorded to their products when, in 1903, they stood back to admire the first fully-mobile fruits of their labors. As so often seems to be the case with individuals and companies that later go on to achieve great fame, there were no shining beacons, flashes of light or thunderclaps of inspiration at the beginning of Harley-Davidson's history, no indications as to what might happen in the future. Few could have foreseen a time when decisions concerning the future of Harley-Davidson would be taken by no less a personage than the President of the United States, so great would be the importance attached to what had by the 1980s become one of the most sacrosanct of America's national institutions.

Interestingly enough, although Harley-Davidsons have always been ranked right up alongside apple pie and bald eagles in terms of their 'American-ness' – even the corporate logo is an unashamed clarion call to patriotism – the American lineage of both Harley and Davidson could hardly have been shorter. William Harley was born in Milwaukee in 1880, son to one of the many couples who had emigrated from England (in Harley's case, from

Left: Walter Davidson Snr with one of the early singles which helped build H-D's reputation as a manufacturer of sturdy (if somewhat unadventurous) machines in the early part of this century.

Right: Bill Harley's engineering skills were honed in a Milwaukee pedal cycle factory before he made the big jump to motorisation. This early publicity shot, taken outside Hirsch's Harley dealership in Seattle, acknowledged and paid homage to this heritage.

Previous page: If the lack of brakes didn't kill them, the punctures caused by wood splinters probably would. . . . American board-racing velodromes in the 1910s and '20s were battlegrounds for only the bravest Harley men.

the industrial north-west) at around that time. Arthur Davidson's American antecedence was just as shallow, his parents having shipped out from Aberdeen, Scotland only ten years before his birth in 1881. His was a family of three boys and two girls; all three brothers would go on to become founder members of the Harley-Davidson Motor Company.

But that was later. In the beginning, it was Arthur Davidson and Bill Harley who fired up the operation. With hindsight, bearing in mind their shared interests in bicycles and in the still new four-stroke internal combustion engine, it was perhaps inevitable that they would form a partnership to produce motorcycles. And yet, in another of these strange and unexpected twists which shape the genesis of great companies and institutions, it appears from the scanty records extant from this period that boats came before bikes in the history of Harley-Davidson.

The crucial turn of fate which effectively ushered in the H-D dynasty was Bill Harley's decision to sharpen up his fitter's skills (which up to then had been put to good use in one of Milwaukee's bicycle works) by taking up a draftsman's apprenticeship at the nearby Barth Manufacturing Company. Already holding down a patternmaker's job at the same metalworking shop was Arthur Davidson.

Their schoolboy friendship was quickly rekindled, as was their mutual interest in the outdoor life. Lying on the western banks of lake Michigan, hard by many other smaller lakes, Milwaukee was a handy base of keen anglers like Bill and Art. The two teenagers made numerous fishing trips together in a small rowboat, regretting only the fact that their sphere of activity was necessarily limited by their boat's restricted range. The prime fishing areas, in the outlying tributaries and deep water zones, were always out of reach.

At this time, in the final years of the nineteenth century, the dominant and most copied automotive engine was the seminal four-stroke single created in 1895 by Frenchmen Count Albert de Dion and Georges Bouton. Also at this time, as luck would have it, another (rather less well-known) European was working at Barths. There was nothing particularly extraordinary or remarkable about Emil Kruger. He was German, but then so were many of the men who had left Europe in the late nineteenth century to look for fame and fortune in America's 'boiler room', the north-central industrial heartland of Wisconsin, Illinois and Michigan.

What made Kruger interesting to the two young men from Milwaukee was the fact that he had brought with him some detailed construction plans for a De Dion-type engine from Aster, his previous employers in Paris. With Kruger's cooperation, Harley and Davidson set to work building a short series of motors, culminating in one which turned out to be a more than adequate power source for their fishing boat.

Although this was their first and last direct involvement in the marine world, the watery connection did not disappear entirely. While working on separate freelance engineering assignments prior to the formation of the Harley-Davidson Motor Co., Arthur Davidson collaborated extensively with another young engine 'nut' by the name of Ole Evinrude. The Evinrude badge would later become synonymous with powerful outboard motors for sports and leisure marine craft.

Back in 1900, having cracked the fishing problem, Harley and Davidson were turning their attentions back towards dry land, and specifically towards the commercial potential of a motorised bicycle. Reasoning, with some justification, that they were unlikely to reach a standard any lower than that already being displayed by a disturbingly large number of 'get-rich-quick' manufacturers, whose expertise seemed to lie more in the fields of charlatanry and intrigue than in engineering, Bill and Arthur began to develop their own engines, based once more on Kruger's Aster/De Dion plans.

Arthur's parents proved supportive of their son's ambitions. This was fortunate, since all the development work was going on inside their respectable middle-class Milwaukee home. Art's elder brother Walter, up to then working as a railroad machinist in the great empty wastes of the central United States, got wind of all the feverish activity and decided in 1902 to return to the homestead for a piece of the action, albeit in a part-time role. This 50 percent boost to the staff complement was both helpful and at the same time awkward, since it put near-intolerable extra strain on the already cramped working conditions.

Harley was able to come up with some temporary relief in the shape of a friend's workshop. That was enough to bring about the existence, in the spring of 1903, of the first fully-functioning cycle powered by a Harley-Davidson motor — or at any rate, by a motor bearing the name of Harley-

Above: A typical 5-35 type single, as produced in considerable numbers (and with little modification) between 1904 and 1918. Relatively good silencing and a conservative paint scheme earned it the nickname 'Silent Gray Fellow'.

Right: Indian's high-tech racers were a thorn in Harley's flesh for decades. This confident pilot is about to try his luck at Brooklands in 1911.

Davidson on its crankcase. The engine broke no new ground; it was a conventional single, featuring the so-called 'atmospheric' valve arrangement typical of the day (the valves' function being controlled purely by the movement of gases inside the combustion chamber). It displaced around 400cc. This power unit was fitted into its guinea-pig cycle frame by the simple expedient of bolting it into the space beneath the crossbar, a logical design whose precedent had been successfully set one year before by George Hendee and Oskar Hedstrom in Springfield, Massachusetts in the construction of the first 'Indian' motorcycle.

Although the concept was admirable in its simplicity, it soon became clear to the H-D men that an arrangement where the power source was considerably more potent than that of the average human being's leg muscles invariably brought destructive forces to bear on the bicycle's now-overstressed parts. Breakages were frustratingly frequent in the early stages of testing, and the situation was in no way improved by the imperfect condition of American roads at the time.

Assuming they were of serious intent, and wishing to sell machines in the long as well as the short term, would-be motorcycle builders at the beginning of the century had little choice but to embrace the worthy principles of strength and simplicity. Apart from the obvious need to build something that would survive for more than a few minutes, there was precious little else in the way of foundations on which to build. The automotive industry in general was still in its nascent stage, with only minimal technological trickle-down to the even younger two-wheeled market. The best that an honest motorcycle maker could hope for was to acquire a reputation for reliability in a world scourged by appalling road surfaces and infested by fly-by-night shysters out for a quick buck.

That first Harley-Davidson was designed by chief engineer Bill Harley (the only college graduate among the founders), and built up by Walter Davidson, using patterns made by his brother Arthur. Though much effort was put into getting the machine up and running, an apocryphal tale still persists to the effect that this cycle was not immediately regarded by its creators as the progenitor of a long line of motorcycles intended for sale to the general public. Indeed, legend has it that the partners only began to see the commercial

possibilities when a mutual acquaintance asked them to build another 'Harley-Davidson' for his personal use.

Given the single-minded and concerted fashion in which the three men went about their task, with literally months of experimentation, fabrication and aggravation being capped by a not insignificant testing program on local roads, this admittedly attractive yarn is difficult to credit. The hard-headed approach displayed in later years by the company in regard to business matters tends to confirm the alternative that the founders knew exactly what they were doing all along. It is also a fact that both Bill Harley and Arthur Davidson were avid consumers of whatever information they could find within the covers of automotive and scientific journals. Harley in particular, with his level-headed attitude and better education, would certainly have been all too aware of the shortcomings of contemporary motorcycles and, by extension, of the yawning gap in the market that was so obviously waiting to be filled by a workmanlike and reliable offering.

The major problem with the first H-D machine was the fact that it was a compromise, designed and built as a motorised bicycle rather than as a true motorcycle. The drawbacks of this concept became all the more apparent when a more powerful, 25 cubic inch (420cc) version of the first engine was shoehorned into the by now severely overstressed frame. Still, the new motor proved to be a powerful and reliable enough base unit on which to build for the next three years, and was initially installed in H-D's first 'proper' motorcycle chassis which made its debut in the latter part of 1903.

Only one example of this, Harley-Davidson's first real motorcycle, was built. Although the original machine has long been lost to posterity, reconstructions still exist in museums. The most obvious advantages this revised model had over the prototype were in the area of wheelbase dimension (sensibly extended for better stability), and in the general beefing-up of the steering head and wheel bearings, the frame tubes, and the wheels. Final drive fol-

lowed the fashion of the day, being a leather belt which could be tightened or slackened by the rider in order to modulate the degree of grip on the large diameter rear sprocket (thereby altering the rate of forward progress).

The fuel tank hung from the crossbar, again an utterly conventional move. George Hendee's 1902 Indian, by contrast, featured a gas tank mounted in a novel position atop the rear fender. Throughout the fifty-year rivalry between H-D and Indian, the Milwaukee products would always be cast in the durable, slightly plodding role, while the Springfield machines had an altogether more glamorous and sporty image. The tortoise eventually triumphed over the hare, however, the 1953 demise of Indian bringing to an end that firm's glittering record of race wins and technological innovation.

Upon completion of the first 'real' Harley-Davidson, things suddenly began to happen. Over the winter of 1903-04, orders for two more models were fulfilled by the Davidsons, now operating out of a soon-to-be-enlarged 15ft by 10ft shed which had been erected by their father in his own back garden. Walter Davidson committed himself full-time to the fledgling business, and four more part-timers were taken on in early 1904 to help cope with the steadily increasing flow of orders. Bill Harley meanwhile had gone back to school to the University of Wisconsin in order to brush up on and redirect new engineering techniques back into the motorcycle's development process.

By 1905, production was up to eight machines a year, and even the extended shed was proving impossibly small. Once again, the Davidson family came to the rescue, the cost of a purpose-built factory site in Milwaukee being met by an uncle, James McLay. This was the turning point in H-D's history. From eight bikes in 1905, production shot up to 49 bikes in 1906, and tripled every year thereafter until 1910, at which point well over 3000 machines per annum were passing through what eventually became known as the Juneau Avenue works.

Below left: Ohio's 980cc Flying Merkel V-twins occasionally split the warring H-D and Indian racers in the 1910s. Braking systems were regarded by some as unmanly. . .

Right: . . .particularly on board racers like this H-D twin, where every pound shaved off the weight meant a little more speed. This example might be thought a trifle over-restored.

By this time, the only Davidson brother still remaining outside the family firm had also joined up. William A Davidson, the eldest of the three, had already acquired a reputation for hard but fair treatment of the men who had been working under him in his previous position as a foreman on the Chicago & Milwaukee Railroad. His new job at H-D of Vice President and Works Manager helped free up more of Arthur Davidson's time, allowing him to move into the increasingly vital area of sales promotion, where he spared no efforts in exploiting the public's hunger for mobility at a time when motor cars were still prohibitively expensive.

He was also able to make some capital out of the fact that Harley had concentrated on refining and improving the solitary model in their 'range', rather than taking the risky route attempted by some other manufacturers – often with disastrous results – of wholesale development and release of several models at one time. The inevitable consequence of such a shortsighted policy was that the image of motorcycling as a whole suffered, with riders often to be seen marooned at the side of the road, let down by poor quality machinery.

Not helping with this image problem was the inadequate silencing tacked onto many of the big single-cylinder bikes of the age. Here was one area in which Harley-Davidson had been especially careful, reasoning (again, quite rightly) that customers were more likely to be attracted by silence than scandal. If they wanted to soup up their machines later on by sawing a length off the exhaust pipe, well, that was their choice. But Harley-Davidsons would all chuff along quietly when they came out of the factory; that was the management's choice. As was the color, an inoffensive swathe of grey relieved only by the founders' names and the odd pinstripe, a scheme which gave rise to the H-D's popularly adopted sobriquet of 'The Silent Gray Fellow.' This nickname stuck with the factory for many years.

Despite the factory's efforts to promote its cycle as nothing more than a rugged and reliable mode of transport, many of the more intrepid owners were using these valuable attributes to good advantage in the excitingly new and challenging arena of motor sport. Although H-D did not actually frown on this practice, neither did they do anything to encourage it. The factory attitude to competition in general eventually evolved into a high state of mean-spiritedness, and became the cause of much disgruntlement among those private racers who were expert enough to bring favorable publicity to the marque without so much as a cent's worth of works assistance.

Nonetheless, the company was not averse in the early days to putting its own products to the test. In 1908 Walter Davidson, who by this time had been appointed President and General Manager of the recently incorporated company (Bill Harley being the Chief Designer and Engineer, and Arthur Davidson the Secretary and General Sales Manager) decided to have a bash at the newly-formed Federation of American Motorcyclists' inaugural 'Endurance Run.' The route began at Catskill, New York, and took in Brooklyn, before finishing with a circumnavigation of Long Island. Plodding along in typically methodical style, Walter completed the course with a perfect score, beating 83 other riders on 21 other marques in the process. He then went on to take part in the FAM's Economy Run on the same machine, recording no less than 188mpg en route to victory.

The original 3 horsepower H-D had by then been on the streets for some six years. Bill Harley, returning from his successful spell at university, announced that it was time for an upgrade. By boring and stroking the motor to a new capacity of 35 cubic inches (around 575cc) and reinforcing the sprung front forks, Harley had his upgrade ready in time for a 1909 launch. It went under the model name of 5-35, reflecting the new horsepower rating as well as the piston displacement.

More significant by far, however, was Harley's other project, which involved the grafting onto the 5-35's crankcases of a second cylinder, at a 45 degree angle to the first. The V-twin idea was not a new one; the first Isle of Man TT race, held two years earlier in 1907, had been won very easily by Rem Fowler on a Peugeot-engined Norton employing this same format. Harley-Davidson had immediately noted the potential of such a layout, and had been tinkering with a mule engine of their own since Fowler's victory, but difficulties with the atmospheric inlet valve system had delayed the entry of a feasible production model.

By 1909, a solution had been reached with the fitment of mechanically activated valves – and the way was suddenly made clear for a whole new chapter to open up, not just for Harley-Davidson, but for motorcycling itself.

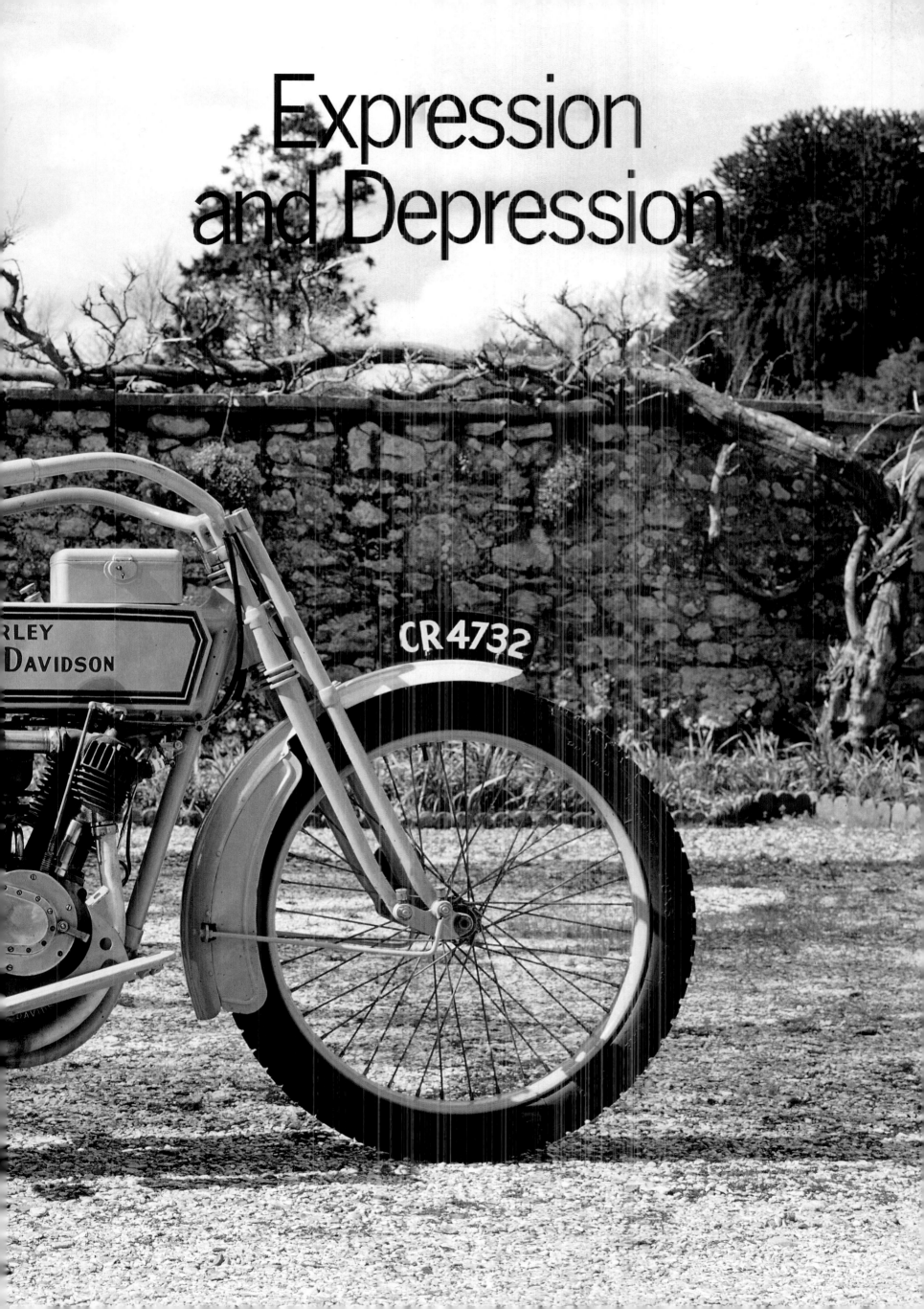

Expression and Depression

The heart of any motorcycle is generally held to be its engine. Before the current era of fully-enclosed machines, it was always the art of motorcycle designers not just to integrate the power unit into the bike's overall styling, but to highlight it, draw attention to it, and turn it into a statement of the company's philosophy.

No manufacturer has succeeded so well in this totemisation game as Harley-Davidson. Harley equals V-twin; V-twin equals Harley: it's taken as read. Hardly surprising, considering the fact that V-twins have been exiting Milwaukee in an unbroken stream since 1909, first with the F and then in 1911 with the renowned J.

The appeal of the V-twin was clear enough in those early days. In exchange for a relatively small weight penalty, the single-cylinder engine's power capability could be increased by as much as 100 percent. In North America, with its vast travelling distances and thinly scattered law enforcement agencies, this feature alone was enough to convince motorcycle showroom browsers (many of whom were young and devil-may-care) that V-twins were the only way to go.

There was no shortage of choice in the market by the time Harley-Davidson moved into it. All the big domestic manufacturers – Indian, Excelsior, Flying Merkel – had at least one big 45 degree vee on their books, and all were doing well by them. There were disadvantages associated with this format, quite apart from the extra weight (which in any case was seen as a plus point by riders all too accustomed to being bounced out of the saddles of their lightweight singles).

The major negative was undoubtedly the V-twin's inherent vibration at higher engine speeds. By way of compensation, the excellent low-end performance more than made up for this shortcoming. With high gearing fitted to maximise the easy cruising properties of a luxuriant torque curve, the vibration could, to all intents and purposes, be relegated to the status of a minor annoyance.

With one cylinder lying directly behind the other, and hence out of the cooling airstream, the provision of copious finning on the cylinder barrels was even more critical on the V-twins than it had been on the singles. The practical effect of this was to restrict the potential for engine enlargement via the normal route of increasing the cylinder bores; there simply was not sufficient room between the pots to expand in that direction. Instead, significant capacity increases could only be gained by the more involved method of lengthening the stroke, a technique which certainly resulted in even better bottom end response, but only at the expense of a rather limited ability to rev out at the top end. Almost all of the American companies quickly came to the conclusion that the best compromise between smoothness and power in a V-twin was to be had in an engine capacity of 61 cubic inches (1000cc) – a size which remains popular for V-twins even now.

Previous page: The J model was perhaps Harley's best-liked. Its 18-year production run ended in 1929.

Right: A closer look at the J's 61 cubic inch (1000cc) engine, here shown in a 1915 model. The classic 45-degree angle between the cylinders is still a major feature of Harleys going into the 1990s.

Below: A 1920 advertisement for the J from Britain's *Motor Cycle* magazine.

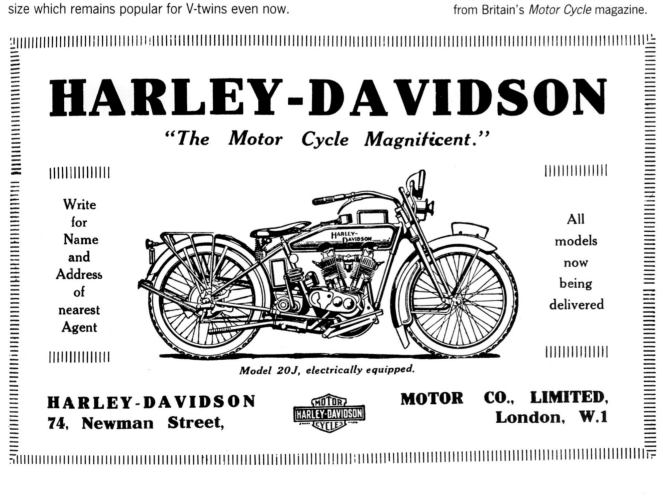

Left: Smooth-running four cylinder machines like this 1914 Henderson posed a threat to Harley's vibey twins, but H-D chose not to respond with a four of their own.

Going into the second decade of the century, the mushrooming popularity of competitive motorcycle sport, particularly on the new board tracks and dirt ovals, underlined the timeliness of H-D's move into big twins. Not that the factory officially approved of this trend, of course; at least, not if sponsorship was being requested. Their support remained confined to the more sedate world of reliability trials and the like, highlighting with some justification the less overtly sporting strengths of their motorcycle.

Number one rivals Indian, meanwhile, were profiting from H-D's reticence, enjoying success after success on racetracks around the world. Events in 1911 were symptomatic of the two firms' different attitudes. While Indian were sweeping the board at the Isle of Man Tourist Trophy races in June, the feathered headdress emblems shining proudly on the fuel tanks of the first three machines home, Harley-Davidson were busy putting the finishing touches to a primitive 'idler' mechanism, designed to allow manual disconnection of the drive to the rear wheel at temporary halts.

Although H-D were publicly criticised by dealers and racers alike for what was seen as their unenterprising and poor-spirited policy of non-involvement in racing, the fact of the matter was that H-D's ordinary street machines were – like every other manufacturer's, if they were honest enough to admit it – in sore need of basic development. Advances like the idler mechanism were of direct benefit to the ordinary H-D rider, who up to that point had been obliged to pedal-restart his machine after all but the very briefest of stops.

Nonetheless, the factory's view that a dollar spent on research and development in the workshop was better than a dollar spent on funding the antics of a bunch of speed-crazy fools, was one that was destined to change, in spite of the unyielding dogmatism which was being displayed by H-D's founders at this time.

More useful advances were made in 1912, particularly in the transmission department. The inclusion in the specification of a multiplate clutch allowed the factory to replace the 8E V-twin's unreliable old leather belt (which nevertheless continued to appear on the single until 1914) with a far more trustworthy chain.

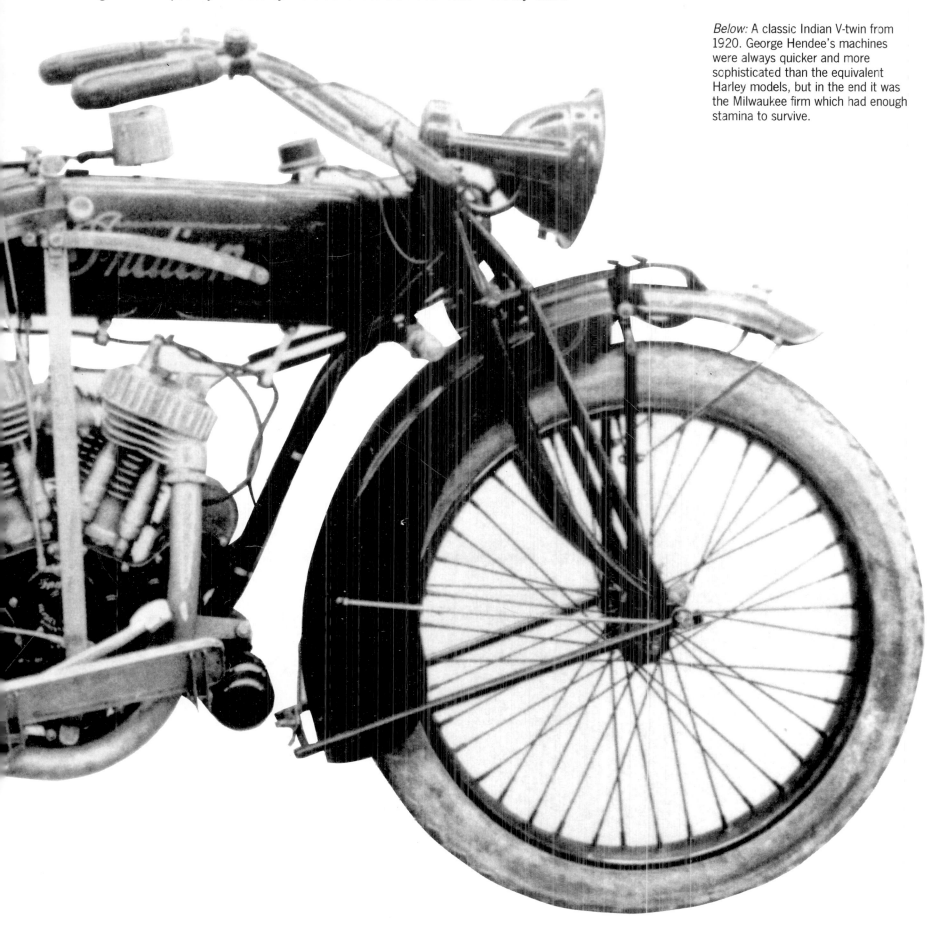

Below: A classic Indian V-twin from 1920. George Hendee's machines were always quicker and more sophisticated than the equivalent Harley models, but in the end it was the Milwaukee firm which had enough stamina to survive.

Meantime, the Milwaukee factory was continually growing to keep pace with the public's apparently insatiable demand for cheap transport. Sidecars were particularly popular. By 1912, annual production was up to more than 10,000 machines, and Arthur Davidson's unstinting efforts to build up a comprehensive dealer network were beginning to bear fruit, with Harleys becoming increasingly common on roads in the more remote parts of the United States.

Inevitably, booming sales of street bikes only served to stimulate still further the activity on the nation's racetracks. Harley-Davidson's detached stance in this area was becoming more and more inappropriate; so much so that in 1913 the founders were finally forced to accept the need for change. They engaged the services of William Ottaway, ostensibly as Assistant Engineer under Bill Harley, but in reality as the head of a newly created racing department.

Ottaway's credentials were impeccable. Up to that time he had been responsible for the production of the highly competitive 'White Thor' racers for the rival Thor Motorcycles group. His new brief at Milwaukee was to extract more power from H-D's existing engines, while Bill Harley addressed the long overdue matter of designing the two-speed gearbox that would be essential for racing. Ottaway quickly vindicated the founders' decision to hire him, not only by bumping up the 1000cc V-twin's power output, but also by putting together an all-new, limited edition competition bike – the 11K. This machine, incorporating all of Ottaway's tuning modifications in a purpose built light-weight chassis, went on to thrust Harley-Davidson straight into the forefront of motorcycle racing – quite a jump for a company which had up to that point shown no interest in such frippery.

The 11K almost made a sensational debut at the inaugural 300 Mile Classic race on Dodge City's two-mile track in July 1914, H-D's works rider Walter Cunningham storming into the lead at the 100-mile point ahead of well-established riders on rather more distinguished machinery. Glen Boyd prevented the upset by taking the chequered flag on one of George Hendee's all-conquering eight-valve Indians, but only after Cunningham had been sidelined by chain and spark plug problems while still in the lead. The well-drilled Harley teamsters continued to show good form in the remaining 1914 season races, doing everything bar actually winning. That pleasure would have to wait until 1915, a year which marked the start of a long spell of success by the works 'Wrecking Crew' team, sweeping all before them on Ottaway-designed eight-valve versions of the 11K racer.

It was a shame that H-D's overdue blossoming as a performance-orientated motorcycle company coincided with two epochal events which shaped the destinies of ordinary people all over the world. Despite its name, the first of these events – the World War – in some ways had less direct effect on the American people than did the second, which was full implementation of production line techniques by the automobile manufacturer Henry Ford. Almost overnight, motor cars became affordable for the common man; at the same time, warning bells began to sound for those motorcycle manufacturers

Top: Harleys were used extensively by the American forces of law and order, often because they were somewhat cheaper than rival machinery. This is a typical 1916 squad.

Left: In the same year, the US Expeditionary Force found a use for Harleys in Mexico, for the pursuit of famed bandit Pancho Villa.

Right: One of Milwaukee's less popular releases, the fore-and-aft 584cc 'W' flat twin, which ran from 1919 to 1922.

Left: Though the 'W' Sport Twin was a reasonable attempt at cashing in on a format which was popular in Europe, it proved too unexciting for the power-hungry USA market.

Right: Harley's big Milwaukee plant on Juneau Avenue, seen here in the latter part of the 1920s, was the subject of many expansion programs after its humble start in 1906.

Below right: Claude Temple enjoyed many successes on H-Ds outside of his own career as a motorcycle manufacturer. He won this 1921 Brooklands race at an average speed of 92.37mph.

whose prosperity had been founded on the relative cheapness of their products. The gradual weeding-out process affecting the weaker American marques gathered pace as war conditions severely restricted the importation from Europe of ancillary items not then produced by the native industry.

Indian, at that time the biggest motorcycle firm in America, suffered greatly in the war from self-inflicted wounds caused by the commitment of too great a proportion of their total output to military motorcycle production. In keeping with their conservative traditions, Harley-Davidson adopted a more circumspect posture. By offering a much smaller portion of their output to the government, they were able to maintain a healthy home market. Indeed, by exploiting Indian's short-sightedness, H-D were able to expand their agency network by poaching many of the Springfield company's under-supplied and understandably disaffected dealers.

When the war ended in 1918, Indian's home market had been effectively plundered. Harley-Davidson had improved their own position relative to Indian, such that the two companies were now very much on an equal footing with around 1000 dealers each. Detecting a bright future ahead, H-D's founders authorised another factory expansion programme in readiness for what they expected to be a doubling up of production from their sub-20,000 annual output during the straitened war years.

To take maximum advantage of the new trading conditions, the faithful old Model 9 single, the 'Silent Gray Fellow', was discontinued in 1918, to be replaced in 1919 by a totally new model. The horizontally-opposed 37 cubic inch (600cc) Model W 'Sport Twin' was a Douglas lookalike, aimed squarely at Indian's highly rated Scout lightweight.

Unfortunately, and not for the last time, the market had been misjudged by Harley-Davidson. American motorcyclists were still in love with the big, fast 'Model J' V-twin. The Sport Twin was not what they wanted at that time, being rather slow and uninspiring. It sold reasonably well in H-D's recently created European export market, its abstemious consumption of fuel being perfectly suited to the depressed post-war conditions, but the home market dictated its early demise in 1922 – a year which turned out to be one of the worst in the American motorcycle industry's short history.

As the 1920s began, Henry Ford's master plan to swamp the country in a tidal wave of black Model Ts was already well advanced. Waking up to the threat, the other big players in the US auto industry launched a counterwave of competing econo-cars. This was all very bad news for the bike firms, whose fortunes immediately nosedived as precipitously as Ford's had soared. The problem was that the role of motorcycling had suddenly changed from that of essential transport provider into a far less crucial one based on leisure. The sea-change was partly attributable to the bike manufacturers' own realignment towards competition in the mid-1910s. Many of Harley-Davidson's older and wiser employees predictably saw this as a belated vindication of Harley's much-criticised pre-war position on non-involvement. Nobody had foreseen the threat from Ford, nor the transformation it wreaked on the world of transport; accordingly, nobody had made any plans to reposition the motorcycle in the marketplace.

Ironically enough, Harley-Davidson's race team were by this stage breaking records at board and oval meetings all over the country, including the posting of the first ever 100mph-plus team victory at the Fresno, California track in early 1921. The 'Crew' also won the fifth Dodge City 300 Mile event in that same year. But the parlous economic conditions, combined with the futility (and expense) of attempting national domination over the still-strong Indian and Excelsior-mounted opposition, finally forced H-D to pull out of racing altogether at the end of 1921. The announcement was made by President Davidson in a circular release to Harley dealers: 'We find that we have become engaged in two distinct businesses at the factory; one, the business of racing, with a complete separate organisation, and the other, the legitimate business of making and selling motorcycles.'

A ruthless program of cost-cutting came into immediate effect, not just in the racing department, whose staff were literally disowned in the middle of a race meeting, but right throughout the entire company. If H-D were badly off, Indian were in a terrible state, their 1920 production figure of 20,000 being slashed to less than 7000 the following year. Both firms somehow staggered through to 1922, albeit in a severely trimmed state.

To avoid further blood-letting, a truce was arranged between the two companies. Over lunch in New York's Astor Hotel, Arthur Davidson and Indian's general manager Frank Weschler agreed to standardise the prices of competing models, so as to kill off the potentially ruinous effects of price-cutting. Nowadays, such an arrangement would, if uncovered, be vilified under the heading of cartel price-fixing; in 1922, it was the natural solution to a simple problem, and one which allowed both parties to make sensible plans for the future without having to keep looking over each other's shoulders. These price-fixing meetings went on to become an indispensable annual appointment for the managers of Indian and Harley-Davidson.

Having established the rules of the game in the most gentlemanly fashion, the two motorcycling giants then went away to lay plans for each other's destruction. For their part, Harley-Davidson's sales strategy was based on the

Left: Legendary British ace Freddie Dixon had good cause to grin after yet another win (this time at the 1923 Clipstone Speed Trials) on his modded JD racer.

Right: Douglas Davidson (no relation), here pictured at Brooklands in July 1921, had achieved a place in the record books one year earlier by becoming the first British rider to top 100mph.

Below right: Freddie Dixon again, making one schoolboy's dream come true in 1921.

launch of the JD, a larger-engined version of the faithful 1000cc J V-twin. Although the 1200cc JD was primarily aimed at the heavy duty three-wheeler commercial market, which still persisted despite the car-induced demolition of the private sidecar market, the new motor's extra power struck a sympathetic chord among the new breed of enthusiast motorcyclists moving in to fill the vacuum left behind by the Model T defectors. In this connection, the '74' (the JD's capacity in cubic inches) was also a useful response to the Chief, Indian's highly capable and well-favored entry in the heavyweight stakes. Looking back, the 74 could certainly be deemed a success, as this engine size and type featured in the Harley-Davidson lineup right up to 1980, and thereafter (in Sporster format) until the present day.

Following the success of their talks the previous year, Arthur and Walter Davidson arranged another meeting with Indian's Frank Weschler in 1923. The subject this time was the ejection from H-D and Indian sales showrooms of all other motorcycling marques, such as Excelsior, Cleveland and Reading Standard. Although Weschler was reportedly less than keen on this idea, having enjoyed the benefits of business cooperation and personal friendships with the representatives of these 'second division' companies for many years, the Davidsons finally prevailed upon him to agree to their proposal. The aim was to establish true solus franchises; the human consequence of this ruthless scheme was, inevitably, the demise of many smaller makes.

Another consequence of this pact was the creation of conditions suitable for a consolidation of Harley-Davidson's position at home, in Europe, and even Japan, where they established a foothold to challenge Indian's already firmly rooted Tokyo-based operation. This Japanese connection would eventually result in the setting up of a Harley-producing subsidiary in the Ginza district, which was in fact the first motorcycle manufacturing plant in Japan. Given the state of enmity which now exists between Harley riders and the Japanese 'opposition,' it is extraordinary and not a little ironic to think that the first motorcycles to be built on a commercial basis in Japan were Harley-Davidsons sold under the Rikuo badge.

In the mid-1920s, the transportation demands of America's forces of law and order were such that firms could make a healthy contribution to their own balance sheets by securing contracts to supply police motorcycles. The vibration problem that was an inbuilt design fault of big V-twins led many police officers to prevail upon their employers to let them use the much

smoother four-cylinder offerings of Henderson and Ace. The 1924 disappearance of Ace from the motorcycling scene cut down the choice somewhat, and naturally aroused the interest of Harley-Davidson, who could see big potential sales in the offing for any firm willing to put up a viable alternative to the Henderson.

Recognising that they did not possess the in-house expertise to produce an all-new engine, H-D immediately employed Ace's now redundant chief design engineer, Everett DeLong, on a brief to come up with a cheap new four-cylinder unit. Working in secret, DeLong quickly penned what he and the few others who were privy to the project considered to be a commercially worthy design. Effectively two sleeved-down J 74 twins laid side by side, the DeLong motor seemed to meet H-D's criteria. Bill Davidson, however, was not convinced; using his power as the company's leading shareholder, he vetoed the project on the grounds that it would have been too expensive to produce. Shortly afterwards, DeLong left the company to work for Cleveland, and all traces of the stillborn four-cylinder Harley-Davidson were destroyed.

The founders thus had to content themselves with a simple cosmetic revamping of the justly popular but by then old-fashioned J. Their options were necessarily limited by the fact that the J was their only high-profile model throughout the period of 1922-1929, after the Sport Twin's extinction in 1922 and before the arrival of the 45 cubic inch (750cc) model D in 1929. The improvements made to the J included a few welcome modifications to the engine, specifically to the valvegear and lubrication system, which were enough to ensure continuing loyalty among the 74's large and devoted band of followers.

Another continuing trend, and a somewhat less pleasant topic for discussion at H-D board meetings, was the apparently inexorable waning of motorcycling's popularity in the mid 1920s. Harley-Davidson were obliged to move into the ancillary parts business because of the fact that so many of their suppliers were being forced into closure by the prevailing economic circumstances. Their total output of machines was running at pre-war levels, only around 12,000 bikes being built in 1924. Even so, that made Harley-Davidson the biggest American manufacturer, with Indian producing approximately half as many machines as H-D. The only other manufacturer of note, Excelsior, was running at about half Indian's capacity, relying heavily on its police sales of Henderson fours.

Left: Harleys were designed to run best on America's ultra straight freeways, but that didn't stop this 1920's group from tackling the crookedest street in San Francisco.

Right: From 1922, the 1000cc 'J' had a big brother, the 1200cc 'JD'. Gray had turned to olive by then too.

Below: The 350cc Peashooter, available in both side valve and ohv formats, was campaigned on American tracks to great effect by Joe Petrali.

In 1925, Indian and Cleveland attempted to revitalise their flagging fortunes by launching lightweight single-cylinder bikes of 21 cubic inch (350cc) capacity. This engine size was extremely popular in England, home of the world's biggest motorcycle market at that time, so the American firms' decision to try and break into that field was a logical one. Equally predictable was Harley-Davidson's response the following year, in the shape of two separate 350cc singles. Model A was a sidevalve plodder capable of around 50mph (assuming that the piston could be persuaded to hold together at such a giddy speed). Model B differed in that it featured overhead valvegear, which endowed it with a considerably higher and more reliably obtainable top end of around 65mph.

The Harley dealership network, bred on a steady diet of fast V-twins, was less than enthusiastic about the new singles. But, after cynically dubbing the bikes 'Peashooters,' the same dealers were later required to eat their words. Although sales success was not instant in the US, where riders were not especially bothered about the 350's economy (its most obvious selling point), its race successes in the national series specially created for this class

Previous page: A long-track specification overhead valve Harley racer of the Great War period.

Left: Swedish daredevil Erik Westerberg did 104mph on his Harley on the ice of Stockholm's Edsviken Bay – without studs or spikes. . .

Below: Speedway was a popular sport in England in the late 1920s. Harley's Peashooter variant (foreground) had its work cut out against BSAs like the background example.

Right: Motorcycle sport of all kinds was incredibly well supported in the 1920s. This hillclimbing Harley sidecar entry looks like a family affair.

of machine were more difficult to ignore. The heroic feats of Joe Petrali on America's new 'flat track' circuits and on the notorious 'widowmaker' hill climbs were to assure him of a position of honor in the annals of Peashooter and, indeed, Harley-Davidson history.

Pressing home their advantage, H-D delighted their big twin fans with the announcement in 1927 of the JH (61ci) and JD-H (74ci) variants, scheduled for production in 1928. The most notable and attractive feature of these new roadburners was the utilisation of twin camshafts to operate the valves. Although aimed at the very top end of the market, with a suitably lofty price ticket nearly 20 percent higher than that of the ordinary J, the twin cammers were sufficiently impressive machines to earn themselves the reputation as

the best Harleys ever made. It was unfortunate that the factory chose to wait so long before indulging itself in such a commendable upgrading exercise, since the worthy but venerable J was by this time fast reaching the end of its run.

There was about to be a major shakeup in the Harley range, in fact, with the launch of two new models in 1929 and 1930. The first new model was destined to underwrite the company's future for the next twenty years; the second one nearly damaged the company's reputation beyond repair.

And in between the two launches, events on Wall Street threatened to bring about the ruin not just of Harley-Davidson, but of every other company, corporation and conglomerate in the industrialised world.

Indian Troubles

At the close of the last chapter, mention was made of Harley-Davidson's launch of two new models at the end of the 1920s.

In fact, *three* machines were announced by the factory in 1929, but only two of these were to play a significiant role in the company's history. Moreover, two of these three machines were all but identical, and hence could almost be classified as one model – though this was far from being the image the factory was trying to portray. At a casual glance, these two machines were practically indistinguishable from one another. The fact that one was powered by a 500cc single, and the other by a 750cc V-twin, was indicative of the extraordinary simplistic thinking behind Harley-Davidson's model range policy at this time.

With or without hindsight, it now seems astonishing that any motorcycle company could simultaneously offer such an ill-considered pair of models as the 45 cubic inch (750cc) D V-twin and the 30.5 cubic inch (500cc) C single for sale to the general public. In this case, not for the first time, Harley-Davidson's almost fanatical concern with keeping costs down nearly led to their undoing.

The notion this time was, quite simply, a brazen attempt to make two motorcycles out of one. The 750cc D started off badly by being encumbered with a torquey but over-lazy and decidedly underpowered sidevalve motor. While contemporary equivalents from Indian and Excelsior were easily capable of speeds approaching 80mph, Harley's supposedly competitive 45 could not even touch 60mph. Worse yet, it had a nasty tendency to destroy itself if the frustrated rider decided to fly in the face of reason by attempting to keep up with the rapidly-departing opposition.

Other compromises had had to be built into the D, for no other reason than that H-D had wanted to make use of exactly the same frame and cycle parts for the C. Of necessity, these frame components had to be beefy enough to contain the bigger and more powerful engine of the two. The inevitable consequence was that the C's rather feeble 500cc single motor had a decidedly hard job pushing the excess weight of a 750cc-sized chassis along the road. The whole ill-conceived exercise was a classic example of over-rationalisation, a felony which was then compounded by inadequate development.

The only saving grace on either machine was the provision of a front brake, a feature which, somewhat incredibly, had made its first appearance on Harleys only one year earlier on the 61 and 74 cubic inch V-twins. Even then, it had been regarded with some skepticism by those who thought of themselves as true Milwaukee men. These riders considered front brakes to be abominations and the work of the devil. In a curious way, applying this idea to Harley-Davidsons in isolation, they were half right.

Previous page: A beautifully kept 1936 61-E Knucklehead.

Right: The tough WLA army bike gave sterling service in the testing conditions of World War II, where the Harley's reliability and ease of servicing were of key significance. Some 89,000 were produced.

Below: The wheel has come full circle, with H-D now offering a springer-forked model for the '90s, but this is an original springer, with gold-plated custom touches.

With the notable exception of the XLCR Cafe Racer in 1977, Harley-Davidsons for the street have always been designed along cruising rather than racing lines. As such, they have traditionally featured riding positions which require the rider to maintain a straight back and forward-extended limbs, in a posture not too dissimilar to that assumed when driving a car. Such a posture has the effect of biasing the overall weight distribution towards the rear of the cycle, which in turn permits enthusiastic use of the back brake without too much risk of wheel lockup. Even today, a certain degree of care is advisable when using H-D front brakes, particularly on models featuring skinny 'custom' front tyres. The distrust of Harley's 1928 customers (riding on somewhat less tenacious rubber) was, therefore, not wholly unjustified.

In the event, buyers of the 1929 D and C sidevalve models had other things to worry about, thanks to the factory's failure to put either model through a serious development program. The nature of the shared frame meant that, while there was no problem fitting the single-pot C motor, serious difficulties were encountered when it came to shoe-horning in the much bigger twin. Although the basic engine went in all right, there was insufficient clearance for the 45's generator to be sited in its usual V-twin location, ahead of the crankcase. Instead, provision had to be made for it to be fitted slightly ahead and to the left of the vee made by the cylinders. From a distance, bystanders observing the passage of a D mistook the large cylindrical generator for an extra cylinder; the unsurprising result was that the D quickly acquired a 'three-cylinder Harley' misnomer.

It took even less time for this unfortunate machine to acquire a hatful of less innocent nicknames, bestowed upon it by angry dealers and their customers once it had become obvious that the generator's botched-up bevel gear drive was not strong enough to hold together under pressure. Worse still, the clutch components (which were already in service on the small capacity A and B singles, as well as on the new C model) were plainly inadequate for use in a motor twice the size – even if it was almost certainly less than twice as powerful. Harley-Davidson were not inclined to release horsepower figures at this time, probably with good reason in the 45's case.

Besieged by complaints, the factory hurriedly revamped the D, fitting bigger bearings in the generator drive and, in an attempt to rectify the performance shortcomings, including a larger bore carburetor in the specification. This modification hauled the 45's top speed over the 60mph mark, hardly an earth-shattering tune-up but a step in the right direction at least. The new 'performance' image was further enhanced by a quick restyle of the fuel and oil tanks. Despite all its initial teething problems, the 45 eventually became the backbone of Harley's model range, continuing in production as the power unit for solo mounts until 1953, and in the role of commercial slave in Harley's three-wheel Servicars right up until 1974.

The C proved rather less resilient. America's predilection for big-inch cruisers had already been firmly established long before the end of the 1920s. The much smaller market for European-style singles was by definition more difficult to satisfy, but having opted to compete in that market, H-D's approach was then inexplicably casual.

There was sales resistance even before the C was launched. The so-called 'Baby Harley' was far from being a worthy example of the sports single genre, combining as it did the twin failings of unexciting performance and unremarkable reliability. When it was unveiled, weighing in at a hefty 365 pounds, it seemed that the motorcycling public's advance appraisal of the machine was uncomfortably accurate. Like the D, it was hard pushed to reach the 60mph claimed for it by its manufacturers; also like the D, it proved itself to be fragile right out of the crate. Cooling was its weakness. The piston displaying an alarming propensity to eat itself in the hands of anyone who felt inclined to test its open-throttle behavior.

By 1931, the Baby Harley had lost its relatively lightweight Model B-derived frame, in favor of the 45's by then revised chassis. In the process, the C gained over 60 pounds and became even more sluggish than before. Though it did not officially disappear from the H-D catalog until 1937 (thanks in large part to its popularity as a commercial hauler in Japan of all places), sales in the USA had never been anything other than desultory.

If the C was bad, then the all-new 74 cubic inch V-twin revealed in August 1929 was a disaster. While Harley-Davidson's strong following might have allowed them to commit one *faux pas* in what was for them an unfamiliar market in small singles, a similar failure in their own specialist niche of

Left: The 'Twin Cam' JD and JDH big twins were only produced for a short time at the end of the 1920s, but were an instant hit with sports-minded riders.

Right: Charles Lindbergh, the first man to fly the Atlantic, was an enthusiastic Harley man in his spare time.

Below: The 45 cub c inch DLD of 1929 was known as 'the three-cylinder Harley' because of its unusual generator placement, but this more modern mutant (spotted at Daytona) really does have three cylinders.

V-twins — coming so soon after the 45's inauspicious debut — should have been unthinkable.

And yet, unbelievably, it appeared that the company had not learned its lesson. The new VL, put forward as the long-overdue replacement for the 15-year-old J, was a 74 cubic inch (1200cc) lookalike of the 45ci D. With a new frame and stronger forks, it was nearly 25 percent heavier than the J at around 550 pounds fully wet, and offered little in the way of innovation, other than quickly-detachable wheels and the option of a more contemporary style of sidecar. In fact, the main 'advance' claimed by the factory was not an advance at all, but simply a retention of existing sidevalve technology. The most often-quoted benefit was that maintenance would be made easier by dint of the fact that the engine could be left in the frame during routine top-end work. Retention of the total-loss lubrication system was further evidence of the VL's conservative specification.

On the face of it, the VL did not look like the kind of machine that might upset H-D's traditionally conservative clientele. Quality of construction had never been a problem at Milwaukee, and the VL was no exception to that rule. The bike's deficiencies were as much conceptual as mechanical.

Ricardo-designed heads, in conjunction with unusually small flywheels, were intended to pep up the engine's performance. These flywheels certainly enhanced the bike's low-speed pickup and accelerative qualities, but only at the cost of severely diminished top-end power. The VL's output turned out to be no greater than that of the J, and such power as it did have seemed to vanish altogether at higher engine speeds, a disappearing trick signalled all

Right: The 74 cubic inch VL sidevalve twin did not represent much of a step forward for Harley-Davidson. It was discontinued in 1936.

Below: Harleys have always been very popular in Japan. In fact, the first recorded importation took place as early as 1912. The three-wheeled Servicar derivative found especial favor in crowded Tokyo.

too painfully by the coincident commencement of serious vibration. The fly-wheels were too small, a fact pointedly brought to the factory's attention by disappointed dealers and owners worldwide. Once again, Harley-Davidson had released a machine for public consumption without having put it through any sort of serious test program.

New crankcases incorporating bigger flywheels were hastily fabricated and shipped out to H-D dealers, along with newly enlarged frames, with the instruction that these items should be retro-fitted to all VLs either sold or still on the showroom floor – a total of over 1300 cycles. Power-increasing alter-ations to the camshaft and valves were handed down at the same time. No financial assistance was offered to the dealers to help them in this massive clean-up operation, with the result that more than a few tore up their Harley franchises in protest. Other dealers who pleaded with the company to put the much-loved J back into production were also disappointed by H-D's negative response.

Additional pressure was put on the already struggling dealer network in 1929 as a result of a misguided decision by America's newly-elected Presi-dent Hoover to erect import barriers in order to protect the nation's farmers from the ruinous effects of cheap imports and rising inflation at home. Faced with the prospect of having to negotiate Hoover's tariff hurdles, foreign governments predictably retaliated by hoisting import barriers of their own. America's exporting potential was strangled at a stroke, obliging companies like Harley-Davidson to streamline their home marketing in order to survive. Dealers were whipped into action in search of turnover in the civilian and (in-creasingly important) police sales areas, competing furiously against Indian and Excelsior/Henderson.

The extra effort looked like it might pay off, with signs of a slight upturn in the domestic motorcycle market despite the launch fiascos perpetrated by Harley-Davidson. But then, in October 1929, came the stock market crash on Wall Street. Suddenly there was unemployment on a massive scale as first banks and then businesses went under. The value of transportation fell through the floor as Americans across the country found themselves strug-gling to stay alive. Gasoline became a luxury item. Cars became next to worthless. Sales of motorcycles, at the bottom of the heap, began a down-ward slide which was to bottom out for Harley-Davidson in 1933, when just over 3300 units were sold – only slightly above the equivalent figure for 1910.

H-D's founders were in no position materially to assist their rapidly-shrinking dealers. All they could do was encourage them to greater efforts in the fight to take as big a proportion as possible of whatever market remained open to them. That effectively meant squeezing out their main competitor, Indian. Going into 1930, this was a prospect which seemed on the cards, as the Springfield company had been slowly bleeding to death for years at the hands of successive incompetent managers.

But in April of 1930, Harley-Davidson's plans received a setback when the fabulously wealthy industrialist E. Paul du Pont bought a majority stake in Indian, announcing at the same time his intention to ensure the firm's con-tinuing involvement in the production of motorcycles. Excelsior, meanwhile, were capitalising on Harley's discomfiture over the VL (which had led to the cancellation of many police force orders), increasing production of their own Hendersons to fill the gap. Fortunately for H-D, however, this additional threat to their position was dissipated almost immediately by Excelsior themselves with their suicidal decision to fit cheaper – and considerably less reliable – ignition systems to their police-specification machines. An import-ant order by the Californian Highway Patrol was botched by Excelsior as a re-sult, and marked the beginning of their withdrawal from the motorcycle in-dustry.

It was now a straight fight between Harley-Davidson and Indian for control of the American market. H-D had their gloves off right from the start, out-raging motorcyclists nationwide with a scheme which encouraged their dealers to scrap any non-Harleys which were brought into their shops as part-exchanges for (very attractively priced) VL police specials. This dubious policy had the effect of decimating the number of Indians on the road, and lifted the state of rivalry between the two firms to such a pitch that ordinary civilian riders of Harleys were turned away from Indian dealerships, and vice versa. So much rancour was caused that even the ruthless H-D management felt morally obliged to discontinue the offer, dropping it six months after its introduction.

Great damage had been done to the public images of both manufacturers

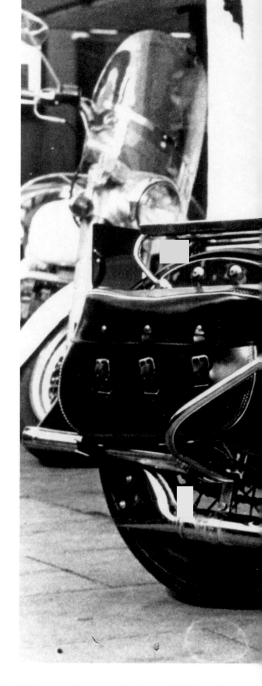

One of Harley's longest-lived and most successful models was the sidevalve '45', a docile plodder in the best H-D tradition. Thousands of 45s are still in use today; this one has been the subject of much tender loving care.

by then. Nonetheless, the annual price-fixing conferences between H-D and Indian continued to take place. The cosiness of the 1932 meeting was dis-turbed by the surprise attendance of E. Paul du Pont, who took the oppor-tunity to lecture the Davidson brothers Walter (President) and Arthur (Sales Manager) on the subject of business ethics in general. Du Pont was espe-cially caustic on the subject of H-D's seeming duplicity in the case of the VL police bikes deal, the details of which had of course not been divulged to Indian's representative at previous meetings.

Recovering from their initial shock at du Pont's outburst, the Davidson's calmed a potentially explosive situation by apologising to the French-born in-dustrialist, and citing the need for desperate measures in a desperate situa-tion. By this time, the 45 had been revamped, with a new frame (which allowed the troublesome generator to be sited in its proper place, ahead of the front cylinder) and a new purpose-built transmission. The 74ci VL had also benefitted from the upgrading of its previously suspect clutch. By 1932, both twins had secured a measure of public trust. They may not have been the world's most exciting motorcycles, but at least they were reasonably re-liable.

This image of Harley-Davidsons as rather prosaic, functional motorcycles seems at odds with the marque's currently glamorous profile, but the re-putation of the Milwaukee products was undoubtedly built on humble foun-dations. The Servi-car, launched in 1932, exemplified this practical aspect. Although this curious looking three-wheeled contraption has strong Harley associations, Indian had actually pre-empted H-D in the States with their own three-wheeler, the 'Dispatch-Tow', a device whose purpose was to facil-itate the delivery of motor cars to and from garages by providing transport for the driver before and after such deliveries (the Dispatch-Tow being hitched behind the car).

The Servi-car/Dispatch-Tow format had already been a common sight on Japanese roads for some time before the Indian appeared, in the shape of H-D single-powered commercial 'rear cars'. In the States, the Servi-car soon found a niche as a light-duty delivery vehicle, and also as a means of transport for parking penalty officers. Because of the easy starting capability of the D 45ci engine, motorcycling experience was not a necessary prerequisite for would-be meter attendants; indeed, many of them were women.

By 1933, Harley-Davidson's model lineup was beginning to look quite respectable, although Indian's competing machinery was still dynamically superior in most respects. It was a pity that the full effects of the national recession were biting at their hardest at this time. Motorcycle production was troughing out, and racetrack activity had just about ground to a halt. In a desperate attempt to inject some life back into the sport, the American Motorcyle Association instigated a new racing framework.

The most significant feature of the new setup was the formation of Class C racing, aimed primarily at private riders on 45 cubic inch motorcycles. Harley-Davidson were initially not displeased by this turn of events, since it would pitch their revamped 45 against Indian's discontinued – but still fast – 101 Scout 750. Their confidence was to be undermined in 1935, however, by the reappearance of a new and still better Scout. Only through the expert ministrations of ace tuner Tom Sifton were H-D able to keep their 45 in the running for honors against the lighter and more maneuverable Indians.

Through a quirk in the rules, Class C also allowed overhead valve 500cc machines to compete. This provision had little immediate impact, but it would ultimately lead to friction within the American motorcycle industry with the arrival from England of Norton's astonishingly successful International. Harley's own 21 and 30.5ci singles were coincidentally withdrawn

from the home market in 1934, the factory having accepted that their future lay in big, powerful V-twins. Four-stroke singles would not resurface in the model range until 1961.

At the other end of H-D's product line-up, the 74ci VL was maturing into the kind of motorcycle which would reaffirm the public's faith in Harleys as solid and reliable mounts. For the 1936 model year, it was bored out to 80 cubic inches (1340cc), not to make it any quicker especially, but to endow it with even more lugging power for commercial and sidecar applications. An optional transmission with three forward gears and a reverse was included in the catalog with these duties in mind. The new 80 (factory designation VLH) displayed an advanced tendency to vibrate and/or overheat – sometimes to the point of seizure – if it was subjected to extended hard use, but other than that it was a workmanlike machine with much to recommend it over Indian's now slower and often cantankerous Chief.

H-D widened the appeal of their cycles in the mid-1930s with the invention of the 'buddy seat', a foreshortened dual seat which allowed the Harley man to take his girl for an outing. The outing would for preference be short, however, or the girl of a very friendly disposition, since a buddy seat placed the two riders in very close contact with one another. One is forced to the conclusion that there are indeed many friendly girls in the US, since the buddy-style seat (admittedly rather more spacious now) still figures on modern-day Harleys.

1936 was one of the most important years in Harley-Davidson's history, ushering in as it did a new age of overhead valve V-twins. First in what was to become a 16-year line of highly-regarded ohv machinery was the 61 cubic inch (1000cc) model E, an all-new, 36 horsepower, duplex framed blockbuster aimed squarely at the sporting rider. As the 61E gradually moved into Harley-Davidson's hall of fame, its distinctively shaped rocker covers eventu-

The 61E of 1936 was a pivotal machine in Harley-Davidson's often troubled history. As their first overhead valve V-twin, the 'Knucklehead' led the way forward into a fifty-year dynasty of overhead valve-engined motorcycles which now shows every sign of propagating itself right into the 21st century.

Looking back at the E's launch, however, it is all too easy to imagine a very different set of consequences which, if they had been allowed to happen, and given the teetering state of H-D's economic position at the time, might well have jeopardised the existence of the company itself. Only the dogged resilience of the founders – coupled with their already well-known firmness with dealers – saved the Knucklehead from sudden and ignominious death.

It was not long after the release of the 61E before the inadequacy of the new bike's valvegear was discovered by dealers and customers. Public confi-dence in the factory's ability to produce reliable machinery, already dented earlier by the equally unimpressive debuts of the 45 and 74ci VLs, took another severe knock. The feeling of *deja vu* experienced by Harley's long-suffering customers was further underlined when the factory followed pre-vious custom and practice by hastily sending out a revised valvegear kit for the E, to be fitted to all 1900-odd machines produced during 1936.

Upon completion of the restitution programme, the factory asked their works rider Joe Petrali to make an attempt on the Daytona Beach mile re-cord with a modified and lightened 61E, in an effort to reassure any remain-ing doubters. Petrali duly obliged, setting a new record of 136.18mph, and in the process stamping the E as the performance model in Harley's range. The E was a significant trend-setter for H-D in another way; it was the first Harley-

Previous page: Babe Tancrede, veteran Rhode Island Harley campaigner, takes another victory, this time in the Laconia 100 Mile Road Race in June 1947.

Left and right: This superbly restored 1942 model WLA 45 is one of a select group of motorcycles considered worthy of exhibit in Britain's National Motor Museum at Beaulieu, a reflection of the esteem accorded it by a war-torn generation.

Below: Harley's attack on the World Land Speed record in March 1936 was meant to have been launched by Joe Petrali on this streamlined knucklehead, but in fact his record-breaking speed of 136.18mph was set without this bodywork, as it was found to upset the handling.

Davidson to feature a large and easily-read speedometer on a console between the two halves of the fuel tank. This styling touch has been retained on F series Harleys to this day.

More importantly, the 61E had at last put Harley-Davidson one step ahead of their long-time rivals, Indian. There was no equivalent 1000cc machine in the 'Iron Redskin' range. Their 1200 Chief was actually cheaper, but then so was Harley's own identically priced 74. The ohv 61 was in its own exclusive niche, a sports machine embodying what was, for Harley at least, modern engine technology. In late 1940, a bored and stroked 74 cubic inch version of the E was launched to run alongside the existing 61ci model. This, the first F series Harley-Davidson, showed itself to be considerably more powerful than the seminal 61, with a top speed in the region of 100mph; the extra performance was only obtained at the cost of exacerbated vibration, but with careful running-in and a reasonably realistic attitude, most enthusiasts were agreed that the gains were greater than the losses.

Three years beforehand, with depression-hit sales still languishing at around 10,000 units annually, H-D had been very much concerned with consolidation rather than experimentation. Trading on their humble origins, the founders announced two more sidevalve twins for the '37 season. The 74ci UL and its 80ci brother, the ULH, were unashamedly aimed at the conservative end of the market, being rather heavy and plodding in the old Harley tradition. With the future so uncertain, the company's cautious approach was both rational and excusable. The UL line ran successfully until 1941, proving especially popular for sidecar and police work, and fulfilling an essential function in helping to drag H-D out of the thirties depression.

The trusty old 45 was still battling on too, improved for 1937 with enhanced lubrication, cooling, and styling. In truth, it was still outshone by Indian's dynamically superior Scout, but the D's supporters came to value its solid dependability, a virtue of arguably greater importance in those straitened times. For those who wished to compete in 750cc Class C races, H-D offered the DLDR, a somewhat ersatz machine which did not really answer the enthusiasts' demands for a hotted-up thoroughbred worthy of doing dirt-track battle with the Indian Scout. Not until the arrival of the heavily-tuned WLR in 1941 would these demands be met.

Back in 1937, however, there was an unexpected crisis with the death in April of William Davidson. This was a big loss to both workforce and management. In his role of Production Head, Davidson had assumed a larger-than-life reputation on the shop floor. He had earned the respect of the ordinary men on the line, who saw him as 'one of them.' Like them, he enjoyed the simple pleasures of life, and also like them, he did not stint in the indulgence of his trencherman's appetites.

His death was coincident with a growing movement towards unionisation in the American automobile industry, a process to which 'Big Bill' was bitterly opposed. When the union's spotlight was finally turned upon the Juneau Avenue factory, Davidson's bull-headed decision to fight against the inevitable was a policy doomed to failure. Davidson's successor, William Ottaway, quickly recognised the futility of confronting the powerful United Auto Workers union, and agreed to the principle of negotiating with the union's representatives on the question of wages and conditions.

By the late 1930s, American motorcycling at the top end had taken on all the trappings of a lifestyle pastime, exemplified by the increasing profusion of clubs which went in for regular meetings, runs, social events, and bike shows. At this time, Harley-Davidson had a strong vested interest in the

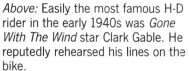

Above: Easily the most famous H-D rider in the early 1940s was *Gone With The Wind* star Clark Gable. He reputedly rehearsed his lines on the bike.

Left: Excellent machine though it was, the 61-E faced stiff competition from England in the shape of bikes like this 1939 Triumph Speed Twin.

Right: WLA-derived 'rat bikes' run for ever and never lose their value.

Left: Harley-Davidson fought hard to secure and retain police contracts, pitching prices very low to squeeze the competition.

Right: The founders examine their new baby for 1947, the 125cc Hummer two-stroke, an unashamed copy (like BSA's Bantam) of the German DKW.

Below right: Another proud patrolman, this time on a Servicar trike. These models were popularly used on parking violation duties.

American Motorcycle Association, contributing most of the funds necessary for the organisation's continued existence. Through the AMA, H-D had noted the propensity of bike club members to embellish their machines with all manner of accessories. The era of the 'dresser' motorcycle had arrived. Clubs were encouraged to become affiliated to the AMA, and awards were sponsored by H-D for the 'Best Equipped' bikes at shows. The money-spinning potential of a factory-supplied accessory market was not lost on H-D's management; winning machines at club shows tended to be selected on the basis of quantity of items fitted rather than quality, owners being especially profligate in the attachment of chrome-plated running lights front and rear. This aftermarket aspect of Harley's business was a not insignificant factor in the company's road back to profitability during the late thirties and early forties.

America's national economic position in general was looking brighter by the start of the 1940s, but motorcycling was still very much a minority interest. There was a war going on in Europe, but far from plunging the States back into depression, the conflict helped to fuel the economic upturn by bringing big orders to American firms. Soon after the start of the war, both Harley-Davidson and Indian were asked to supply 5000 motorcycles by the British government following the destruction by the German air force of Triumph's factory near Coventry.

Harley's offering was the WLA, a kitted-out variant of the low-compression 45 which by then had been in production for ten years. Designed to withstand abuse, the WLA featured protective bash-plates underneath the engine and chain, high-clearance mudguards, bigger engine-cooling fins and a heavy duty air cleaner. Leather panniers, ammunition boxes and a rifle holster on the front forks completed a well-adapted package which proved itself to be perfectly suited to the rigorous demands of a wartime application.

A less effective warbike bearing the Harley-Davidson name came about as a result of the US Government's request in 1942 for H-D to produce shaft-drive flat twin military bikes along the lines of the BMW boxers which were then in widespread use by the German forces in Europe and Africa. Complying with the request, H-D came up with the sidevalve 750cc XA, only to find – not for the first time – that their new engine suffered from top-end lubrication problems. Before these almost customary faults could be rectified, a shift in the war's emphasis put a premature end to the production run after just 1000 XA's had been built. In total, Harley-Davidson produced some 88,000 motorcycles during the war, the vast majority of them WLAs, WLBs and WLCs (the Canadian version), supplemented by a smattering of 74s and 61s for police and shore patrol duties on the home front.

In the middle of the war, and within the space of less than two years, two more of the company's founders had died. President Walter Davidson's death in February 1942, at the age of 65, was from liver problems complicated by overwork. His position at the head of the boardroom table was taken by 'Big Bill's' son, William H Davidson, a long-term employee of broad experience within the managerial structure of the firm and, thanks to his late father's foresight, the biggest company shareholder also.

Then, in September 1943, William S Harley suffered a fatal heart attack at the age of 62. Harley, who was as happy photographing birds as he was designing and riding Harley-Davidsons, was succeeded as Chief Engineer by Bill Ottaway; Harley's son, William J, moved into the vice president/ engineering berth. Ottaway took up his new post just in time to witness the downward turn of H-D's sales graph from its war-inspired peak years of 1942 and 1943. As the focus of the war moved to the Pacific in 1944-45 in answer to the Japanese threat, the American government cancelled its orders for military motorcycles. These machines, including some 15,000 Harley WLA's, found their way back onto both home and export markets in 1945, but they could only be sold at a government-stipulated price of $450 each.

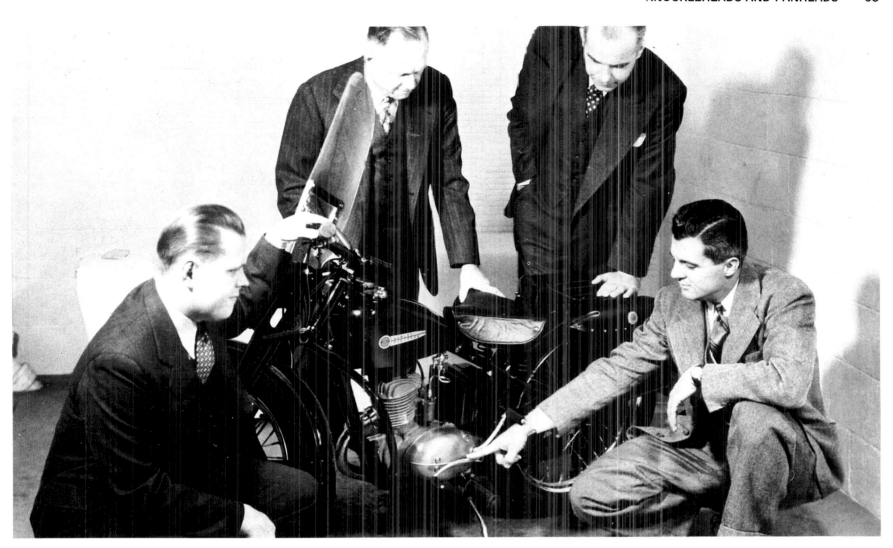

New Models and Economic Problems

That Harley-Davidson should so regularly have been able to release such palpably imperfect new models as the K for public consumption, while still somehow managing to retain such a loyal hard core following, is a topic which almost merits a separate volume of its own. If nothing else, it is certainly eloquent testimony to the marque's magnetic appeal.

As has already been mentioned, the 1952 K looked right. It undoubtedly represented a quantum leap forward from the uninspiring twenties styling of the D it was meant to replace. The powerplant was a letdown, however. Although its unit construction gave it a modern facade, the mundane side-valve format marked it down as very much the son of its father. Norton, along with a whole host of equally successful road and race machines from Italy, had proved the inherently superior power-producing capabilities of the overhead valve arrangement. Harley-Davidson themselves had sixteen years of ohv experience with the 61 and 74 big twins, but for the 45ci K they still elected to go down what was evidently expected to be an even safer flathead route.

It should have been a safer path. Extraordinary though it may seem, despite all the lessons learned in the past, the Harley engineers still had not cottoned on to the importance of proper product development. The KR racing version fell victim to early problems in the clutch department, notwithstanding the fact that its engine was actually no more powerful than its established predecessor, the WR. The straight K was revealed to be disappointingly sluggish, hard pressed to hit a top speed of 80mph. With a posted output of no more than 30bhp, it was patently lacking in the kind of lugging power demanded by those touring riders who preferred to travel two-up with luggage.

The K also suffered from its share of mechanical niggles, most notably a tendency to break gear teeth. Tuning parts were available to hoist the performance up to a more satisfactory level, and there were a few KK models produced in 1953, created by the insertion of the KR's hotter cams, polished ports and ball bearing crank into the K streetbike. By all accounts, these KKs were everything that the ordinary Ks should have been.

1953, Harley's 'Golden Anniversary' year, was celebrated with a bang: K panniers could now be ordered in the wonder material of white plastic, as well as in the usual fringed leather. In spite of this and many other anniversary temptations, the Ks continued to languish on showroom floors, kept company only by a larger version of the DKW-derived 125cc Hummer two-stroke. This, the new Teleglide, displaced 165cc, and sat in a chassis featuring rudimentary telescopic forks. The new machine rekindled a smoldering interest in the small strokers, and led to the reintroduction of the 125 in 1955. Both machines then ran alongside one another in the range up to and including 1959.

The lightweight end of H-D's range might have looked reasonably healthy, but by 1954, it was painfully obvious to all – including Harley's management – that the 750cc K was desperately in need of more power. This was achieved by the commonly-used Harley expedient of lengthening the stroke by three-quarters of an inch, to give a new displacement of 54ci (883cc). The new model, designated KH, also benefitted from revisions to the clutch and transmission, and breathed more easily through larger valves. Again, there was a street/racer hybrid, the KHK, and again, this was considered to be *the* K model to buy, if only because the 'racing' innards endowed it with performance to trade punches with quite ordinary imported sports machines.

Previous page: Fred Mork gives his Aermacchi-Harley single a run out at Daytona in 1985. These machines were still competing successfully at big events like the Isle of Man TT races right through until the mid 1980s.

Below left: The advent of the factory 'dresser' in the mid 60s, in the shape of the Electra Glide, legitimised a rebellious splinter group of the 50s.

Right: It didn't take long for the customisers to start work on the Duo-Glide.

Below: By the 1980s, diehards were harking back to the image, if not the lifestyle, of the 50s rebels.

Left: Another KR750 racer, this time the short-circuit version. It was also available in long track, short track, TT oval and off-road formats, a truly versatile (and eventually quite competitive) clubman racer.

Below: The Chevrolet Stingray of motorcycling in the '60s, Harley's ohv Sportster featured unit construction, light weight, short-range touring ability – and lots of image.

Let down by the factory's timidity in the choice of engine format, the K series was by no means an unqualified success for Harley-Davidson. In their defense, H-D did experiment in the mid fifties with an all-aluminum engined replacement for the K, the KL, and even got as far as testing a running prototype before guillotining the project. This error was to be put right in 1957, one year after the KH's discontinuation, with the resounding arrival of the XL Sportster.

Before that happened, however, in 1955 the 74ci Panhead's bottom end was beefed up with sturdier main bearings, leaving the motor wide-open for the ex-works horsepower enhancement. To reflect this new 'high perform-ance' aspect, the designation for the F was changed to FLH, a letter-code which is still used today to denote definitive big twin Harleys.

The spark of excitement thus lit among H-D disciples grew to fever pitch two years later, with the 1957 launch of the XL Sportster. In reality, it was nothing more than a logical development of the KH. Practically identical to it in most respects, it differed only in one major aspect: the provision of a decently powerful overhead valve engine. Although there were few visible differences between the old and the new engines, the Sportster reflected rather more advanced thinking in regard to the extraction of a more refined kind of power. Reverting to the original 750cc K's shorter stroke, the XL achieved the KH's extra displacement of 883cc by an increase in the bore. This approach, now widely accepted in modern tuning applications, allowed a higher rev ceiling by virtue of a decrease in piston speed, which in turn had been made possible by the shortening of the stroke. While low-down torque was compromised by this tuning method, the bonus came in the form of en-hanced smoothness at high rpm. Bigger pistons also allowed for bigger valves on the Sportster, improving engine breathing. The overall result was 40 horsepower at 5500rpm, figures which on a Harley-Davidson sales bro-chure must have seemed quite staggering.

Complaints concerning the inaccessibility of the old Ks transmission com-ponents led H-D's engineers to fit a 'trapdoor' in the Sportster's gearcase. The gears themselves were shifted by a lever under the rider's right foot, a

Above left: The ingenuity of the custom Harley builder knows no bounds. This fully street-legal double-engined shovelhead was spotted at Daytona.

Above: The engine has always been the focal point of any custom Harley. This 74 features exquisite engraving.

Left: The racing version of the ohv Sportster went under the XLR model name. With 82bhp from its 883cc, it won races both on its native dirt tracks and on some European road circuits.

nod in the direction of the British bikes that were still prevalent in sporting circles at that time. Although the new machine's image was overtly sporting, the factory endeavored to spread the Sportster's appeal by offering such factory options as panniers, screens and luggage racks. By this unsubtle device, Harley-Davidson hoped to cast the Sportster as a multi-purpose machine which might possibly be perceived as a smaller version of the FLH tourer.

In the event, this role-modelling fooled no one. It was plain that the Sportster had at last tapped into the potentially rich sportbike seam which had theretofore eluded Harley-Davidson. At long last, here was a home-grown, 100mph American motorcycle capable of overpowering the upstart Triumphs – in a straight line, anyway. Soggy coil suspension at the rear and inaccurate steering at high speed tended to confine Sportster riders' exuberance around corners. The package was nonetheless an instant hit.

For the 58 season, power was lifted still further for the new XLH model, by raising the compression ratio from an innocuous 7.5:1 to a rather more purposeful 9:1. and by the fitment of still larger valves. But America's excited motorcycling enthusiasts wanted even more; the XLCH was Harley's answer. Magneto ignition, high-level separate exhaust pipes and a small 'peanut' fuel tank distinguished the 'Competition Hot' XL from its humbler cousins. Strangely, the 1959 XLCH came with semi-knobbly off-road type tires, even though its true milieu was plainly the street. Factory publicity shots of the time show gritted-teeth company representatives hurling XLCH's up and down hills, presumably in an effort to persuade buyers that the Sportster's potential market extended all the way out to dirt riders. Needless to say, few buyers of what was after all still a heavyweight machine (nearly 500 pounds) cared to take up the off-road option.

By 1959, all XL derivatives had been given higher performance camshafts, hiking horsepower up to a claimed 55bhp. This period in American motorcycling history was marked by a general demand for more and more horsepower, to be used not only on the streets but also on the quarter-mile drag strips that were becoming increasingly popular towards the end of the 1950s. Harleys were especially handy for this latter purpose, being eminently susceptible to both weight-trimming and tuning. 'Hot' engine parts were readily available from any one of a myriad of aftermarket outlets which had been set up specifically to attend to the needs of those heretics who insisted on modifying their H-Ds. Harley-Davidson frowned upon this practice,

The Best Harleys Ever?

Left: The only real drawback with the Softail Springer, in the wet at any rate, was the limited grip offered by its skinny front tire.

Right and below: The Heritage Softail, featuring a solidly-mounted Evolution engine, hearkened back to the hardtail Hydra Glide of the 1950s.

base model Sportster, with all the shortcomings that that entailed. XR1000 production ran for a couple of years and then faded away, a sad end to what could so easily have been a great bike.

Willie G Davidson's evident willingness to spend time with and listen to the people who were buying his motorcycles was also beginning to show dividends in the mid-1980s. Taking an ever greater role in all aspects of product design, Davidson quickly identified a nostalgic element in the aspirations of customers both old and young, potential or existing. The FX 'Softail' of 1984 was the first tentative realisation-in-the-metal of this apparent yearning.

Embodying the styling appeal of the old rigid-rear-ended classics of the forties and fifties, and the comfort and sophistication of a hidden underframe suspension system, the Softail offered the best of old and new in a single attractive package. Originally sold with a four-speed transmission and kick-start lever so as to emphasise its traditionalism, even these sops to the die-hards were abandoned after the 1985 model year in favor of five speeds and an electric foot. Additional transmission sophistication was brought to bear on the 80-inchers in mid-1984, with the incorporation of a wet multiplate clutch. The solid engine mounts remained on some models, however (including the Softail), making available the dubious pleasure of Harley's equally 'traditional' hammering vibrations to anyone who cared to explore the upper reaches of the engine's rev range.

Diversification was the name of the game in the mid 1980s, with the purchase of a three-wheel sports car manufacturer (Trihawk) in '84 and the securing of various contracts to make gunshell casings for the US Navy. While the Trihawk connection is at the time of writing still to be exploited in any obvious way, the munitions contracts have proved very lucrative, allowing H-D to move into yet more areas outside motorcycling. Their purchase of the highly profitable Holiday Rambler motorhome group in 1986 was perhaps the most visible example of these new-found acquisitional activities, although British enthusiasts will doubtless also recall Harley's takeover of the Armstrong off-road motorcycle specialists in 1988.

1986 was notable for the unveiling of the Evolution-powered Sportsters, available once more in the old 883cc capacity as well as in 1100 and (later) 1200cc alternatives. The transmission ratios were closed up a little too, but the real solution – a five-speed box – is yet to make an appearance. The ultimate expression of H-D's nostalgia-driven return to prosperity did make its appearance in 1986, however.

The Heritage Softail was an unashamed replica of Harley's 1949 FLH Hydra Glide, complete with pseudo-hardtail frame, deeply valanced mud-guards, and optional fringed leather panniers. Sensibly, white plastic panniers were *not* on offer this time. Though priced at the top end of the range, the superbly detailed Heritage soon found a ready market. Fitted with performance add-ons from the company's recently introduced 'Screaming Eagle' selection of tuning parts, the Heritage could even be made to move with what many might consider to be indecent haste for such a gentlemanly conveyance.

Rather more curious was the company's 1988 decision to reintroduce springer forks on the FXSTS Springer Softail, a full eighty years after their first appearance on the front of a Harley-Davidson and, more significantly perhaps, forty years after they had made an unlamented departure in favor of telehydraulic forks. Although almost universally praised in its homeland, some non-American testers found the Springer's skinnily-tired front end to be a trifle unpredictable, not to say skittish, in damp conditions. Such criticisms as there were went largely unnoticed amid another enthusiastic take-up by the growing numbers of motorcyclists in search of something a bit different.

Niggles aside, the Springer is an appropriate machine on which to wrap up this condensed history of one of the world's most charismatic automotive marques, for it typifies the weird dichotomy behind Harley-Davidson's current success. The idea of putting new wine in distinguished-looking old bottles might sound less than honest, but if the wine is good enough to carry off the subterfuge, who are we to complain? And, like fine wines, Harley-Davidsons possess a unique capacity to improve with the passing of the years. Long may the vintages continue to be laid down.

Insignia and artefacts are an inseparable part of the Harley-Davidson experience, and identify the wearer as a believer in the true way. Again, the factory has legitimised this aspect of the sport by producing its own range of highly profitable geegaws. You can even buy removable tattoos now for that street-credible look in the bars at Daytona Beach.

Engraving, gold plating, even jewel-encrusting – there are no limits, either aesthetic or financial, to what some Harley owners will do to their trusty steeds. In the modern age of factory-prepared 'customs', it is becoming increasingly difficult to make your own personal statement, but that doesn't mean you can't try. . .

There is no doubting the talent of
many customisers, particularly in the
United States, where there exists a
wide and sophisticated range of
painting and plating facilities. One
positive upshot of the factory's
recognition of these customer desires
has been a continual rise in the
quality of their own painting, which is
now second to none.

Every February, thousands of motorcycling enthusiasts from all over the world congregate in Daytona, Florida. Ostensibly, the event is a week long series of road races held inside the Daytona speedbowl, but in practice the vast majority of spectators are there for the social scene, to cruise downtown bars. . . or simply to watch one another.

Selected Specifications

	JD/JDH 61 & 74 cu.in.	61-E	Hydra-Glide	XL Sportster	Duo-Glide	Electra-Glide	FX Super Glide
First Year of Manufacture	1928	1936	1949	1957	1958	1965	1971
Engine Type	Twin Cam	Knucklehead	Panhead	XL-Shovel	Panhead	Panhead (1965) Shovelhead (1966 on)	Shovelhead
Capacity	1000/1200cc	1000cc	1200cc	883cc	1200cc		
Bore and Stroke (inches)	3.31×3.50/ 3.41×3.50	3.31×3.50	3.43×3.96	3.00×3.81	3.43×3.96	1200cc	1200cc
Horsepower Rating (claimed)	8.68hp/9.5hp	40bhp	55bhp	40bhp	55bhp	3.43×3.96	3.43×3.96
Transmission	3 speed	4 speed	4 speed	4 speed	4 speed	60bhp	65bhp
Weight (wet)	575lbs	600lbs	600lbs	500lbs	600lbs	4 speed	4 speed
Top Speed (est)	90mph	98mph	100mph	85mph	100mph	780lbs	575lbs
						97mph	99mph

	XR 750 (Alloy)	FXS Low Rider	FLT Tour Glide	FXB Sturgis	FXRS Low Glide	FXST Softail
First Year of Manufacture	1972	1978	1980	1980	1982	1985
Engine Type	XL-Shovel	Shovelhead	Shovel/Evo	Shovelhead	Shovel/Evo	Evolution
Capacity	750cc	1200cc	1340cc	1340cc	1340cc	1340cc
Bore and Stroke (inches)	3.12×2.98	3.43×3.96	3.50×4.25	3.50×4.25	3.50×4.25	3.50×4.25
Horsepower Rating (claimed)	90bhp	65bhp	65bhp	65bhp	65bhp	65bhp
Transmission	4 speed	5 speed	5 speed	4/5 speed	5 speed	4 speed
Weight (wet)	320lbs	640lbs	795lbs	630lbs	640lbs	650lbs
Top Speed (est)	130mph	100mph	98mph	100mph	102mph	108mph

Left: The ultimate expression of luxury touring – the FLT Tour Glide.

Index

Page numbers in *italics* refer to illustrations